Regulation of access to gas networks in Russia in comparison with the energy law of Germany and the EU

VERÖFFENTLICHUNGEN DES INSTITUTS FÜR ENERGIE- UND REGULIERUNGSRECHT BERLIN

Herausgegeben von Franz Jürgen Säcker

Band 65

PETER LANG

Nino Kobadze

Regulation of access to gas networks in Russia in comparison with the energy law of Germany and the EU

PETER LANG

Bibliographic Information published by the Deutsche Nationalbibliothek
The Deutsche Nationalbibliothek lists this publication in the Deutsche Nationalbibliografie; detailed bibliographic data is available online at http://dnb.d-nb.de.

Library of Congress Cataloging-in-Publication Data
A CIP catalog record for this book has been applied for at the Library of Congress.

Zugl.: Berlin, Freie Univ., Diss., 2017

Printed by CPI books GmbH, Leck

D 188
ISBN 978-3-631-74685-1 (Print)
E-ISBN 978-3-631-76119-9 (E-PDF)
E-ISBN 978-3-631-76120-5 (EPUB)
E-ISBN 978-3-631-76121-2 (MOBI)
DOI 10.3726/b14366

Peter Lang - Berlin · Bern · Bruxelles · New York · Oxford · Warszawa · Wien

This publication has been peer reviewed.

www.peterlang.com

ჩემს მშობლებს

Preface

This thesis was submitted to the Free University of Berlin as a doctoral dissertation in the winter semester 2016/2017. Case law and literature as of October 2016 have been taken into account.

Various people have encouraged my research and writing. First and foremost, I would like to thank my doctoral supervisor Professor Dr. Dr. Dres. h.c. Säcker for awakening my interest towards energy law and for supporting the idea behind this thesis with great enthusiasm from the outset. I have immensely benefited from his great oversight and the independence he allowed me during the process of writing. I am also very grateful to the second supervisor of my thesis, Professor Dr. Breig, for his assessment and valuable comments.

I owe a special debt to Uwe Salaschek for encouraging and prompting me to accomplish this project, including with his various promises of rewards where necessary. I would like to warmly thank him for all his help with the review and for his patience. I would also like to express my gratitude to Juliane Mendelsohn for her great and timely support with proofreading and for providing her comments. I am very grateful to my friends, Eleni-Aristea (Elvira) Alevizou and Lina Berezgova for the inspiring discussions and their support at all times.

Any achievement comes at a cost to those around oneself and this thesis is no exception, as it would never have been completed or even started without the enormous effort of my parents to support my studies and their belief in me. I dedicate this thesis to them.

Contents

List of abbreviations

1. Legal acts

Administrative Regulations of the FTS – Order of the FTS approving the administrative regulations concerning the performance by the FTS of the state function of establishing and managing the register of natural monopolies, which are subject to state regulation and control [Prikaz Federalnoy sluzhbi po tarifam Ob utverzhdenii administrativnogo reglamenta ispolneniya federalnoy sluzhboy po tarifam gosudarstvennoy funktsii po formirovaniyu i vedeniyu reestra subyektov yestestvennikh monopoliy, v otnoshenii kotorikh osushchestvlyayutsya gosudarstvennoye regulirovaniye i kontrol] N 417-e of 30.08.2010, published in BNA of 20.12.2010, N 51, repealed by the Order of the FAS on repealing some orders of the FTS [Prikaz FAS Rossii o priznanii utrativshimi silu nekotorikh prikazov federalnoy sluzhbi po tarifam] N797/16 of 21.06.2016

Civil Code of Germany – Civil Code [Bürgerliches Gesetzbuch] of 02.01.2002 (BGBl. I p. 42, 2909; 2003 I p. 738), last amended through Art. 1 of the Law of 20.07.2017 (BGBl. I p. 2787)

Civil Code of Russia – Civil Code of the RF, Part 1, N 51-FZ 30.11.1994 [Grazhdanskiy kodeks RF, Chast 1], published in SZ of 05.12.1994, N 32, p. 3301, last amended on 26.07.2017, effective from 06.08.2017

Code of Administrative Offences of Russia – Code of administrative offences of the RF [Kodeks RF Ob administrativnikh narusheniyakh] N 195-FZ of 30.12.2001, published in RG of 31.12.2001, N 256, last amended on 30.10.2017

Constitution of Russia – Constitution of Russia of 12.12.1993 [Konstitutsiya Rossiiskoy Federatsii ot 12.12.1993], as amended on 30.12.2008, 05.02.2014 and 21.07.2014, published in SZ of 04.08.2014, N 31, p. 4398

Criminal Code of Russia – Criminal Code of the RF [Ugolovniy Kodeks RF] N 63-FZ of 13.06.1996, published in SZ of 17.06.1996, N 25, p. 2954, last amended on 26.07.2017, effective from 06.08.2017

Decree on anti-monopoly and tariff regulation – Decree of the President of RF on several issues of public administration and control in the area of anti-monopoly and tariff regulation [Ukaz Prezidenta RF O nekotorikh voprosakh gosudarstvennogo upravleniya v sfere antimonopolnogo i tarifnogo regulirovaniya] of 21.07.2015 N 373, published in SZ of 27.07.2015, N 30 p. 4571

Decree on ensuring the operation of the Unified Gas Supply System – Decree N 538 of 01.06.1992 of the President of the RF on ensuring the operation of the Unified Gas Supply System [Ukaz Prezidenta RF Ob obespechenii deatelnosti Edinoy sistemi gazosnabzhenia strani], published in 'Journal of Congress of People's Deputies and Supreme Soviet of the RF' of 11.06.1992, N 23, p. 1271

Decree on Structural Reforms – Decree of the President of the RF on fundamental provisions of the structural reform in the sectors of natural monopolies [Ukaz Prezidenta RF Ob osnovnikh polozheniyakh strukturnoy reformi v sferakh estestvennikh monopoliy] N 426 of 28.04.1997, published in SZ of 05.05.1997, N 18, p. 2132, last amended on 23.07.2001

Decree on the system and structure of federal executive bodies – Decree of the President of RF on the system and structure of federal executive bodies [Ukaz Prezidenta RF O sisteme i strukture federalnikh organov ispolnitelnoy vlasti] N 314 of 09.03.2004, published in RG of 12.03.2004, N 50, abolished on 28.09.2017

Decree on the transformation of Gazprom State Gas Concern into Russian Joint Stock Company Gazprom – Decree N 1333 of 05.11.1992 of the President of the RF on the transformation of Gazprom State Gas Concern into Russian Joint Stock Company Gazprom [Ukaz Prezidenta RF O preobrazovanii gosudarstvennogo gazovogo koncerna 'Gazprom' v Rossiyskoe aktsionernoe obshchestvo 'Gazprom'], published in 'Collection of acts of the President and the Government of the RF' of 09.11.1992, N 19, p. 1607, last amended on 12.05.1997

Decree on the transformation of state undertakings, associations and organisations of fuel and energy complex into joint stock companies – Decree N 922 of 14.08.1992 of the President of the RF on peculiarities of transformation of state undertakings, associations and organisations of fuel and energy complex into joint stock companies [Ukaz Prezidenta RF Ob osobennostyakh preobrazovaniya gosudarstvennikh predpiyatiy, obyedineniy, organizaciy toplivno-energeticheskogo kompleksa v aktsionernie obshchestva], published in 'Collection of acts of the President and the Government of the RF' of 31.08.1992, N 9, p. 591

Decree on the transformation of state undertakings and voluntary associations of state undertakings into joint stock companies – Decree N 721 of 01.07.1992 of the President of the RF on organisational measures of transforming state undertakings and voluntary associations of state undertakings into joint stock companies [Ukaz Prezidenta RF Ob organizatsionnikh merakh po preobrazovaniyu gosudarstvennikh predpriyatiy, dobrovolnikh obyedineniy gosudarstvennikh predpriyatiy v aktsionernie obshchestva], published in 'Collection of acts of the President and the Government of the RF' of 06.07.1992, N 1, p. 3, last amended on 31.12.1992

Decree on the transformation into joint stock companies and privatisation of undertakings, associations and organisations of the gas industry of RF – Decree N 1559 of 08.12.1992 of the President of the RF on the transformation into joint stock companies and privatisation of undertakings, associations and organisations of the gas industry of RF [Ukaz Prezidenta RF O preobrazovanii v aktsionernie obshchestva i privatizatsii gosudarstvennix predpriyatiy, obyedineniy i organizaciy gazovogo khozyaistva RF], published in 'Collection of acts of the President and the Government of the RF' of 21.12.1992, N 25, p. 2224, last amended on 12.05.1997

EnWG – German Energy Act [Energiewirtschaftsgesetz] of 07.07.2005 (BGBl. I p. 1970, 3621), last amended through Art. 2 para. 6 of the Law of 20.07.2017 (BGBl. I p. 2808)

Gas Directive 1998 – Directive 98/30/EC of the European Parliament and of the Council of 22 June 1998 concerning common rules for the internal market in natural gas, OJ L 204, 21.07.1998, p. 1-12

Gas Directive 2003 – Directive 2003/55/EC of the European Parliament and of the Council of 26 June 2003 concerning common rules for the internal market in natural gas and repealing Directive 98/30/EC, OJ L 176, 15.07.2003, p. 57-78

Gas Directive 2009 – Directive 2009/73/EC of the European Parliament and of the Council of 13 July 2009 concerning common rules for the internal market in natural gas and repealing Directive 2003/55/EC, OJ L 211, 14.08.2009, p. 94-136

Gas Regulation 2005 – Regulation (EC) No 1775/2005 of the European Parliament and of the Council of 28 September 2005 on conditions for access to the natural gas transmission networks, OJ L 289, 03.11.2005, p. 1-13

Gas Regulation 2009 – Regulation (EC) No 715/2009 of the European Parliament and of the Council of 13 July 2009 on conditions for access to the natural gas transmission networks and repealing Regulation (EC) No 1775/2005, OJ L 211, 14.08.2009, p. 36-54

GasNZV – Regulation on access to gas supply networks [Gasnetzzugangsverordnung] of 03.09.2010 (BGBl. I p. 1261), last amended through Art. 1 of the Regulation of 11.08.2017 (BGBl. I p. 3194)

GWB – Act against Restraints of Competition [Gesetz gegen Wettbewerbsbeschränkungen] of 26.06.2013 (BGBl. I p. 1750, 3245), last amended through Art. 10 para. 9 of the Law of 30.10.2017 (BGBl. I p. 3618)

Judgment on application of the anti-monopoly legislation – Judgment of the Plenum of the Supreme Commercial Court of the RF on several questions raised in relation to the application of the anti-monopoly legislation by the commercial courts [Postanovleniye Plenuma Visshego Arbitrazhnogo Suda RF o nekotorikh voprosakh, voznikayushchikh v svyazi s primeneniyem arbitrazhnimi sudami antimonopolnogo zakonodatelstva] N 30 of 30.06.2008, published in VVAS of August 2008, N 8, last amended 14.10.2010

Law on Competition – Federal Law on protection of competition [Federalniy zakon O zashchite konkurentsii] N 135-FZ of 26.07.2006, published in RG of 27.07.2006, N 162, last amended on 29.07.2017

Law on Gas Supply – Federal Law on gas supply in the RF [Federalniy zakon O gazosnabzhenii v RF] N 69 of 31.03.1999, published in SZ of 05.04.1999, N 14, p. 1667, last amended on 26.07.2017

Law on Natural Monopolies – Federal Law on Natural Monopolies [Federalniy zakon O estestvennikh monopoliyakh] N 147-FZ of 17.08.1995, published in SZ of 21.08.1995, N 34, p. 3426, last amended on 29.07.2017

NDAV – Ordinance regarding general conditions of the network connection and its use for the gas supply at low pressure [Niederdruckanschlussverord nung] of 01.07.2006 (BGBl. I p. 2477, 2485), last amended through Art. 8 of the Law of 29.08.2016 (BGBl. I p. 2034)

Provisions of territorial bodies of the FAS – Order of the FAS on the approval of the provisions of territorial bodies of the Federal Anti-monopoly Service [Prikaz FAS Rossii Ob utverzhdenii polozheniya o territorialnom organe Federalnoy Antimonopolnoy sluzhbi] N649/15 of 23.07.2015, last amended on 05.04.2017

Provisions of the FAS – Regulation of the Government of RF on the approval of the provisions of the Federal Anti-monopoly Service [Postanovleniye Pravitelstva RF Ob utverzhdenii Polozheniya o Federalnoy antimonopolnoy sluzhbe] N 331 of 30.06.2004, published in RG of 31.07.2004, N 162, last amended on 01.07.2016, amendments of 17.10.2016 effective from 01.01.2017

Provisions of the FTS – Regulation of the Government of RF on the approval of provisions of the Federal Tariff Service [Postanovleniye Pravitelstva RF Ob utverzhdenii Polozheniya o Federalnoy sluzhbe po tarifam] N332 of 30.06.2004, published in RG of 15.07.2004, N 150, last amended on

02.11.2013, repealed by the Regulation of the Government of RF of 04.09.2015 N 941

Provisions on access to distribution networks – Regulation of the Government of the RF on the approval of provisions on ensuring access of undertakings to local distribution networks [Postanovlenie Pravitelstva RF Ob utverzhdenii Polozheniya ob obespechenii dostupa organizatsiy k mestnim gazoraspredelitelnim setyam] N 1370 of 24.11.1998, published in SZ of 30.11.1998, N 48, p. 5937, last amended on 08.08.2013

Provisions on review of issues related to access to distribution networks by the FEC – Regulation of the Federal Energy Commission of RF on the approval of provisions regarding the review order of issues related to the access of undertakings to local distribution networks [Postanovleniye federalnoy energeticheskoy komissii RF Ob utverzhdenii Polozheniya o poryiadke rassmotreniya voprosov, svyiazannikh s dostupom organizatsiy k mestnim gazoraspredelitelnim setyiam] N 6/1 of 19.02.1999, published in RG of 18.05.1999, N 94, repealed by the Order of the FTS of 18.05.2011 N 111-e7

Regulation on access to the GTS-UGSS – Regulation of the Government of the RF on ensuring access of independent undertakings to the gas transmission system of JSC Gazprom [Postanovlenie Pravitelstva RF Ob obespechenii dostupa nezavisimikh organizaciy k gazoratransportnoy sisteme otkritogo aktsionernogo obshchestva Gazprom] N 858 of 14.07.1997, published in SZ of 21.07.1997, N 29, p. 3525, last amended on 19.06.2014

Regulation on information disclosure – Regulation of the Government of the RF on the approval of standards of information disclosure by natural monopolies providing services of gas transportation through pipelines [Postanovleniye Pravitelstva RF Ob utverzhdenii standartov raskritiya informatsii subyektami estestvennikh monopoliy, okazivayushimi uslugi po transportirovke gaza po truboprovodam] N 872 of 29.10.2010, published in SZ of 08.11.2010, N 45, p. 5855, last amended on 30.12.2013

Regulation on Prices for gas, Tariffs for transportation services and Fees for connection of gas-powered equipment – Regulation of the Government of the RF on state regulation of prices for gas, tariffs for services of its transportation and charges for technical connection of gas-powered equipment to gas distribution networks in the territory of the RF. [Postanovlenie Praviteslstva RF O gosudarstvennom regulirovaniy tsen na gaz, tarifov na uslugi ego transportirovke i plati za tekhnologicheskoe prisoedinenie gazoispolzuyushchego oborudovania k gazoraspredelitelnim setyam na teritorii RF] N 1021 of 29.12.2000, published in SZ of 08.01.2001, N 2, p. 175, last amended on 17.05.2016

Regulation on State Control of Regulated Prices and Tariffs – Regulation of the Government of the RF on state control (supervision) in the field of regulated state prices (tariffs), as well as amending and repealing several acts of the Government of the RF [Postanovlenie Pravitelstva RF O Gosudarstvennom kontrole (nadzore) v oblasti reguliruemikh gosudarstvom tsen (tarifov), a takzhe izmenenii i priznanii utrativshimi silu nekotorikh aktov Pravitelstva RF] N 543 of 27.06.2013, published in SZ of 08.07.2013, N 27, p. 3602, last amended on 05.02.2016

Rules on access to the services of electricity distribution – Regulation of the Government of RF on the approval of Rules of non-discriminatory access to the services of electricity distribution and provision of these services, Rules of non-discriminatory access to the services of operative-dispatching control in electrical energetics and provision of these services, Rules of non-discriminatory access to the services of administrator of whole-sale trade system and provision of these services and Rules of technical connection of the applications of electricity customers, objects of electricity generation and objects belonging to distribution undertakings and other persons [Postanovleniye Pravitelstva RF Ob utverzhdenii pravil nediskriminatsionnogo dostupa k uslugam po peredache elektricheskoy energii i okazaniya etikh uslug, pravil nediskriminatsionnovo dostupa k uslugam po operativno-dispecherskomy upravleniyu v elektroenergetike i okazanie etikh uslug, pravil nediskriminatsionnovo dosputa k uslugam administratora torgovoy sistemi optovovo rinka i okazanie etikh uslug i pravil tekhnologicheskovo prisoedeneniya energoprinimayushikh ustroistv potrebiteley elektricheskoy energii, obyektov po proizvodstvy elektricheskoy energii, a takzhe obyektov elektrosetevovo khozyaystva, prinadlezhashchikh setevim organizatsiyam i inim litsam] N 861 of 27.12.2004, published in SZ of 27.12.2004, N 52 (part 2), p. 5525, last amended on 28.07.2017

Regulation on the establishment of the Russian Joint Stock Company Gazprom – Regulation of the Government of the RF N 138 of 17.02.1993 On the establishment of the Russian Joint Stock Company Gazprom [Postanovlenie Soveta Ministrov _ Pravitelstva RF Ob uchrejdenii Rossiyskogo aktsionernogo obshchestva Gazprom], published in 'Collection of acts of the President and the Government of the RF' of 01.03.1993, N 9, p. 738, last amended on 28.12.2005

Rules on Gas Consumption – Regulation of the Government of the RF on the approval of Rules on gas consumption and provision of services of gas supply in the RF [Postanovlenie Pravitelstva RF Ob utverzhdenii Pravil polzovaniya gazom i predostavleniya uslug po gazosnabzheniyu v RF] N 317 of 17.05.2002, published in SZ of 20.05.2002, N 20, p. 1870, last amended on 19.06.2017

Rules on Gas Supply – Regulation of the Government of the RF on the approval of Rules on gas supply in the RF [Postanovlenie Pravitelstva RF Ob utverzhdenii Pravil postavki gaza v RF] N 162 of 05.02.1998, published in SZ of 09.02.1998, N 6, p. 770, last amended on 04.02.2017

2. Cases from the case law in Russia

Astrakhan case – case N A06-2960-8/03 consisting of 4 decisions: Decision of the Commercial Court of Astrakhan Oblast of 11.02.2004 [Resheniye Arbitrazhnovo Suda Astrakhanskoy oblasti]; Judgment of the Appellate Court of 29.03.2004 [Postanovleniye apelyatsionnoy instantsii]; Judgment of the Federal Commercial Court of Cassation of Volga Federal District of 17.06.2004 [Postanovleniye kassatsionnoy instantsii Federalnovo Arbitrazhnovo Suda Povolozhskovo okruga]; Judgment of the Presidium of the Supreme Court of the RF of 05.04.2005 N 11857/04 [Postanovleniye Arbitrazhnovo Suda RF], published in VVAS 2005, N 7

Chelyabinskgazcom case – Judgment of the 18th Commercial Appellate Court N 18AP-468/2013 of 26.03.2013 [Postanovleniye Vosemnadtsatogo Arbitrazhnogo Suda], case N A76-17481/2012

FAS vs. Gazprom (NGK/SibEvroGaz) – Judgment of the 9th Commercial Appellate Court of 17.04.2006 [Postanovleniye devyatogo Arbitrazhnogo Suda], case N 09AP-16028/05-AK

Gazprom vs. FAS (Real-Gaz) – Judgment of the Federal Commercial Court of Moscow District N A40-69840/12-79-654 of 27.02.2013 [Postanovleniye Federalnogo Arbitrazhnogo Suda Moskovskogo Okruga]

Gazprom vs. FAS (Tatarstan) – Judgment of the Federal Commercial Court of Moscow District of 29.10.2009 N KA-A40/11185-09 [Postanovleniye Federalnogo Arbitrazhnogo Suda Moskovskogo Okruga], case N A40-83706/08-2-160

Gazprom vs. FAS (Transgaz) – Judgement of the 9th Commercial Appellate Court on examination of lawfulness and reasonableness of the decisions of commercial courts not entered into force [Postanovleniye devyatogo Arbitrazhnogo Apelyatsionnogo Suda po proverke zakonnosti I obosnovannosti reshenii arbitrazhnikh sudov, ne vstupivshikh v zakonnuyu silu], case N 09AP-8871/2007-AK

Omskgazset case – Judgment of the Federal Commercial Court of West-Siberian District of 26.09.2013 [Postanovleniye Federalnogo Arbitrazhnogo Suda Zapadno-sibirskogo Okruga], case N A46-597/2013

Real-Gaz vs. Gazprom – Judgment of the 9th Commercial Appellate Court of N 09AP-29781/2014 of 15.08.2014 [Postanovleniye Devyatogo Arbitrazhnogo Apellyatsionnogo Suda], case N A40-45333/13

Trans Nafta case – Decision of the Federal Anti-monopoly Service in relation to JSC Gazprom and LLC Novosibirskgaz [Resheniye Federalnoy Antimonopolnoy Sluzhbi Rossii], case N1 10/21-08 of 13.05.2008

Trans Nafta vs. Kaspiigazprom – Judgment of the Federal Commercial Court of North Caucasus Federal District dated 20.02.2002 [Postanovleniye Federalnogo Arbitrazhnogo Suda severo-kavkazkovo okruga], case N A15-91/2001-9

3. Journals and newspapers

BGBl.	Das Bundesgesetzblatt [Federal Law Gazette]
BNA	Byuletin normativnikh aktov federalnikh organov ispolnitelnoy vlasti [Bulletin of Normative Acts of the Federal Bodies of executive power]
BR-Drs.	Bundesratsdrucksache [Printed matter of German Bundesrat]
ELJ	European Law Journal
NiG	Neft i Gaz [Oil and gas]
OJ	Official Journal of the European Union
RG	Rossiyskaya gazeta [Russian Gazette]
RGBl	Reichsgesetzblatt [Reich Law Gazette]
SZ	Sobranie zakonodatelstva RF [Collection of Legislation of the RF]
VVAS	Vestnik Visshego Arbitrazhnogo Suda RF [Bulletin of Supreme Commercial Court of the RF]
WiRO	Wirtschaft und Recht in Osteuropa [Economy and law in east Europe]

4. Miscellaneous

BDI	Bundesverband der Deutschen Industrie [Federation of German Industries]
BGW	Bundesverband der deutschen Gas- und Wasserwirtschaft [Federal Association of German gas and water industry]
cf.	compare
CoA	Cooperation Agreement

CODD	Central Operations and Dispatch Department of JSC Gazprom
diss.	dissertation
e.g.	for example
EBRD	European Bank for Reconstruction and Development
ed.	editor; eds. editors
etc.	and so forth
f./ff.	following page/following pages
FAS	Federal Anti-monopoly Service of Russia
FEC	Federal Energy Commission of Russia
fn.	footnote
FTS	Federal Tariff Service of Russia
GDS	Gas distribution systems of Russia
GDU	Gas distribution undertaking of Russia
GTS-UGSS	Gas transmission system of the Unified Gas Supply System of Russia
i.e.	in other words
JSC	Joint Stock Company
LLC	Limited Liability Company
LNG	liquefied natural gas
N	number
OECD	Organisation for Economic Cooperation and Development
p.	page
para.	paragraph
pt.	point
RF	Russian Federation
RGSS	Regional Gas Supply Systems of Russia
RJSC	Russian Joint Stock Company
sec.	section
sent.	sentence
t.	tome
TPA	third party access
UGSS	Unified Gas Supply System of Russia
VIK	Verband der Industriellen Energie- und Kraftwirtschaft [Association of the Industrial Energy and Power Industry]
VKU	Verband kommunaler Unternehmen [Association of Local Utilities]
vol.	volume

Introduction

This research comparatively examines the regulation of access to gas networks in Russia in the light of developments in the EU and the experiences in Germany in this area.

The regulation of network industries is expected to perform a balancing test, which should ensure the least onerous decision for the public good. It should, on the one hand, guarantee the security of supply and on the other hand, keep these industries attractive for investments as well as provide qualitative goods and services for competitive prices. The introduction of competition is the main tool for balancing out the regulation in the upstream and downstream markets of network industries. However, competition may not exist without access to the network, duplication of which is economically unviable and access to which is indispensable for entering the market and operating in the sector. Therefore, access to networks on non-discriminatory conditions is the most important precondition for introducing competition. This is where regulation is required in order to prescribe rules for such access. Regulation is especially crucial in areas like the gas sector where the whole value chain historically used to be, and in Russia still is, in the hands of a single vertically integrated undertaking.

One of the most important accomplishments of introducing competition in the gas sector is that gas suppliers can have their gas carried over existing networks at non-discriminatory terms and conditions. The negotiated and later the mandatory and regulated access of newcomers to the networks of incumbents has consequentially become the core of the EU natural gas Directives, which gave rise to the liberalisation of the gas markets in the EU. Competitive access to transport facilities has always been and still remains the most important precondition for competition in the gas sector.

In spite of fundamental differences in the organisation of the gas sector, as well as deviations in legal acts, a structured comparison with the legislation of Germany and the EU framework of the gas network regulation is extremely interesting for Russia from a doctrinal point of view. Furthermore, a comparative representation of these different regulatory regimes would contribute to the interests of all parties in the view of existing and potential cross-border investments and investment protection issues, as well as the trade with gas.

In the legal doctrine and practice of Germany, the topic of pro-competitive regulation of access to the natural gas network has been researched extensively. In Russia, on the other hand, despite the existence of the legislative basis and some case law, many legal details have still not been disputed, most notably the question of whether the existing regulatory regime actually guarantees non-discriminatory and effective access to the gas networks has not yet been resolved. Moreover, in Russia, where effective unbundling has not yet been introduced and thus vertically integrated undertakings still have incentives to discriminate against their competitors, the enforcement of non-discriminatory network access is even more important as it is one of the few means of introducing competition into the sector.

The central question of this research is to assess whether and to what extent the existing regulation of access to the gas networks of Russia actually contributes to the goal of creating competitive gas markets. Furthermore, areas in need of improvement will be pointed out where appropriate and the approach for legislative amendments framed respectively. The issue of network charges will be addressed only at those points where they are substantial for analysing the question.

In view of the above, this research will proceed as follows: in the first part, the framework of the regulation of access to the gas networks in the EU and the rules of network access in Germany will be outlined. Since this presentation will serve as a basis for the following legal comparison, it will be focused mainly on those points that are important for the later discussion. The second part will discuss the historical development and current organisation of the gas industry and legislation regulating access to natural gas networks in Russia from a comparative perspective. The relevant rules will be presented in a structured way according to the topics and following the systematics of the EU law, as far as is feasible. When dealing with single aspects of the gas network regulation a parallel will be drawn with relevant provisions of the energy law of Germany and the EU, where appropriate. The conclusions regarding the principal results of the comparative assessment will be summarised in the last chapter of the second part.

A. Regulation of access to gas networks in the EU and in Germany

I. Overview of the gas industry in Germany prior to the first Energy Package

The first time gas was used for street lighting in Germany dates back to 1826.[1] The local production of gas from coal dominated the gas market in the beginning of the 20th century and predominantly the communities controlled local gas supplies through municipal gas works.[2] The first long-distance gas pipelines were built by companies of coal industry, which were established to enable supplies of gas to neighbouring communities.[3] From the middle of the 1960s Germany started to increase imports of natural gas, which gradually replaced gas production from coal and made the rapid construction of long-distance gas pipelines indispensable.[4] Apart from gas pipelines, for purposes of import high pressure gas networks are also represented on a regional level within Germany.[5]

The first German Energy Act of 1935 legitimised the monopoly positions of the local energy supply undertakings, gained through concession and demarcation agreements with energy suppliers of other communities, obliging the parties not to supply to the territories of one another.[6] For several decades the competition policy of Germany in the field of energy relied on the central idea "to prevent the effects of competition that are detrimental for national economies".[7] Only after the 4th amendment of the Act against Restraints of Competition of Germany in 1980 did the competition authority obtain the right to intervene in the activities of energy supply companies with a limited scope. Since the change of paradigms in the beginning of the 1990s, however, it is assumed that supply-side competition in the field of production and sales of gas as well as electricity is possible and contributes to efficiency increase.[8] Therefore, competition has to be actively promoted, inter alia, by means of ensuring a non-discriminatory access

---

1 See *Kemper*, Access to gas networks in Germany and in Spain, p. 21 ff.
2 See *Säcker*, in: Säcker, Handbook of German-Russian energy law, p. 2 ff.
3 See *Körting*, History of the German gas industry, p. 488 ff.
4 See *Barbknecht*, in: Säcker, Handbook of German-Russian energy law, p. 83 f.
5 See ibid.
6 See *Kemper*, Access to gas networks in Germany and in Spain, p. 22 f.
7 See Preamble of the German Energy Act of 1935 (RGBl I p. 1451).
8 See *Timofeeva*, Unbundling in the Russian electricity industry, p. 5 with further sources; see also Säcker/Schönborn, in: Säcker, Berlin Commentary on energy law, t. 1, p. 444, para. 2 f.

to gas networks, which are still considered as natural monopolies for the reason that construction of new parallel gas networks are not, as a rule, economically feasible.[9] The realisation of a non-discriminatory access to gas networks can in turn be only achieved through an effective unbundling of network operation from other activities of vertically integrated gas undertakings.[10]

Gas network is divided into transmission and distribution levels. In order to enable transport of gas on long distances, high pressure pipelines are deployed on the transmission level.[11] Distribution of gas to end consumers takes place through lower pressure pipelines on the distribution level.[12] Germany as well as the EU is in principle dependent on the imports of natural gas.[13]

---

9 See *Timofeeva*, Unbundling in the Russian electricity industry, p. 5 with further sources.

10 See *Säcker*, in: Säcker, Handbook of German-Russian energy law, p. 168 ff.

11 See *Monopolkommission*, Electricity and Gas 2007, para. 427. See also *Wendt*, Capacity Congestions, p. 7.

12 See ibid.

13 See ibid.

II. Legal framework of access to gas networks in the EU and Germany

1. Development of the EU legal framework of access to natural gas networks

In the following, the EU legal framework of access to natural gas networks will be described. Along with the development of network access regulation by the Energy Packages, changes in unbundling requirements will also be emphasised.

a) Gas Directive 1998

The liberalisation process of the gas industry of Germany started out from the EU level with the first Directive 98/30/EC[14] (hereinafter Gas Directive 1998). With regard to access to the network, the Gas Directive 1998 aimed at the creation of a non-discriminatory access regime. This would in turn lead to a sufficient and comparable level of opening-up of markets in different Member States.[15] Specifically, the Gas Directive 1998 obliged the Member States to introduce either or both procedures of negotiated and regulated access to gas networks in their national laws.[16] Further, the Gas Directive 1998 introduced mandatory unbundling of accounts for natural gas transmission, distribution and storage activities of integrated natural gas undertakings[17] as well as confidentiality requirements (informational unbundling).[18]

From the options offered by the Gas Directive 1998, Germany transposed both procedures of network access, however, in practice the negotiated access[19] was applied far more frequently due to the existence of the

---

14 Directive 98/30/EC of the European Parliament and of the Council of 22 June 1998 concerning common rules for the internal market in natural gas, OJ L 204, 21.07.1998, pp. 1–12.

15 See Recital 23 of the Gas Directive 1998.

16 Art. 14 to Art. 16 of the Gas Directive 1998.

17 Art. 13 of the Gas Directive 1998.

18 Art. 8 para. 1 and Art. 11 para. 1 of the Gas Directive 1998; see also *Säcker/Schönborn*, in: Säcker, Berlin Commentary on energy law, t. 1, p. 445, para. 4.

19 The German version of Art. 15 para. 1 of the Gas Directive 1998 refers to the term 'Netzzugang auf Vertragsbasis', i.e. network access on a contractual basis. See *Büdenbender*, Commentary on EnWG, p. 187, para. 37.

so-called Associations Agreements (*Verbändevereinbarung*), which, inter alia, regulated the formation of the network access charges.[20] The attempt to create competition in energy networks without state regulation had only had limited success and was terminated by the adoption of the second energy package.[21]

b) Gas Directive 2003

The Gas Directive 1998 was repealed by the Directive 2003/55/EC[22] (hereinafter Gas Directive 2003), which imposed on the Member States the transposition of a wider range of provisions as compared with its predecessor.[23] As a supplement to the Gas Directive 2003 and part of the so-called second energy package, the Regulation 1775/2005[24] (hereinafter Gas Regulation 2005) entered into force on 01.07.2006.

With regard to access to the network, the Gas Directive 2003 revoked the option of the Member States to set up the negotiated access and obliged them to "ensure the implementation of a system of third party access to the transmission and distribution system, and liquefied natural gas (hereinafter LNG) facilities based on published tariffs, applicable to all eligible customers, including supply undertakings, and applied objectively and without discrimination between system users".[25] The option of the negotiated access was kept only with regard to access to storage facilities and linepacks, as well as upstream gas pipelines.[26] In order to be able to implement the prescribed obligation, the Gas Directive

20 See *Säcker/Boesche*, in: Säcker, Berlin Commentary on energy law, t. 1, p. 1230, para. 3. The legislator of Germany was criticised by the European Commission for introducing legally unbinding Associations Agreement Gas within the framework of implementing the Gas Directive 1998. See *Kemper*, Access to gas networks in Germany and in Spain, p. 33 f. with further sources.

21 See *Theobald/Zenke/Dessau*, in: Schneider/Theobald, Law of energy industry, para. 82, p. 893 f.

22 Directive 2003/55/EC of the European Parliament and of the Council of 26 June 2003 concerning common rules for the internal market in natural gas and repealing Directive 98/30/EC, OJ L 176, 15.07.2003, pp. 57–78.

23 See *Kemper*, Access to gas networks in Germany and in Spain, p. 35 f.

24 Regulation (EC) No 1775/2005 of the European Parliament and of the Council of 28 September 2005 on conditions for access to the natural gas transmission networks, OJ L 289, 03.11.2005, pp. 1–13.

25 Art. 18 para. 1 of the Gas Directive 2003.

26 Art. 19 and Art. 20 of the Gas Directive 2003. See also *Johnston/Block*, EU Energy Law, para. 4.31 ff., p. 83 ff.

2003 also required the Member States to establish a wholly independent regulatory authority at least responsible for, inter alia, ensuring non-discrimination, effective competition and the efficient functioning of the market. This also involved fixing or approving the methodologies used to calculate or establish the terms and tariffs for the connection and access to transmission and distribution networks, prior to their entry into force.[27]

Moreover, in Art. 21 para. 1 the Gas Directive 2003 stipulated the grounds for refusal of access, namely: lack of capacity, public service obligations, as well as serious economic and financial difficulties with take-or-pay contracts. In order to revoke any of these grounds of refusal, duly substantiated reasons have to be provided. In any event, take-or-pay contracts cannot be deemed as a legitimate ground for refusal of access, unless an approval from the responsible regulatory authority is sought.[28] Member States have been empowered by the Gas Directive 2003 to take necessary measures to ensure that a natural gas undertaking, which refuses access because of the lack of capacity, makes the necessary enhancements, as long as it is economic to do so or a potential customer is willing to pay for them.[29] By way of harmonising lack of network capacity, when duly substantiated, as a possible ground of refusal of access it should be avoided that network operators (i) refuse granting access to capacity available ('capacity hoarding'), (ii) offer capacity in a less useful manner ('capacity degradation') and (iii) strategically limit investment in their pipeline system ('strategic underinvestment').[30]

For the purpose of promoting investments, the Gas Directive 2003 left the possibility to exempt major new gas infrastructures[31], i.e. interconnectors between Member States, LNG and storage facilities, upon request, from the application of some provisions, including Art. 18 which introduced the mandatory regulated third party access.[32] The exemption may be granted by the regulatory authority under several conditions, namely, if the investment enhances competition in gas

27 Art. 25 para. 1 and para. 2 of the Gas Directive 2003.

28 Art. 27 of the Gas Directive 2003. See also *Waloszyk*, Law and Policy of the European gas market, p. 108 f.

29 Art. 21 para. 2 of the Gas Dircetive 2003. See also *Johnston/Block*, EU Energy Law, para. 4.56 ff., p. 89 ff.

30 See COMP/39.315, ENI para. 43. See also *Kruimer*, Non-discrimination Obligation of Energy Network Operators, p. 121 ff.

31 The Gas Directive 2003 in Art. 2 para. 33 defined "new infrastructure" as an infrastructure not completed by the entry into force of the Directive.

32 Art. 22 para. 1 of the Gas Directive 2003.

supply and security of supply; the level of risk attached to the investment is such that the investment would not take place, unless an exemption was granted; the infrastructure is owned by a natural or legal person which is separate at least in terms of its legal form from the system operators in whose systems that infrastructure will be built; charges are levied on users of that infrastructure; the exemption is not detrimental to competition or the effective functioning of the internal gas market, or the efficient functioning of the regulated system to which the infrastructure is connected.[33] The rationale of the exemption possibility is that some investments may be so significant and risky that they would not take place under the regulated third party access regime, as the investors would be too uncertain about their payback and would rather wish to reserve part of the capacity for their own use.[34]

Further, the Gas Directive 2003 focused on the enhancement of the unbundling provisions through introducing legal and functional, i.e. operational unbundling, in addition to detailing requirements of informational unbundling and separation of accounts. Namely, the operators of transmission and distribution systems, which were parts of vertically integrated undertakings, had to be independent from other activities of the undertaking at least in terms of their legal form, organisation and decision making.[35] The Directive relied on the idea that the operation of the transmission and distribution systems through legally separate entities was necessary to ensure efficient and non-discriminatory network access.[36] The Gas Directive 2003 left the only option for Member States not to introduce the legal and functional unbundling in relation to distribution system operators of the integrated gas undertakings serving less than 100,000 connected customers.[37]

The second energy package was transposed by Germany through the adoption of the German Energy Act[38] (hereinafter EnWG) in 2005, the initial basic structure of which is still being maintained.[39]

33 Art. 22 para. 1 and para. 3 of the Gas Directive 2003.

34 See *Bernaerts*, in: Vinois, EU Energy Law, p. 29.

35 Art. 9 para. 1, Art. 13 para. 1 and Art. 15 of the Gas Directive 2003.

36 See Recital 10 of the Gas Directive 2003.

37 Art. 13 para. 2 sent. 3 of the Gas Directive 2003.

38 German Energy Act [Energiewirtschaftsgesetz] of 07.07.2005 (BGBl. I p. 1970, 3621), last amended through Art. 2 para. 6 of the Law of 20.07.2017 (BGBl. I p. 2808).

39 *Säcker/Boesche*, in: Säcker, Berlin Commentary on energy law, t. 1, p. 1229 f., para. 2.

c) Gas Directive 2009

The Gas Directive 2003 was repealed by the Directive 2009/73/EC[40] (hereinafter Gas Directive 2009), which aimed at further promotion of non-discriminatory network access and an equally effective level of regulatory supervision in each Member State.[41] Another component of the so-called third energy package in relation to natural gas market, the Regulation No 715/2009[42] (hereinafter Gas Regulation 2009) repealed the Gas Regulation 2005 and introduced detailed rules of regulated access to natural gas transmission systems and LNG and storage facilities.

With regard to access to gas networks, the Gas Directive 2009 did not entail any significant changes as compared with its predecessor. The only possibility of regulated access to natural gas transmission and distribution systems and LNG facilities, as well as an option of negotiated access to storage facilities persisted in the Gas Directive 2009 too.[43] The exemption regarding new infrastructure was also maintained.[44] An important novelty of the third energy package in relation to gas markets was the introduction of detailed binding rules for storage system operators concerning the services to be offered by them, as well as the principles of capacity allocation mechanisms and congestion management procedures to be complied with by storage system operators.[45]

The central novelty of the third energy package was rather the introduction of the three options of unbundling of transmission from other activities of a vertically integrated undertaking with the purpose of effective separation of supply and production activities from network operations, which could not be achieved by the rules on legal and functional unbundling provided for by the predecessor of the Gas Directive 2009.[46] It is considered that when the market players controlling transmission or distribution systems are also active on the production or supply side of the gas market, they tend to prevent third party

---

40 Directive 2009/73/EC of the European Parliament and of the Council of 13 July 2009 concerning common rules for the internal market in natural gas and repealing Directive 2003/55/EC, OJ L 211, 14.08.2009, pp. 94–136.

41 See Recital 4 of the Gas Directive 2009.

42 Regulation (EC) No 715/2009 of the European Parliament and of the Council of 13 July 2009 on conditions for access to the natural gas transmission networks and repealing Regulation (EC) No 1775/2005, OJ L 211, 14.08.2009, pp. 36–54.

43 Art. 32 para. 1 and Art. 33 para. 1 of the Gas Directive 2009.

44 Art. 36 of the Gas Directive 2009.

45 Art. 15 and Art. 17 of the Gas Regulation 2009.

46 See also Recital 7 of the Gas Directive 2009.

access (hereinafter also TPA) to networks or to allow such access in exchange for excessive tariffs paid for network use.[47] Unbundling is therefore seen as a kind of universal remedy.[48]

The Member States were entitled to opt for one of the following three unbundling-models for transmission system operators: ownership unbundling, according to which a system is owned and operated by the same undertaking (formal ownership-unbundling[49]), and the same persons are not entitled to exercise control over an undertaking performing the function of either production or supply and over a transmission operator (material ownership-unbundling[50]);[51] the independent-system-operator-model (ISO-model[52]), according to which the transmission system still belongs to a vertically integrated gas undertaking, but for the operation, maintenance, development of the network, and for provision of access services an independent system operator is designated, with a sufficient degree of independence from the owner of the transmission system in view of ownership as well as staff;[53] the independent-transmission-operator-model (ITO-model), which implies only a legal unbundling of transmission system operators from vertically integrated undertakings, however, with stricter requirements for operational independence as compared to the predecessor model introduced by the Gas Directive 2003.[54] Like the Treaty on the Functioning of the EU, the third energy package is neutral regarding either public or private ownership of transmission operators.[55]

In addition, the Gas Directive 2009 also introduced the mandatory legal and functional unbundling of those storage facilities that are technically and/or economically necessary for providing efficient access to the system for the supply

47 See *Waloszyk*, Law and Policy of the European gas market, p. 27. See also COMP/39.316, GDF gas foreclosure and COMP/39.317, E.ON gas foreclosure.

48 See *Busch*, in: Ehricke, Expectations towards the new energy law, p. 120.

49 See *Säcker/Mohr*, in: Säcker, Berlin Commentary on energy law, t. 1, p. 609, para. 14.

50 See ibid.

51 Art. 9 of the Gas Directive 2009.

52 Also referred to as 'deep-ISO-model'. For further details as well as difference from the so-called 'shallow-ISO-model' see *Säcker/Mohr*, in: Säcker, Berlin Commentary on energy law, t. 1, p. 667 f., para. 3 f. See also *Säcker*, The independent system operator, p. 37 ff.

53 Art. 14 of the Gas Directive 2009; see *Kemper*, Access to gas networks in Germany and in Spain, p. 43 f. with further sources.

54 Art. 17 of the Gas Directive 2009; see *Kemper*, Access to gas networks in Germany and in Spain, p. 44 with further sources.

55 See *Bernaerts*, in: Vinois, EU Energy Law, p. 23.

of customers.[56] In relation to distribution system operators, the Gas Directive 2009 kept the minimum requirement of legal and functional unbundling.[57]

First set of tertiary rules, developed on the basis of the third energy package also harmonised the rules on congestion management procedure in order to maximise transmission capacity of interconnection points.[58] According to Art. 2 para. 1 N 5 of the Gas Regulation 2009, congestion management means management of the capacity portfolio of the transmission system operator with a view to optimal and maximum use of the technical capacity and the timely detection of future congestion and saturation points.

2. Legal framework of connection and access to gas networks in Germany

In the following, the current legal framework of connection and access to gas networks in Germany will be described, as it has been transposed based on the requirements of the EU Gas Directives. First, the unbundling rules applicable to the undertakings of Germany operating in the gas sector will be addressed, followed by the legal basis of connection and access to gas networks.

a) Unbundling requirements

As described above, along with the informational unbundling and separation of accounts introduced by the Gas Directive 1998, as well as the legal and functional unbundling imposed by the Gas Directive 2003, the Gas Directive 2009 required from the Member States to transpose one of the three unbundling-models, for the purpose of effective separation of transmission from other activities of a vertically integrated natural gas undertaking.[59]

aa) Unbundling of transmission system operators

From the three options of unbundling of transmission system operators from vertically integrated undertakings, offered by the Gas Directive 2009, the legislator of Germany transposed into EnWG all three of them and offered in its turn to the vertically integrated undertakings to make a choice between these three

56 Art. 15 para. 1 of the Gas Directive 2009.

57 Art. 26 of the Gas Directive 2009.

58 See *Bernaerts*, in: Vinois, EU Energy Law, p. 16.

59 See above A.II.1.c).

forms. Thus, vertically integrated energy supply undertakings[60] may either opt for an ownership-unbundling[61], an ISO-[62] or an ITO-model[63].

However, in order to avoid strengthening of vertical integration, the EnWG stipulated[64] that vertically integrated energy supply undertakings may opt for ISO- or ITO-models only in the cases where these undertakings owned the network in question as of 03.09.2009.[65] As a result of the transposition of unbundling provisions of the Gas Directive 2009 into the national law of Germany, vertically integrated energy supply undertakings have to separate their transmission activities at least according to ITO-model.

bb) Unbundling of distribution and storage system operators

In relation to distribution system operators, the EnWG prescribes a legal (sec. 7) as well as an operational unbundling (sec. 7a), as required by the EU Directives and lays down that vertically integrated energy supply undertakings have to ensure that their distribution system operators (i.e. connected with them in the sense of sec. 3 N 38 of the EnWG) are independent in terms of their legal form, organisation, decision making and operation of networks. An exception from the obligation is foreseen for the vertically integrated energy supply undertakings, to the distribution network of which less than 100,000 customers are directly or indirectly connected.[66] Transmission system owners where the ISO-model has been applied, and storage system operators, which are part of a vertically integrated energy supply undertaking and access to the facilities of which are technically and economically necessary for providing efficient access to the system for the supply of customers, are required to comply with the same conditions of legal and functional unbundling.[67]

---

60 The provisions of EnWG relating to unbundling refer mostly to energy supply undertakings instead of differentiating between gas and electricity.

61 Sec. 8 of the EnWG.

62 Sec. 9 of the EnWG.

63 Sec. 10 and sec. 10a-10e of the EnWG.

64 Sec. 6 sent. 3, sec. 9 para. 1 and sec. 10 para. 1 of the EnWG.

65 BT-Drs. 343/11, p. 144; see also *Säcker/Schönborn*, in: Säcker, Berlin Commentary on energy law, t. 1, p. 660, para. 117 and *Pisal*, Unbundling options, p. 190.

66 Sec. 7 para. 2 and sec. 7a para. 7 of the EnWG.

67 Sec. 7b of the EnWG; cf. also Art. 15 para. 1 of the Gas Directive 2009.

b) Regulation of connection to gas supply networks

In the part 3 "Regulation of network operation" the EnWG draws a distinction between network connection and network access. While network connection (sec. 17 ff. of the EnWG) concerns the physical connection to a certain network, the provisions regarding network access (sec. 20 ff. of the EnWG) regulate the injection of gas (and electricity) into the network as well as the extraction of gas from the network.[68] Sec. 17 and 18 of the EnWG in principle oblige the network operators to grant connection, complemented through entitlement to network access in sec. 20 as the right to use someone else's pipelines with the purpose of injecting, transporting and extracting power.[69] Notably, there is no term in energy law which would be able to consolidate the notions of network connection and access.[70] Moreover, 'use of connection'[71] has to be also differentiated from the two terms.[72]

Sec. 18 of the EnWG entitles any party to the connection to low pressure energy supply networks and is therefore also called the "general obligation to connect".[73] Sec. 17 of the EnWG on the other hand, contains the obligation of the operators of energy supply networks and entitles all other seekers of the connection to high or middle pressure pipelines as well as those that are not entitled to the connection pursuant to sec. 18.[74] For this reason the provision is also referred to as the "specific obligation to connect".[75] However, considering the system of the EnWG, sec. 17 is a general provision and, therefore, the fundamental norm for the network connection right, whereas sec. 18 constitutes a special provision since it merely refers to the entitlement of the end consumers to the connection to low pressure pipelines.[76] Therefore, sec. 17 of the EnWG will be described in the following.

---

68 See *Theobald/Nill-Theobald*, Fundamentals of energy industry law, p. 243 with further sources. See also *Theobald/Zenke/Dessau*, in: Schneider/Theobald, Law of energy industry, para. 34, p. 881.

69 See *Theobald/Nill-Theobald*, Fundamentals of energy industry law, p. 243 with further sources.

70 See *Salje*, in: Baur/Salje/Schmidt-Preuß, Regulation in the energy industry, p. 801 f., para. 2.

71 *Anschlussnutzung*.

72 See *Koenig/Kühling/Rasbach*, Energy law, p. 62 f., para. 4 f.

73 See *Theobald/Nill-Theobald*, Fundamentals of energy industry law, p. 245.

74 See *Hartig*, in: Stuhlmacher/Stappert/Schoon/Jansen, Energy law, para. 50, p. 89.

75 See *Theobald/Nill-Theobald*, Fundamentals of energy industry law, p. 245.

76 See *Salje*, EnWG, p. 500, para. 3. See also *Theobald/Nill-Theobald*, Fundamentals of energy industry law, p. 245.

Sec. 17 para. 1 of the EnWG lists the persons entitled to the connection under this provision. These are the end consumers, defined as natural or legal persons that buy energy for their own use by sec. 3 N 25 of the EnWG; operators of same-level or downstream energy supply networks and pipelines, whereas sec. 3 N 4 of the EnWG defines the operators of energy supply networks as operators of electricity and gas networks; and operators of production and storage facilities.

According to the prevailing opinion, the right to connect to the network does not constitute a statutory obligatory relationship itself, in which case the person seeking for the connection would have to be granted such connection directly based on the law.[77] Instead, the legislator has introduced an obligation to contract[78], according to which sec. 17 para. 1 as well as sec. 18 para. 1 entitle to the conclusion of a network connection contract.[79] Thus the legal relationship between network operators and connection seekers is specified only through the network connection contract, the contents of which are in many cases prescribed by various regulations.[80] Technically, the connection to the network can be implemented by the network operator as well as by a third party, however under condition that the technical requirements of the network operator are duly respected.[81] The relationship of connection to the network encompasses not only setting up of the connection itself but also its further operation so that the network operator would violate its obligation to grant connection to the network if it disrupts the connection.[82]

---

77 See *Theobald/Nill-Theobald*, Fundamentals of energy industry law, p. 245. See also *Theobald/Zenke/Dessau*, in: Schneider/Theobald, Law of energy industry, para. 37, p. 881 f., *Bourwieg*, in: Britz/Hellermann/Hermes, EnWG, p. 585, para. 8, *Salje*, in: Baur/Salje/Schmidt-Preuß, Regulation in the energy industry, p. 803 f., para. 8, *Säcker/Boesche*, in: Säcker, Berlin Commentary on energy law, t. 1, p. 1074, para. 6.

78 Regarding difference between statutory right and obligation to contract in relation to network access right see *Britz*, in Fehling/Ruffert, Regulatory Law, p. 450, para. 38.

79 See *Theobald/Nill-Theobald*, Fundamentals of energy industry law, p. 245. See also *Theobald/Zenke/Dessau*, in: Schneider/Theobald, Law of energy industry, para. 37, p. 881 f.

80 See *Theobald/Nill-Theobald*, Fundamentals of energy industry law, p. 245 f. See also *Theobald/Zenke/Dessau*, in: Schneider/Theobald, Law of energy industry, para. 37, p. 881 f.

81 See *Theobald/Nill-Theobald*, Fundamentals of energy industry law, p. 246.

82 See *Salje*, EnWG, p. 515, para. 32. See also *Theobald/Zenke/Dessau*, in: Schneider/Theobald, Law of energy industry, para. 41, p. 882 f. *Theobald/Nill-Theobald*, Fundamentals of energy industry law, p. 246.

As to conditions of the network connection, sec. 17 para. 1 sent. 1 of the EnWG prescribes that the connection has to be realised under reasonable, non-discriminatory and transparent technical and economic conditions, which are not less favourable than such used by the network operators in comparable cases for the services within the undertaking or towards connected or associated undertakings.

Since all network operators have a general obligation to grant a connection to their networks, a refusal to connect is only permissible in exceptional cases.[83] According to sec. 17 para. 2 of the EnWG, the network operators may refuse to grant connection only if they substantiate that this is not possible or not reasonable on operational or other grounds, taking into account the objectives of sec. 1 of the law. The reasoning of the refusal has to be provided in written form.

Based on sec. 17 para. 2 sent. 3 of the EnWG, the reasoning in the case of lack of capacity has to contain sound information concerning the measures and costs necessary for the construction of the network, which would enable the connection. Thus, a mere formulaic explanation would not suffice.[84]

According to sec. 17 para. 2 sent. 4 of the EnWG, the network operator may demand a compensation for providing the reasoning, as long as it has pointed to the arising of costs beforehand. However, the fee to be paid by the connection seeker should not be in excess of the half of the costs incurred by the network operator for providing the explanation.

The right to connect to the network can be enforced in the ordinary court through the action demanding performance[85] on the one hand.[86] On the other hand, refusal to connect to the network without a legitimate ground constitutes an abuse of market position by the network operator pursuant to sec. 30 para. 1 N 1 of the EnWG, according to which the violation of the provisions of chapters 2 and 3 of the EnWG (including sec. 17 and 18) by a network operator represents an abusive conduct. Such conduct is prohibited as per sec. 30 para. 1 sent. 1 of the EnWG. The persons and groups of persons, whose interests have been substantially affected by the conduct of a network operator, may file an application to the regulatory authority pursuant to sec. 31 para. 1 of the EnWG. The regulatory authority has a number of powers, which it can employ in order to

83 See *Theobald/Nill-Theobald*, Fundamentals of energy industry law, p. 246.

84 See *Theobald/Zenke/Dessau*, in: Schneider/Theobald, Law of energy industry, para. 49, p. 884 f.

85 *Leistungsklage*.

86 See *Salje*, in: Baur/Salje/Schmidt-Preuß, Regulation in the energy industry, p. 805, para. 14.

effectively remedy the abuse, including ordering connection to the network as well as adjustment of the conditions or alteration of network connection fees.[87]

c) Regulation of access to gas supply networks

From the legal point of view, access to the network is the purchase of the rights to use the pipeline system belonging to a third party and serving the supply.[88] The statutory right of access to energy supply networks[89] is also called third party access, constitutes an exception from private autonomy principle[90] and is an indispensable prerequisite of introduction of competition.[91] In German legal doctrine the statutory obligation to grant access to networks is also referred to as a type of obligation to contract (a relative or an indirect obligation to contract).[92]

In the legislation of Germany access to energy supply networks is primarily regulated through sec. 20 of the EnWG. The provision prescribes whether and how to grant access and equally concerns gas as well as electricity supply networks.[93] According to sec. 20 para. 1 sent. 1 of the EnWG, operators of energy supply networks have to grant non-discriminatory network access to everyone according to objectively justified criteria.

In addition, the practical implementation of access to gas supply networks is enabled by the Regulation on access to gas supply networks[94] (hereinafter GasNZV), adopted on the basis of sec. 24 of the EnWG.

---

87 See also *Theobald/Zenke/Dessau*, in: Schneider/Theobald, Law of energy industry, para. 35, p. 881.

88 See *Salje*, in: Baur/Salje/Schmidt-Preuß, Regulation in the energy industry, p. 801 f., para. 2.

89 Also referred to as 'network access right under private law', see *Britz*, in Fehling/Ruffert, Regulatory Law, p. 449, para. 37, as well as 'statutory obligatory relationship to be defined contractually', see *Höppner*, Regulation of network structure, p. 197.

90 See *Höppner*, Network changes in access concept, p. 33.

91 See *Säcker/Boesche*, in: Säcker, Berlin Commentary on energy law, t. 1, p. 1233, para. 11.

92 *Kontrahierungszwang*. See *Busche*, Private autonomy and obligation to contract, p. 117 f. and 299 ff.

93 See the definition in sec. 3 N 16 of the EnWG, according to which gas as well as electricity supply networks constitute energy supply networks.

94 Regulation on access to gas supply networks [Gasnetzzugangsverordnung] of 03.09. 2010 (BGBl. I p. 1261), last amended through Art. 1 of the Regulation of 11.08.2017 (BGBl. I p. 3194).

aa) Entitlement to network access

According to sec. 20 para. 1 sent. 1 of the EnWG, the obliged parties of granting TPA to gas supply networks are the operators of gas supply networks, i.e. natural or legal persons, or legally non-independent organisational entities of a vertically integrated energy supply undertaking, operating gas supply networks.[95] However, the operator of the gas network does not necessarily coincide with the owner of the network.[96] The notion of 'gas supply networks' cover gas transmission and distribution networks, as well as LNG and storage facilities, necessary for access to transmission, distribution or LNG facilities.[97]

According to the wording of the provision, 'everyone' can make use of the TPA right.[98] Gas suppliers,[99] wholesalers[100] and other network users[101] come into consideration as the holders of the right of access to gas supply networks.[102]

Further, even though the wording of the provision does not mention this condition, it follows from its ratio legis that, in order to successfully claim the TPA right, the access seeker has to be dependent on the access to the network for the participation in the competition on the supply or production side.[103] Dependency on the access means that the access seeker has no other sufficient and reasonable possibility, to which it could switch in order to supply its customers.[104]

The wording of the provision, in accordance with the Gas Directive 2009[105], refers to 'granting network access', i.e. the obligation of the network operator to open its network to third parties and to let them use it for the purpose of supplying their customers.[106] Thus, the right of access to the network implies the

---

95 Sec. 3 N 6 of the EnWG.

96 See *Kment*, in: Kment, EnWG, para. 7, p. 474 with more details.

97 Sec. 3 N 20 of the EnWG.

98 The term has been introduced to the EnWG in order to cover also natural persons (as well as pool of individuals) along with legal persons. See *Säcker/Boesche*, in: Säcker, Berlin Commentary on energy law, t. 1, p. 1235, para. 17 and 21.

99 See the definition of a gas supplier under sec. 3 N 19b of the EnWG.

100 See the definition of a wholesaler under sec. 3 N 21 of the EnWG.

101 See the definition of a network user under sec. 3 N 28 of the EnWG.

102 See *Säcker/Boesche*, in: Säcker, Berlin Commentary on energy law, t. 1, p. 1235, para. 17.

103 See *Säcker/Boesche*, in: Säcker, Berlin Commentary on energy law, t. 1, p. 1236 f., para. 22.

104 See ibid.

105 See Art. 32 ff. of the Gas Directive 2009.

106 See *Säcker/Boesche*, in: Säcker, Berlin Commentary on energy law, t. 1, p. 1238 f., para. 24 ff.

right to use the network belonging to a third party.[107] The use of network itself constitutes a statutory obligatory relationship.[108]

Further, sec. 20 para. 1 sent. 1 prescribes that access has to be non-discriminatory and based on objectively justified criteria.[109] First of all, this condition covers granting immediate access without discrimination of extern network users against the ones affiliated with the network operator.[110] Secondly, the conditions of using the network have to be non-discriminatory, especially when defining appropriate charges for use of network.[111] Further, both forms of discrimination, vertical, i.e. unequal treatment of external network users against the ones affiliated with the network operator, as well as horizontal, i.e. unequal treatment of an extern network user against other extern network users, are prohibited.[112]

The requirement of granting access on objectively justified criteria implies an obligation to create reasonable access possibilities so that an efficient network usage is being enabled.[113] Unnecessary or disproportionate technical requirements on the part of network operator should be avoided and transaction costs should be kept at minimum.[114]

bb) Obligation of publishing information

Network operators have to publish the conditions of network access, model contracts, concession fees, as well as the charges for use of the network on the internet.[115] Further, network operators have to provide the network users with the information necessary for an efficient network access.[116]

---

107 See *Säcker/Boesche*, in: Säcker, Berlin Commentary on energy law, t. 1, p. 1238, para. 26.

108 See *Thole*, in: Säcker, Berlin Commentary on energy law, t. 1, p. 1271, para. 132.

109 This standard has to be understood as a uniform one since objective justification cannot be rationally separated from the principle of non-discrimination. See *Säcker/Boesche*, in: Säcker, Berlin Commentary on energy law, t. 1, p. 1243, para. 39.

110 See *Säcker/Boesche*, in: Säcker, Berlin Commentary on energy law, t. 1, p. 1243, para. 39.

111 See ibid.

112 See *Säcker/Boesche*, in: Säcker, Berlin Commentary on energy law, t. 1, p. 1243 f., para. 40 f.

113 See *Kment*, in: Kment, EnWG, para. 11, p. 475.

114 See ibid.

115 Sec. 20 para. 1 sent. 1 of the EnWG.

116 Sec. 20 para. 1 sent. 4 of the EnWG.

The most important information for the network user subject to publication is the amount of fees for use of the network, which has to be approved by the regulatory authorities in advance and thus, the parties are not free to negotiate.[117] On the contrary, model contracts do not have the same level of importance on which the implementation of the rights of network users would depend since it is not mandatory to conclude the contract according to a model; still, their publishing contributes to overall transparency.[118] As to the extent of the difficulty of the information provided, the EnWG in sec. 20 para. 1 sent. 5 contains a requirement that the rules concerning network access have to be suitable for the masses, i.e. clear and understandable. Standardisation and simplification will add to the further automatisation of the procedure for network access in future.[119]

The scope of the obligation of gas supply network operators concerning publishing information is prescribed in more detail in sec. 40 of the GasNZV. The information concerning available transport capacities as well as expected capacity congestions, i.e. the situations where the capacity is insufficient to satisfy the entirety of the demand, has to be communicated only upon request of a potential network user since these data can be disclosed with reference to a concrete time period and a relevant geographic section of the network.[120] Upon request access seekers have to be informed about the suitable quality of gas which may be injected into the network since this information is also dependent on the various criteria (point of the planned injection, point of extraction, duration etc.).[121]

The regulatory authorities may impose fines on network operators in the case of a failure to meet the obligation of publishing information.[122]

cc) Obligation of cooperation

Network operators are obliged to cooperate with each other to the extent necessary for provision of efficient network access.[123] In particular, gas supply network

117 See *Säcker/Boesche*, in: Säcker, Berlin Commentary on energy law, t. 1, p. 1244 f., para. 44 f.

118 See *Säcker/Boesche*, in: Säcker, Berlin Commentary on energy law, t. 1, p. 1245, para. 45.

119 See *Kment*, in: Kment, EnWG, para. 19, p. 476 f.

120 See *Säcker/Boesche*, in: Säcker, Berlin Commentary on energy law, t. 1, p. 1247, para. 51.

121 See *Säcker/Boesche*, in: Säcker, Berlin Commentary on energy law, t. 1, p. 1247, para. 52.

122 Sec. 31 in conjunction with sec. 30 para. 1 sent. 1 and sec. 95 para. 1 N 4 of the EnWG.

123 Sec. 20 para. 1 sent. 3 of the EnWG.

operators have to enter into a binding cooperation with each other to the extent that is necessary for the implementation of gas transport for a transport customer[124] through several networks only with an entry and exit contract, unless the cooperation is technically impossible or economically unreasonable.[125] The aim of the obligation of cooperation is to arrange access to networks as uncomplicated and as free of barriers as possible.[126]

dd) Obligation to enhance network

According to sec. 11 para. 1 sent. 1 of the EnWG, operators of energy networks are, apart from their obligation to operate[127], bound to optimise, enhance and expand the network needs-based, as far as it is economically feasible for them to do so. This obligation can be enforced by the regulatory authority on its own initiative as well as upon request of an access seeker, however the provision does not foresee a possibility of enforcement under private law since it aims predominantly at protection of public interest and those of private persons play a secondary role.[128] Moreover, pursuant to sec. 15 para. 3, transmission as well as distribution network operators[129] are obliged, among others, to contribute to the security of supply through corresponding transport capacities and reliability of their networks.

ee) Arrangement of access to gas supply networks

In Germany the Associations Agreements constituted the first regulations for arranging gas network access, which, however, were not of a statutory nature but a sort of self-commitment of the gas industry.[130] The last Associations Agreement

---

124 Sec. 3 N 31b of the EnWG: A transport customer [Transportkunde] is a wholesaler, a gas supplier including trading division of a vertically integrated undertaking and a final consumer in the gas sector.

125 Sec. 20 para. 1b sent. 5 of the EnWG.

126 See *Säcker/Boesche*, in: Säcker, Berlin Commentary on energy law, t. 1, p. 1248, para. 56.

127 I.e. obligation to operate a secure, reliable and efficient energy supply network in a non-discriminatory manner (sec. 11 para. 1 sent. 1 of the EnWG). See also *Höppner*, Regulation of network structure, p. 202.

128 See *Wendt*, Capacity Congestions, p. 155 ff.

129 Even though sec. 15 para. 3 of the EnWG refers to only transmission network operators, sec. 16a declares the provision also applicable to distribution network operators.

130 See *Thole*, in: Säcker, Berlin Commentary on energy law, t. 1, p. 1262, para. 98.

Natural Gas II[131] was based on the concept of point-to-point-transmission, the so-called 'contract path model'.[132] In this model the transport customer had to conclude separate contracts with each network operator managing the relevant section of the network in the route from the entry to the exit point.[133] The calculation of charges was made according to the distance based on the system of point numbers on the transmission level and based on the stamp tariff on the distribution level.[134]

After the introduction of the mandatory regulated access to gas networks on the EU level, leaving the determination of the concrete model of arrangement of access to the Member States, Germany, after a lengthy and controversial legislative process, decided to incorporate the so-called 'entry-exit model' in the law.[135] In addition, the Cooperation Agreement[136] (hereinafter CoA) concluded between gas supply network operators is simultaneously applicable[137] and regulates the process of cooperation between the gas supply network operators in order to meet the obligations imposed on them by virtue of sec. 20 para. 1 sent. 3 as well as para. 1b of the EnWG (obligation of cooperation).

(1) Entry-exit model of network access

The entry-exit model of network access foresees the arrangement of network access based on only two contracts, entry and exit contracts, irrespective of the quantity of networks concerned by the transport.[138] This model, also called 'two-contract principle', is stipulated in sec. 20 para. 1b sent. 2 and 3, according to

131 *Verbändevereinbarung Erdgas II*, concluded on 03.05.2002 between BDI, VIK, BGW, and VKU with the duration until 30.09.2003.

132 See *Thole*, in: Säcker, Berlin Commentary on energy law, t. 1, p. 1262, para. 99.

133 See ibid.

134 See ibid.

135 See *Thole*, in: Säcker, Berlin Commentary on energy law, t. 1, p. 1264 ff., para. 107 ff. See also *Brodt*, Gas network access model, p. 43 ff.

136 Cooperation Agreement between operators of gas supply networks located in Germany [Kooperationsvereinbarung zwischen den Betreibern von in Deutschland gelegenen Gasversorgungsnetzen], as last amended on 30.06.2016, entry into force on 01.10.2016, available at: http://www.bdew.de/internet.nsf/id/DE_Kooperationsvereinbaru-Gas.

137 For more details on the negotiations concerning the CoA see *Thole*, in: Säcker, Berlin Commentary on energy law, t. 1, p. 1267 ff., para. 116 ff.

138 See *Thole*, in: Säcker, Berlin Commentary on energy law, t. 1, p. 1266, para. 114. See criticism of the model at the stage of discussing the legislative initiative in *Barbknecht*, in: Ehricke, New law of energy industry, p. 72.

which access to gas supply networks is implemented through an entry contract[139] on entry capacities with the network operator, to the network of which the gas has to be injected, and an exit contract[140] on exit capacities with the network operator, from the network of which the gas has to be extracted. Since there are large numbers of different ownership and management relations to the gas supply networks, the operators are obliged to further organise the transport internally in order to comply with the two-contract principle.[141] For the purpose of simplifying the process of supplying a number of end-customers in the same network, the exit contract can be concluded as a framework exit contract with a distribution network operator.[142] The two-contract model has significantly enhanced competition since the network users have to conclude only two contracts and the gas injected for transportation is not identical with the gas factually extracted, apart from the volume.[143]

The legal definition of the entry-exit model is stipulated in sec. 20 para. 1b sent. 10 of the EnWG, according to which transmission network operators are obliged to arrange the rights on booked capacity in such a manner that they entitle the transport customers to supply gas at any entry point for the off-take at any exit point of their network, or a part of the network in the case of permanent congestions. Since there is usually no congestion on local distribution level, distribution network operators are obliged to make all exit points available for the entry points of their networks.[144] The entry-exit model is further developed to the market-area-model in the GasNZV. According to sec. 20 para. 1 sent. 1 and 2 of the GasNZV, transmission network operators form market areas and designate a market area coordinator for each area. Pursuant to sec. 20 para. 1 sent. 3 of the GasNZV, market area coordinators have to be responsible for the operation of the virtual trading point of the market area, arrangement of balancing group, and acquisition and control of use of balancing energy.

---

139 *Einspeisevertrag* sec. 20 para. 1b sent. 2 of the EnWG.

140 *Ausspeisevertrag* sec. 20 para. 1b sent. 3 of the EnWG.

141 Sec. 20 para. 1b sent. 5 of the EnWG. See *Thole*, in: Säcker, Berlin Commentary on energy law, t. 1, p. 1273, para. 140.

142 Sec. 20 para. 1b sent.4 of the EnWG. See *Thole*, in: Säcker, Berlin Commentary on energy law, t. 1, p. 1273, para. 140.

143 See *Knappke*, in: Stuhlmacher/Stappert/Schoon/Jansen, Energy law, para. 130, p. 160.

144 Sec. 20 para. 1b sent. 11 of the EnWG. See *Thole*, in: Säcker, Berlin Commentary on energy law, t. 1, p. 1272 f., para. 139.

(2) Freely allocable capacities

The principal characteristic and the main advantage of the two-contracts principle is that the transport customers can freely combine (allocate) the entry and exit capacities[145] within a market area.[146] The transport customer is entitled to supply gas volumes within the scope of its booking at any booked entry point for the off-take at any booked exit point of the network or a part of the network, without determining the transport route in advance.[147] The principle of 'free allocability of capacities' (also called 'the principle of non-dependence on transport path') constitutes the basic element of the entry-exit model.[148] The scope of the free allocability of capacities is not limited to the ownership borders of individual networks.[149]

The capacity products have to be designed orientating towards the demand of the transport customers and in conformity with the provisions of efficient and practicable network access.[150] The transmission network operators have to offer the transport customers firm and interruptible capacities.[151] According to the definitions of the Gas Regulation 2009, Art. 2 para. 1 N 13 and N 16, 'interruptible capacity' means gas transmission capacity that may be interrupted by the transmission system operator in accordance with the conditions stipulated in the transport contract, whereas 'firm capacity' means gas transmission capacity contractually guaranteed as uninterruptible by the transmission system operator.[152] Firm capacity may not be interrupted by the network operator, i.e. the transport customer can use it at any time within the scope of its booking.[153] On the contrary, interruptible capacity cannot be used by the transport customer at any time since

---

145 Entry capacity is the maximum volume of gas per hour in standard cubic meters, which can be injected at an entry point to a network or to a part of a network of a network operator in total (sec. 3 N 13a of the EnWG). Exit capacity is the maximum volume of gas per hour in standard cubic meters, which can be extracted at an exit point from a network or from a part of a network in total and which can be booked (sec. 3 N 1a of the EnWG).

146 See *Thole*, in: Säcker, Berlin Commentary on energy law, t. 1, p. 1275, para. 144.

147 Sec. 8 para. 2 sent. 1 of the GasNZV. See Thole, in: Säcker, Berlin Commentary on energy law, t. 1, p. 1275, para. 144.

148 See *Thole*, in: Säcker, Berlin Commentary on energy law, t. 1, p. 1275, para. 144.

149 See *Thole*, in: Säcker, Berlin Commentary on energy law, t. 1, p. 1275, para. 145.

150 See *Thole*, in: Säcker, Berlin Commentary on energy law, t. 1, p. 1278 f., para. 152.

151 Sec. 11 para. 1 of the GasNZV.

152 These capacity products are defined neither in the EnWG nor in the GasNZV.

153 See *Thole*, in: Säcker, Berlin Commentary on energy law, t. 1, p. 1278 f., para. 152.

it may be interrupted by the network operator under certain circumstances.[154] In addition, the probability of an interruption has to be reflected in the demanded charges, which also serves as an informant of the existing risk of interruption for the transport customer.[155] Firm and interruptible capacities are two different capacity products; therefore assignment of interruptible capacities instead of requested firm capacities constitutes a refusal of network access in the sense of sec. 20 para. 2 of the EnWG and not granting of modified access.[156]

The capacity products have to be offered on a yearly, quarterly, monthly, daily as well as intra-day basis.[157] Gas transmission network operators have to auction firm and interruptible capacities through a capacity booking platform in a transparent and non-discriminatory procedure.[158]

(3) Independent usability, tradability and transfer of capacity rights

Entry and exit capacities have to be accessible independently of each other.[159] Independent using means that entry and exit capacities can be booked in different levels and at different times independently from each other.[160]

Further, entry and exit capacities have to be tradable.[161] For the purpose of simplifying trading with capacity rights the operators of capacity booking platforms are obliged to arrange online presence of the platforms.[162]

In the case of a change of supplier, the new supplier can demand from the former supplier the transfer of the booked entry and exit capacities necessary for supplying the customers, if the new supplier is not able to meet its supply obligations otherwise and can substantiate this.[163] With the introduction of this so-called 'rucksack principle' the legislator has freed new suppliers, and hence the desirable change of suppliers, from the insecurity of capacity issues.[164]

---

154 See ibid.

155 See *Thole*, in: Säcker, Berlin Commentary on energy law, t. 1, p. 1278 f., para. 152.

156 See *Thole*, in: Säcker, Berlin Commentary on energy law, t. 1, p. 1279, para. 154.

157 Sec. 11 para. 1 of the GasNZV.

158 Sec. 13 para. 1 sent. 1 of the GasNZV. See for more details *Thole*, in: Säcker, Berlin Commentary on energy law, t. 1, p. 1280, para. 156.

159 Sec. 20 para. 1b sent. 1 of the EnWG.

160 Sec. 8 para. 2 sent. 2 of the GasNZV. See also *Thole*, in: Säcker, Berlin Commentary on energy law, t. 1, p. 1280 f., para. 157.

161 Sec. 20 para. 1b sent. 1 of the EnWG.

162 Sec. 12 para. 4 of the GasNZV.

163 Sec. 20 para. 1b sent. 9 of the EnWG.

164 See *Thole*, in: Säcker, Berlin Commentary on energy law, t. 1, p. 1281, para. 159 f.

(4) Implementation of obligations of cooperation

The network operators have to arrange the physical transport of gas; therefore, the obligation of cooperation concerns not only the number of contracts, but goes much further up to technical and economic issues.[165] In particular, operators of gas supply networks have to cooperate in the following fields: calculation and offering of capacities, provision of system services, passing-on of costs and charges, and development of common standards of contracts.[166] In addition, the network operators have to exhaust the possibilities of the cooperation with each other under consideration of the technical restrictions and economic reasonableness, with the purpose to keep the number of the networks and parts of networks, as well as balancing zones[167] as small as possible.[168]

For the purpose of implementation of the obligations of cooperation, transmission network operators form market areas and designate a market area coordinator for each of them.[169] Market area coordinators have to be responsible for the operation of the virtual trading point of the market area, arrangement of balancing group, and acquisition and control of use of balancing energy.[170] Network operators are also obliged to keep the number of the market areas as small as possible.[171]

Further, the obligations of cooperation are embodied in the CoA, which is divided according to the internal processing and organisation requirements within the market areas as well as beyond their borders.[172] The conclusion of a cooperation agreement is mandatory for all network operators.[173]

165 See *Thole*, in: Säcker, Berlin Commentary on energy law, t. 1, p. 1273, para. 141.

166 Obligations of cooperation of network operators are stipulated in sec. 20 para. 1b sent. 5-8 of the EnWG.

167 According to the definition of sec. 3 para. 10b of the EnWG, balancing zone is the part of one or more networks, the entry and exit points of which can be attributed to a certain balancing group.

168 Sec. 20 para. 1b sent. 7 of the EnWG.

169 Sec. 20 para. 1 sent. 1 and 2 of the GasNZV.

170 Sec. 20 para. 1 sent. 3 of the GasNZV.

171 Cf. sec. 20 para. 1b sent. 7 of the EnWG. See also *Thole*, in: Säcker, Berlin Commentary on energy law, t. 1, p. 1273, para. 141.

172 See *Thole*, in: Säcker, Berlin Commentary on energy law, t. 1, p. 1284, para. 167 ff. with more details and further sources.

173 Sec. 8 para. 6 of the GasNZV.

(5) *Arrangement of contracts*

For the implementation of network access, contracts have to be concluded between the transport customers and the network operators as well as between the network operators among themselves.[174] Contracts concluded between the transport customer and the network operator are entry and exit contracts[175], as well as framework exit contracts[176]. The minimum requirements for general terms and conditions laid down by sec. 4 of the GasNZV have gained significant importance in practice, so that the entry and exit contracts usually stipulate the level and duration of the capacity rights, service and the charges, and for the rest a reference to the general terms and conditions is made.[177] The CoA also prescribes substantial part of the basic conditions of the contracts.[178] Even if publicly modified, every network usage contract, as a civil law contract, has to comply with the general provisions of the Civil Code of Germany[179], especially the requirements concerning the Standard Business Terms pursuant to sec. 305 ff. of the Civil Code of Germany.[180]

The parties to the entry and exit contracts are the transport customer on the one hand, and the network operator on the other hand, in or from the network of which the gas is injected or extracted.[181] The main condition, and therefore the content of both contracts is providing the booked firm or interruptible capacities at the relevant entry or exit point, considering possible constraints of assignment and limits of usage, as well as the obligation of the transport customer to pay respective charges for this performance.[182] The scope of the entry contracts includes the entitlement of the transport customer to use the whole network from the entry point to the virtual trade point; the exit contract entitles

174 See *Thole*, in: Säcker, Berlin Commentary on energy law, t. 1, p. 1285, para. 174.

175 Sec. 20 para. 1b, sent. 2 and 3 of the EnWG. However, there are peculiarities with regard to biogas (sec. 31 ff. of the GasNZV).

176 Sec. 20 para. 1b sent. 4 of the EnWG. More details on the arrangement of the framework exit contracts See *Thole*, in: Säcker, Berlin Commentary on energy law, t. 1, p. 1287 f., para. 185 ff.

177 See *Thole*, in: Säcker, Berlin Commentary on energy law, t. 1, p. 1286, para. 177.

178 See *Thole*, in: Säcker, Berlin Commentary on energy law, t. 1, p. 1286, para. 178.

179 Civil Code [Bürgerliches Gesetzbuch] of 02.01.2002 (BGBl. I p. 42, 2909; 2003 I p. 738), last amended through Art. 1 of the Law of 20.07.2017 (BGBl. I p. 2787).

180 See *Kment*, in: Kment, EnWG, para. 5, p. 473.

181 See *Thole*, in: Säcker, Berlin Commentary on energy law, t. 1, p. 1286 f., para. 180.

182 See *Thole*, in: Säcker, Berlin Commentary on energy law, t. 1, p. 1287, para. 181.

the transport customer to use the network accordingly from the virtual trade point to the exit point up to the end-customer.[183]

As supplements to the CoA, standardised terms and conditions for conclusion of contracts and booking procedure for contracts between transport customers and transmission network operators have been developed.[184] Transport customers have to book capacities of a transmission network operator online in an auction of capacities in a so-called primary capacity platform.[185]

ff) Refusal of access

According to sec. 20 para. 2 sent. 1 of the EnWG, the network operators may refuse the access only if they substantiate that granting access is not possible or not reasonable due to operational or other reasons, taking into account the objectives of sec. 1 of the law. Since according to the content and rationale of the TPA provision, all access seekers are in principle entitled to network access, network operators may refuse it only in exceptional cases.[186] The presence of one of the legitimate grounds has to be exposed and substantiated by the network operator.[187]

In practice, the grounds of lack of capacity or existing valid supply contracts are invoked in most cases of refusal of access on ground of unreasonableness.[188] Access refusal can also be justified with the grounds concerning the person of network user, e.g. insolvency.[189] The case of operational impossibility is practically limited to the case of refusal of access on the ground of different, incompatible gas quality.[190] Grounds of refusal of access can also be classified into absolute and relative grounds of denial.[191]

---

183 Sec. 3 para. 3 sent. 2 of the GasNZV.

184 Supplement 1 to the CoA. See also *Thole*, in: Säcker, Berlin Commentary on energy law, t. 1, p. 1287, para. 183.

185 The joint capacity booking platform of major European Transmission System Operators, available at: https://platform.prisma-capacity.eu/. See also *Thole*, in: Säcker, Berlin Commentary on energy law, t. 1, p. 1287, para. 183.

186 See *Säcker/Boesche*, in: Säcker, Berlin Commentary on energy law, t. 1, p. 1296, para. 220.

187 Sec. 20 para. 2 sent. 2 of the EnWG.

188 See *Säcker/Boesche*, in: Säcker, Berlin Commentary on energy law, t. 1, p. 1296, para. 220.

189 See ibid.

190 See *Säcker/Boesche*, in: Säcker, Berlin Commentary on energy law, t. 1, p. 1296, para. 220.

191 See in detail in *Olbricht*, Network access in the German gas industry, p. 204 ff.

(1) *Impossibility*

An operational, technical ground of refusal of access is e.g. a deficient condition of the network, which could result in a proved threat of operational safety of the network or of the supply, in case the requested access was granted.[192] The same applies if a safe operation of the network cannot be guaranteed temporarily due to an existing insurmountable staff shortage.[193] Hence, the grounds of impossibility related to the network operation are particularly those of deficient technical safety that could result from network facility or from the use of network.[194] In any case, these grounds can justify refusal of access only temporarily since they can be fixed by the network operator.[195] In general terms, it is not conceivable that the use of the network by a third person leads to a greater threat of the network operation than the use of the network by an undertaking related to the network operator.[196]

Another temporary technical ground of refusal of access is the lack of connection to the network.[197] The network operator is in principle obliged to set up the network connection.[198] However, the operator of the facilities that have to be connected to the network has to create appropriate technical conditions for the connection in advance and also, as a rule, bear the costs of the connection.[199]

(2) *Unreasonableness*

The case law as well as the literature has come to the common conclusion that lack of required capacity of the network (lack of capacity) constitutes an eligible ground for refusal of access.[200] Since in the case of lack of capacity, the capacities are 'occupied' by other network users, it constitutes not a technical but an economic or a legal impossibility of access, the examination of which

---

192 See *Säcker/Boesche*, in: Säcker, Berlin Commentary on energy law, t. 1, p. 1296 f., para. 221.

193 See ibid.

194 See ibid.

195 See ibid.

196 See ibid.

197 See *Säcker/Boesche*, in: Säcker, Berlin Commentary on energy law, t. 1, p. 1297, para. 222.

198 Sec. 17 and 18 of the EnWG.

199 See *Säcker/Boesche*, in: Säcker, Berlin Commentary on energy law, t. 1, p. 1297, para. 222 with further sources.

200 See *Säcker/Boesche*, in: Säcker, Berlin Commentary on energy law, t. 1, p. 1297, para. 223. See also sec. 20 para. 2 sent. 3 of the EnWG.

can be most convincing within the scope of unreasonableness.[201] These are above all economic grounds or grounds related to contractual commitments, which can justify refusal of access in the case of lack of capacity under certain circumstances.[202] In these cases it is technically (i.e. factually) still possible for the network operator to grant access to the network even if breaching existing contractual obligations.[203] Thus, two types of congestions can be differentiated: contractual and physical congestions.[204] Contractual congestions are the situations where there is still demand on firm capacities whereas the technical capacities are already fully booked.[205] Within the EU there is substantial contractual congestion in gas networks.[206] Physical congestion refers to a situation where the level of demand for actual deliveries exceeds the technical capacity at some point in time.[207] Physical congestion of gas networks is, at present, unlike contractual congestions, rarely a problem.[208]

Since access can be exceptionally refused only on grounds of an existing full network load, a congestion which possibly arises in the future due to a contractually arranged 'stockpiling of capacities', cannot justify a refusal neither on technical nor on other grounds.[209] Hence, reserving capacities for the future cannot justify refusal of access.[210]

Further, the network operator is not entitled to invoke existing long-term supply contracts as a justification of refusal of access on ground of unreasonableness due to the lack of capacity.[211] The rationale is that ensuring fulfilment of these contracts does not constitute a part of the 'own' interests of network operators.[212]

---

201 See *Säcker/Boesche*, in: Säcker, Berlin Commentary on energy law, t. 1, p. 1297, para. 223.

202 See *Säcker/Boesche*, in: Säcker, Berlin Commentary on energy law, t. 1, p. 1297 f., para. 224.

203 See ibid.

204 See *Wendt*, Capacity Congestions, p. 8.

205 See Art. 2 N 21 of the Gas Regulation 2009.

206 See Recital 21 of the Gas Regulation 2009. For more details see *Höffler*, Congestion Management, p. 82 f.

207 See Art. 2 N 23 of the Gas Regulation 2009.

208 Cf. Recital 22 of the Gas Regulation 2009.

209 See *Säcker/Boesche*, in: Säcker, Berlin Commentary on energy law, t. 1, p. 1298 f., para. 227.

210 See ibid.

211 See *Säcker/Boesche*, in: Säcker, Berlin Commentary on energy law, t. 1, p. 1299 f., para. 229 f.

212 See *Säcker/Boesche*, in: Säcker, Berlin Commentary on energy law, t. 1, p. 1300, para. 230.

Moreover, this is a relationship between the supplier and its customer under the civil law, and the network operator is not entitled to act as a defender of the legal order.[213]

Network operators cannot justify refusal of granting access to the networks to the end-users, which are connected at the low pressure stage, with not having concluded contract for the use of the connection (*Anschlussnutzungsvertrag*) foreseen in the Ordinance regarding general conditions of the network connection and its use for the gas supply at low pressure[214] (hereinafter NDAV).[215] For the rest of the transport customers (e.g. the traders or end-customers connected at the middle or high pressure stage) there are no statutory regulations in this respect.[216]

On the other hand, the fact that a network connection contract (*Netzanschlussvertrag*)[217] has not been concluded, can serve as a reason for the network operator to refuse access to the network since conclusion of such contract is mandatory according to sec. 2 para. 2 of NDAV.[218] However, in this case the network user would be able to defend itself by declaring the obligatory conclusion of the network connection contract as an infringement against effective implementation of network access.[219]

The network operator can neither rely on the non-conclusion of the network usage contract (*Netznutzungsvertrag*) in order to justify the refusal of access since the granting of network access is arranged in the form of a statutory obligatory relationship.[220]

Non-payment of the exchange charges or the charges for determining the meter status cannot be invoked by the network operator as a reason to refuse

213 See ibid.

214 Ordinance regarding general conditions of the network connection and its use for the gas supply at low pressure [Niederdruckanschlussverordnung] of 01.07.2006 (BGBl. I p. 2477, 2485), last amended through Art. 8 of the Law of 29.08.2016 (BGBl. I p. 2034).

215 See *Säcker/Boesche*, in: Säcker, Berlin Commentary on energy law, t. 1, p. 1302, para. 236. See also sec. 3 of NDAV.

216 See *Säcker/Boesche*, in: Säcker, Berlin Commentary on energy law, t. 1, p. 1302, para. 235.

217 See the definition of the network connection contract in sec. 5 of NDAV.

218 See *Säcker/Boesche*, in: Säcker, Berlin Commentary on energy law, t. 1, p. 1304, para. 241.

219 See ibid.

220 See *Säcker/Boesche*, in: Säcker, Berlin Commentary on energy law, t. 1, p. 1304, para. 242.

access.[221] Exchange charges have been previously sporadically deployed in connection with the supplier change and they have been charged as a part of the network usage fee.[222] In this way, the network operators tried to compensate the administrative burden caused by the change of customer.[223] However, such payments constitute an unfair impediment for a new supplier in attracting potential customers; thus the exchange charges could be seen as an infringement of the principle of non-discriminatory network access.[224] Other covered forms of exchange fees through charging metering and transfer prices or fees for determining the meter status would also violate sec. 20 para. 1 sent. 1.[225]

A distribution network operator cannot refuse access to the distribution network claiming unreasonableness of granting access due to an absent balancing group in the sense of sec. 20 para. 1b sent. 5 causing the impossibility of proper allocation of costs.[226] A balancing group serves as a possibility for transmission network operators to allocate costs for the control energy used based on the costs-by-cause principle.[227] Thus, transmission network operators have a legitimate interest to form and develop a properly functioning balancing group, whereas distribution network operators would not succeed in claiming that the absence of a balancing group burdens them the same way as it does in the case of transmission network operators.[228]

Apart from the above reasons for refusal of access on grounds of unreasonableness that are common for gas and electricity network operators, the EnWG prescribes additional grounds specific to access to gas supply networks in sec. 25. According to this provision, granting access to gas networks can be unreasonable if it causes serious economic and financial difficulties to the gas supply undertaking to fulfil the unconditional payment obligations derived

---

221 See *Säcker/Boesche*, in: Säcker, Berlin Commentary on energy law, t. 1, p. 1304, para. 243.

222 See ibid.

223 See ibid.

224 See *Säcker/Boesche*, in: Säcker, Berlin Commentary on energy law, t. 1, p. 1304 f., para. 243 with further sources.

225 See *Säcker/Boesche*, in: Säcker, Berlin Commentary on energy law, t. 1, p. 1305, para. 244 with further sources.

226 See *Säcker/Boesche*, in: Säcker, Berlin Commentary on energy law, t. 1, p. 1305, para. 245 with further sources.

227 See *Säcker/Boesche*, in: Säcker, Berlin Commentary on energy law, t. 1, p. 1305, para. 245.

228 See ibid.

from gas supply contracts. The unconditional payment obligations imply the so-called take-or-pay clauses in gas import contracts, according to which gas importers are obliged to a minimum order and they have to pay irrespective of the volume of gas factually taken.[229] Upon application of the gas supply undertaking concerned, the decision has to be made by the regulatory authority. The gas supply undertaking has to prove whether the requirements of sec. 25 sent. 1 are fulfilled.

(3) Written form and notification of the regulatory authority

According to sec. 20 para. 2 sent. 2 of the EnWG, the grounds of the refusal of access have to be explained by the network operator in writing. Since sec. 126b of the Civil Code of Germany is readily transposable to this provision, an explanation can also be provided in an email or a fax message.[230]

According to sec. 20 para. 2 sent. 2 of the EnWG, the refusal of access has to be immediately notified to the regulatory authority. However, only the notification of the regulatory authority is not sufficient but has to be done additionally besides informing the access seeker.[231] The reporting obligation allows the regulatory authority to address the potential cases of abusive refusal independently, even if the party concerned has not informed the authority and has not filed the corresponding application.[232]

Based on sec. 20 para. 2 sent. 3 of the EnWG, the reasoning in the case of lack of capacity has to contain sound information concerning the measures and costs necessary for the construction of the network, which would enable the access. The purpose of this provision is first of all to prevent the misuse of lack of capacity as the ground for refusal of access.[233] On the other hand, it demonstrates that lack of capacity in the network can only exist transitionally.[234] Finally, the provision clarifies that the argument of lack of capacity directly conditions construction of the network and in that way burdens back the network operator that

229 See *Knappke*, in: Stuhlmacher/Stappert/Schoon/Jansen, Energy law, para. 165, p. 168 f.

230 See *Säcker/Boesche*, in: Säcker, Berlin Commentary on energy law, t. 1, p. 1306, para. 248.

231 See *Säcker/Boesche*, in: Säcker, Berlin Commentary on energy law, t. 1, p. 1306, para. 249.

232 See ibid.

233 See *Säcker/Boesche*, in: Säcker, Berlin Commentary on energy law, t. 1, p. 1306, para. 250.

234 See *Säcker/Boesche*, in: Säcker, Berlin Commentary on energy law, t. 1, p. 1306, para. 250.

relied on the lack of capacity as a ground for refusal of access.[235] Thus, if there are in fact sufficient capacities to grant network access, the network operator is not able to refuse access due to its obligation to state reasons; if capacities are indeed not enough, the network operator is obliged to enhance the network as far as it is economic to do so.[236]

This special obligation of network operators in sec. 20 para. 2 sent. 3 EnWG does not arise automatically but only upon request of an access seeker. The law, however, does not require the written form for such a request, so that an oral explanation of an access seeker will suffice as long as it expresses clearly enough, that the access seeker, whose access to the network has been denied on the ground of lack of capacity, expects an additional explanation from the network operator concerning the further development of the network capacity.[237] According to sec. 20 para. 2. sent. 3 part 2, the access seeker is temporally not limited and does not have to demand the explanation immediately after the refusal.

The network operator has to promptly expose the measures necessary to enable the requested access.[238] These should contain a detailed schedule as well as an explanation in cases where the network operator does not consider that the measure should be implemented despite the existing lack of capacity.[239] Also, if the network operator invokes economic unreasonableness of the measure, it has to clarify in detail on which circumstances it relies.[240]

According to sec. 20 para. 2 sent. 4, the network operator may demand a compensation for providing the reasoning, as far as it has pointed to the arising of costs beforehand. However, the fee to be paid by the access seeker should not be in excess of the half of the costs incurred by the network operator for providing the explanation (e.g. for special network calculations, for obtaining cost estimates etc.).[241] Regarding the extent of the costs, the legislative background of the law suggests that "normal costs of initiation of transaction" should be applied as a standard.[242]

---

235 See ibid.

236 See ibid.

237 See *Säcker/Boesche*, in: Säcker, Berlin Commentary on energy law, t. 1, p. 1306 f., para. 251.

238 BT-Drs. 15/3917, p. 7, 60.

239 See *Säcker/Boesche*, in: Säcker, Berlin Commentary on energy law, t. 1, p. 1307, para. 252.

240 See ibid.

241 See *Säcker/Boesche*, in: Säcker, Berlin Commentary on energy law, t. 1, p. 1308, para. 255.

242 BT-Drs. 15/3917, p. 7, 60.

gg) Congestion management

Congestion management constitutes a form of network safety management, where the network operator takes measures, first of all of a technical nature, to reduce the load of the networks considering the threat of capacity congestions.[243] Congestion management[244] rules together with the obligations of network enhancement facilitate efficient operation of the gas networks.[245] The main challenge in the gas sector is not to overcome specifically arisen physical bottlenecks but rather to avoid the emergence of contractual congestions whilst the factual capacities allow a further allocation.[246]

Even though the EnWG prescribes in sec. 11 para. 1 sent. 1 a general obligation regarding expanding networks[247], no such implicit obligation of the network operator can be derived from sec. 20 in the case of congestion.[248]

Congestion management in gas networks is regulated by the GasNZV.[249] The GasNZV prescribes the rules for auctioning of capacities at the market area borders, subsidiary capacity allocation according to the priority principle, as well as secondary trade and capacity optimisation.

According to Art. 41 para. 9 of the Gas Directive 2009, congestion management of national gas transmission networks, and the implementation of congestion management rules have to be submitted to the regulatory authorities for approval.

(1) Auctioning capacities

As per sec. 13 para. 1 sent. 1 of the GasNZV, the transmission network operators are obliged to auction firm entry and exit capacities through the capacity booking platform in a transparent and non-discriminatory procedure. However,

---

243 See *Säcker/Boesche*, in: Säcker, Berlin Commentary on energy law, t. 1, p. 1298, para. 226. See also the definition of congestion management in Art. 2 para. 1 N 5 of the Gas Regulation 2009, also above part A.II.1.c), p. 10.

244 Concerning the term 'congestion management' see detailed in *König*, Congestion management, p. 43 ff.

245 See more extensively about the interaction between congestion management and network enhancement in *Höppner*, Regulation of network structure, p. 128.

246 See *Arndt/Herzmann*, in: Britz/Hellermann/Hermes, EnWG, p. 767, para. 214.

247 See above part A.II.2.c)dd).

248 See in detail in *Wendt*, Capacity Congestions, p. 160 ff.

249 Gas Regulation 2009 also contains general provisions concerning congestion management mechanisms. On the applicability of the two legal acts see *Wendt*, Capacity Congestions, p. 69 f.

the capacities to be auctioned are limited to the ones at the market area borders since the list of the points, to which pursuant to sec. 13 para. 3 sent. 1 of the GasNZV the provision is not applicable, covers all market-area-intern points.[250] According to sec. 13 para. 1 sent. 4, interruptible as well as intra-day capacities[251] are exempt from the auctioning obligation and have to be allocated based on the chronological order of the respective reservations (priority principle).[252] Auction process is organised according to the 'one-stop-shop' principle exclusively through one platform on the internet.[253]

(2) Subsidiary capacity allocation according to priority principle

As mentioned, intra-day and interruptible capacities, as well as market-area-intern capacities, which are exempt from the obligation to auction, are allocated based on the principle of priority.[254] However, the wording of the respective provisions stipulating the chronological order of the allocation suggest to take into account the date of application in the case of market-area-intern capacities as per sec. 13 para. 3 sent. 2 of the GasNZV on the one hand, and the date of reservation of the capacity as per sec. 13 para. 1 sent. 4 on the other hand. Under 'reservation' purchase of capacities should be understood pursuant to sec. 2 N 6 of the GasNZV. Since there is no rationale behind such difference between the application of the priority principle and the legislator has also not substantiated its approach[255], it should be considered that the chronological order of the applications, and not the date of reservation, is relevant in both cases.[256] However, there is an exception from this principle for transport customer supplying biogas, in which case pursuant to sec. 34 of the

250 Cf. BR-Drs. 312/10, p. 71 f. See also *Wendt*, Capacity Congestions, p. 72.

251 Since there is no definition of the intra-day capacities, it should be understood as capacities for the use on the same day of their allocation. See more details in *Wendt*, Capacity Congestions, p. 73.

252 The provision containing the exemption (sec. 13 para 1 sent. 4 of the GasNZV) was abolished through the recent amendment of the GasNZV on 11.08.2017 effective on 01.04.2018.

253 See *Wendt*, Capacity Congestions, p. 73.

254 The provision containing the exemption (sec. 13 para 1 sent. 4 of the GasNZV) was abolished through the recent amendment of the GasNZV on 11.08.2017 effective on 01.04.2018, so that the allocation of all entry and exit capacities offered by transmission network operators will be subject to the same rules.

255 BR-Drs. 312/10, p. 70.

256 See more details in *Wendt*, Capacity Congestions, p. 77.

GasNZV network operators are obliged to conclude entry and exit contracts with such applicants as a matter of priority. Like auctioning, the allocation of capacities based on the priority principle is arranged through the primary capacity platform.[257]

(3) Secondary trade and capacity optimisation

In order to facilitate more efficient use of network capacities and thus to a functioning competition, the secondary trade of the capacities has been allowed and is being promoted.[258] Pursuant to sec. 12 para. 2 of the GasNZV network users may sell or sublet entry and exit capacities to third parties; however, the transaction has to take place exclusively on the capacity booking platform where the allocation of primary capacities takes place. In order to avoid capacity hoarding with the aim of profitable resale, the fees for the capacities shall not significantly exceed the initial fees to be paid to the network operators.[259]

Since the mere possibility of secondary trade would not contribute to the high rate of returning capacities to the market, the obligation of release of capacities has been introduced additionally.[260] Pursuant to sec. 16 para. 1 sent. 1, network users are obliged to promptly offer partially or entirely unused firm capacities as secondary capacities on the capacity booking platform or place at the disposal of the transmission network operator for the time period and within the scope of the non-utilisation. Moreover, as per sec. 16 para. 3 of the GasNZV in case a transport customer does not make use of its firm capacities during 3 months within the preceding calendar year, the network operator has to withdraw the contracted firm capacities with the term of at least one year, in case contractual congestions exist in its gas network (also referred to as 'use-it-or-lose-it rule'[261]). The network user may object to the withdrawal pursuant to sec. 16 para. 4 of the GasNZV.[262]

---

257 See more details in *Wendt*, Capacity Congestions, p. 78 f.

258 Cf. Art. 16 para. 3 lit. b of the Gas Regulation 2009, according to which network users who wish to resell or sublet their unused contracted capacity on the secondary market shall be entitled to do so.

259 See more details in *Wendt*, Capacity Congestions, p. 84 f.

260 BR-Drs. 312/10, p. 77.

261 See *Arndt/Herzmann*, in: Britz/Hellermann/Hermes, EnWG, p. 770 f., para. 221.

262 See more details in *Wendt*, Capacity Congestions, p. 84 f.

hh) New infrastructure

Access-based policies are ruled by a double dilemma since, on the one hand, the granting of access might lead to an enhancement of the short-term consumer welfare, but through a decrease of investment incentives as a result of lower investment returns. On the other hand, the refusal of access might temporarily stimulate investments, while potentially exerting a detrimental effect on market competitiveness.[263]

Since regulation is expected to perform a balancing test[264], the EnWG[265] as well as the EU Directives[266] foresee a possibility of exempting network operators from the obligation to grant access to their networks in the case of new infrastructure, with the purpose of creating a positive investment climate. Infrastructure is considered to be new, if it is put into operation after 12 July 2005, as defined by sec. 3 para. 29a of the EnWG.

According to sec. 28a of the EnWG, interconnectors between Germany and other states, LNG and storage facilities may be exempt from the application of sec. 8 to 10e as well as sec. 20 to 28 for a limited time if the following conditions are met: 1. the investment enhances competition in gas supply and security of supply; 2. the level of risk attached to the investment is such that the investment would not take place, unless an exemption was granted; 3. the infrastructure is owned by a natural or legal person which is in the sense of sec. 8 to 10e separate from the network operators in whose networks that infrastructure will be built; 4. charges are levied on users of that infrastructure; 5. the exemption is not detrimental to competition or the effective functioning of the internal gas market, or the efficient functioning of the regulated system to which the infrastructure is connected. According to sec. 28a para. 3 of the EnWG, upon the application of the gas supply undertaking concerned, the regulatory authority decides whether the conditions for the exemptions, that have to be attested by the applicant, are present. The first instance had already taken place in the case of the Baltic Sea connecting pipeline OPAL, which has been partially exempted from the regulation by the Federal Network Agency for Electricity, Gas, Telecommunication, Post and Railways (hereinafter Federal Network Agency).[267]

263 See *Waloszyk*, Law and Policy of the European gas market, p. 195.
264 See *Waloszyk*, Law and Policy of the European gas market, p. 187.
265 BT-Drs. 15/3917, p. 87.
266 Art. 22 of the Gas Directive 2003 and later Art. 36 of the Gas Directive 2009.
267 Decisions by the Federal Network Agency of 25.02.2009 BK7-08-009 and BK7-08-010 as well as amending decisions of 07.07.2009. See also *Koenig/Kühling/Rasbach*, Energy law, p. 109, para. 123.

III. Enforcement of the right of access to gas networks

The wording of sec. 20 para. 1 sent. 1 EnWG leaves the question of practical enforcement of the right of access to gas networks open.[268] However, since it is a statutory right, the entitlement to access arises immediately with its application and by virtue of the law.[269] Also, in other, systematically related provisions, like sec. 917 of the Civil Code of Germany, the legislator refers to the term "require". According to this provision, the right of way of necessity does not arise when solely the statutory requirements are met, but only when the entitled person requires it from the neighbours.[270] Since granting network access is a statutory obligatory relationship too, where the question of the "if" of access is already solved[271], the access seekers may refer directly to the ordinary court in order to claim their rights of network access.

On the other hand, according to sec. 30 para. 1 sent. 1 of the EnWG, abuse of market position by the operators of energy networks is prohibited. The persons and groups of persons, whose interests have been substantially affected by the conduct of a network operator, may file an application to the regulatory authority on review of this conduct pursuant to sec. 31 para. 1 of the EnWG. As per sec. 30 para. 1 N 1 of the EnWG, a violation of the provisions of chapters 2 and 3 of the EnWG (which includes sec. 20) by a network operator constitutes an abusive conduct.

268 See *Säcker/Boesche*, in: Säcker, Berlin Commentary on energy law, t. 1, p. 1249, para. 62.

269 See *Salje*, EnWG, p. 600 f., para. 26.

270 For an extensive analysis see *Boesche*, Civil dogmatic structure of the network access right, p. 232 f. See also *Säcker/Boesche*, in: Säcker, Berlin Commentary on energy law, t. 1, p. 1249, para. 62 with further sources.

271 See *Kment*, in: Kment, EnWG, para. 4, p. 473. See also *Busche*, Private autonomy and obligation to contract, p. 299 ff. and 618, who considers that the obligation to grant access to energy networks constitutes a type of obligation to contract (*Kontrahierungszwang*).

1. Regulatory review

a) The competent authority

From the provisions of energy law preceding the adoption of the EnWG, it was not clear whether the energy-law-specific prohibition of discrimination had a priority over the one stipulated in the Act against Restraints of Competition (hereinafter GWB)[272] due to specificity, so that both laws had been applied simultaneously.[273] This duality of the provisions of competition and energy law on network access and discrimination, and the applicability of sec. 19 and 20 of the GWB together with sec. 20 of the EnWG therewith, has been terminated by sec. 111 of the EnWG.[274] According to para. 1 of this provision, sec. 19, 20 and 29 of the GWB are not applicable if explicitly final rulings are made pursuant to the EnWG or the regulations issued based on the EnWG (e.g. GasNZV). According to para. 2 of sec. 111 of the EnWG, the provisions of chapter 3 of the EnWG as well as regulations issued based on this chapter are final rulings in the sense of para. 1 sent. 1 of this provision. The regulation of energy networks constitutes a sector-specific complement to the general competition law and the EnWG takes precedence over the provisions of GWB merely in relation to network regulation.[275] Hence, further duties and competences of the competition authorities, like e.g. merger control, are not affected.

Accordingly, for the cases arisen from the EnWG the duties of the regulatory authority are performed pursuant to sec. 54 of the law by the Federal Network Agency as well as by regional regulatory authorities.

The most important powers of the Federal Network Agency include the competence stipulated in sec. 65 para. 1 of the EnWG, according to which the regulatory authority can oblige undertakings and associations of undertakings to terminate the conduct that contradicts the provisions of the EnWG as well as other statutory regulations enacted on the basis of the EnWG. Apart from this, another crucial power of the regulatory authority with regard to the enforcement

272 Act against Restraints of Competition [Gesetz gegen Wettbewerbsbeschränkungen] of 26.06.2013 (BGBl. I p. 1750, 3245), last amended through Art. 10 para. 9 of the Law of 30.10.2017 (BGBl. I p. 3618).

273 See *Säcker/Boesche*, in: Säcker, Berlin Commentary on energy law, t. 1, p. 1312, para. 266 with further sources.

274 See *Säcker/Boesche*, in: Säcker, Berlin Commentary on energy law, t. 1, p. 1312, para. 266.

275 See *Zeidler*, in: Baur/Salje/Schmidt-Preuß, Regulation in the energy industry, p. 506 f., para. 25.

of network access right is stipulated in sec. 30 para. 2 of the EnWG, according to which the authority may oblige the network operator abusing its dominant position to cease the violation, demand adjustments of the network fees and other conditions of network connection and access, as well as impose granting of network access or connection in the case of an illegitimate refusal. According to sec. 94 of the EnWG, in case network operators do not comply with the decisions, orders and other measures of the regulatory authority, it may enforce compliance, including ordering penalty payments (*Zwangsgeld*).

Pursuant to sec. 75 para. 1 sent. 1 of the EnWG, decisions of the regulatory authority shall be subject to appeal. The high regional court competent for the seat of the regulatory authority has the power to rule on the appeal as per sec. 75 para. 4 of the EnWG.

b) Refusal of access

When the network operator does not make a contract proposal after the access seeker has claimed network access according to sec. 20 EnWG, the situation can be solved based on the statutory character of the right of access to energy networks.[276] This is not a peculiarity of energy law but also characteristic to the law regulating the relationships between neighbours, like the right of way of necessity or the right of encroachment.[277] Thus, if the network operator refuses to offer a contract or to conclude a contract for network usage, the access seeker may claim the right on network access in a civil proceeding.[278] However, in this case it could be more effective to apply for a ruling on abusive practices[279] to the competent regulatory authority pursuant to sec. 31 (special abuse proceeding by the regulatory authority) and sec. 32 of the EnWG (injunctive relief, liability for damages).[280] The same applies to the cases when the network operator illicitly refuses to grant access to the network.[281] The network seeker may file an application to the regulatory authority on review of the conduct of the network

276 See *Säcker/Boesche*, in: Säcker, Berlin Commentary on energy law, t. 1, p. 1250, para. 63.

277 Sec. 912 Civil Code of Germany. See *Säcker/Boesche*, in: Säcker, Berlin Commentary on energy law, t. 1, p. 1250, para. 63.

278 See *Säcker/Boesche*, in: Säcker, Berlin Commentary on energy law, t. 1, p. 1251, para. 65. Cf. sec. 32 para. 1 and 3 EnWG.

279 *Missbrauchsverfügung*.

280 See *Säcker/Boesche*, in: Säcker, Berlin Commentary on energy law, t. 1, p. 1251, para. 65.

281 See ibid.

operator pursuant to sec. 31 para. 1 of the EnWG. According to sec. 31 para. 3 of the EnWG, the authority has to decide on the matter within 2 months after the receipt of the complete application. In the case of illicit refusal of access, the regulatory authority may impose to grant network access pursuant to sec. 30 para. 2 N 2.

Apart from that, sec. 1004 para. 1 sent. 1 of the Civil Code of Germany offers a general principle for claiming removal of the interference for the cases of continuous refusal of network usage on the one hand, and for refusal to pay network fees despite of using the network on the other hand.[282] The general rule of the Civil Code of Germany can also be transferred to the energy-law-specific sec. 32 para. 1 of the EnWG.[283] According to this provision, injunctive relief is applicable not only in cases of removal of an interference consisting in the usage itself but also in cases where the usage of ownership has to be accepted due to objective legal grounds.[284] In these situations, the action for removal of interference is not directed at the usage as such but at the non-remuneration of the usage offered only in return for payment.[285] Hence, the aforementioned provisions offer protection to the network users paying excessive fees for the network usage as well as to the network operators receiving too low or no remuneration against their will for letting the third parties use their property.[286]

c) Dispute concerning conditions

When a gas supplier concludes a contract with a network operator on the use of the network in order to supply its customers ("if"), and on the conditions of the usage, especially the charges for such usage ("how"), there is no need to invoke the statutory obligation of network access.[287] In the case of a dispute concerning the "if" of the network access right, the Federal Network Agency has the authority to rule.[288] The amount of the network usage charges are also defined by the Federal Network Agency within the ex-ante fee approval procedure or according to the

282 See *Säcker/Boesche*, in: Säcker, Berlin Commentary on energy law, t. 1, p. 1250 f., para. 63.
283 See ibid.
284 See ibid.
285 See ibid.
286 See ibid.
287 See *Säcker/Boesche*, in: Säcker, Berlin Commentary on energy law, t. 1, p. 1251, para. 66.
288 See ibid.

principles of incentive regulation.[289] In cases where the dispute concerns the conditions of the contract for network usage, that are not prescribed by the legal norms, the access seeker may opt for a civil claim with reference to sec. 32 para. 1 and 3 EnWG, beside an application to initiate an abuse proceeding.[290]

In the case of refusal of granting network access with reasonable conditions, the prerequisites of sec. 30 para. 1 N 1 of the EnWG are fulfilled (abusive conduct of a network operator through violating the provisions of chapters 2 and 3 of the EnWG).[291] Like in the case of refusal of access, the network user may file an application to the regulatory authority on review of the conduct of the network operator pursuant to sec. 31 para. 1 of the EnWG. According to sec. 31 para. 3 of the EnWG, the authority then has to decide on the matter within 2 months after the receipt of the complete application. Based on sec. 30 para. 2 of the EnWG, the regulatory authority may oblige the network operator to cease the violation as well as demand adjustments, if e.g. the requested network charges deviate from the ones approved or if the conditions of network access do not comply with the statutory requirements.

2. Judicial review

In cases where a network operator refuses to grant the requested access to the network to the access seeker, and no help can be obtained from the Federal Network Agency according to sec. 30 and 31 of the EnWG, the access seeker may do nothing but refer to the ordinary court.[292] The access seeker can either directly ask for enabling the use of network (action demanding performance[293]) or apply for the conviction of the network operator to the issuance of the declaration of acceptance of the offer on the conclusion of the network usage contract submitted by the network seeker.[294] At the same time the access seeker can theoretically initiate actions for acknowledgement as well as for an injunction.[295] However,

289 See ibid.

290 See ibid.

291 See *Säcker/Boesche*, in: Säcker, Berlin Commentary on energy law, t. 1, p. 1252, para. 68.

292 See *Säcker/Boesche*, in: Säcker, Berlin Commentary on energy law, t. 1, p. 1308 f., para. 256.

293 *Leistungsklage.*

294 See *Säcker/Boesche*, in: Säcker, Berlin Commentary on energy law, t. 1, p. 1308 f., para. 256.

295 See ibid.

in the action for acknowledgement according to sec. 256 of the German Code of Civil Procedure[296] only the existence of the obligation to conclude a contract may be ascertained and the parties have to agree on the contents of the contract additionally, which means that in the case of a disagreement the access seeker would have to refer to the court again with an action asking to grant access on the requested terms.[297] Therefore, there is no interest in bringing the action for acknowledgement, unless some peculiarities are present.[298]

For the action demanding issuance of the ruling to implement the right of network access to be compliant with the requirement of precision prescribed in sec. 253 para. 2 N 2 of the German Code of Civil Procedure as well as with the requirements of a functional enforcement procedure, the requested use of network has to be described as detailed as possible in terms of quantity, timing and space.[299] An application of the access seeker should present the main duties of the parties in such detail to make it possible for the court to issue a sufficiently precise ruling for the enforcement procedure.[300] In the majority of the cases the parties represent the same industry and are aware of the ancillary services related to the main duties and the commitments of the network operator as well as the access seeker derived therefrom; thus it is not necessary to stipulate these details in the ruling.[301] The competent court may, however, alter single clauses of the contract proposal, which deviate from the requirements of the law, as far as the alteration concerns not an aliud but a minus in relation to the application filed by the claimant.[302]

While examining the possibility of the enforcement of the statutory right of network access through the action demanding the performance the court has to make sure that the hardship of the access seeker is serious enough to grant

296 Code of Civil Procedure [Zivilprozessordnung] of 5.12.2005 (BGBl. I p. 3202; 2006 I p. 431; 2007 I p. 1781), last amended through Art. 1 of the Law of 11.10.2016 (BGBl. I p. 2222).

297 See *Säcker/Boesche*, in: Säcker, Berlin Commentary on energy law, t. 1, p. 1309, para. 257.

298 See ibid.

299 See *Säcker/Boesche*, in: Säcker, Berlin Commentary on energy law, t. 1, p. 1309, para. 258.

300 See *Säcker/Boesche*, in: Säcker, Berlin Commentary on energy law, t. 1, p. 1310, para. 260.

301 See *Säcker/Boesche*, in: Säcker, Berlin Commentary on energy law, t. 1, p. 1310, para. 260 with further sources.

302 See *Säcker/Boesche*, in: Säcker, Berlin Commentary on energy law, t. 1, p. 1310, para. 261 with further sources.

priority to its request.[303] According to the case law[304], a general difficulty to enter the market does not suffice as a ground for hardship since in this procedure it is only about the individual interests of the parties.[305] In the injunctive procedure for issuing a ruling for access to the network it has to be basically borne in mind that new suppliers have to establish themselves in the structure of energy industry developed over the decades.[306] This may be feasible solely through granting access to the networks since their customers can be supplied only in this way and the refusal of the network operator to grant such access may irreparably damage the market position of the new entrants.[307]

According to sec. 102 of the EnWG, the regional courts have exclusive jurisdictional competence over civil disputes arisen from this law regardless of the value of the subject-matter.

3. Enforcement of other contracts related to realisation of access rights

In relation to the enforcement of contracts, the CoA and other contracts have to be differentiated.[308] For resolution of disputes between the network operators themselves concerning their obligations derived from the CoA, the agreement itself foresees under sec. 58 the arbitration proceeding, and excludes the ordinary legal process. For disputes of the network operators with third persons, e.g. a transport customer or a market area coordinator, with whom the model contracts are concluded, the contract parties may refer to the ordinary legal proceeding, as stipulated in these contracts.[309] In addition, the mentioned third parties have an option to induce an initiation of an abuse proceeding under sec. 31 of the EnWG or a supervisory proceeding under sec. 65 of the EnWG.[310] The

303 See *Säcker/Boesche*, in: Säcker, Berlin Commentary on energy law, t. 1, p. 1310 f., para. 262.

304 Brandenburgisches OLG, Judgment of 24.09.2002, RdE 2003, p. 19 f.; LG Hannover, Judgment of 30.08.2002, RdE 2002, 22 ff.; Judgment of 24.06.2002, RdE 2002, 290 ff.; Judgment of 19.04.2002, RdE 2002, 247 ff.

305 See *Säcker/Boesche*, in: Säcker, Berlin Commentary on energy law, t. 1, p. 1310 f., para. 262.

306 See *Säcker/Boesche*, in: Säcker, Berlin Commentary on energy law, t. 1, p. 1311, para. 263.

307 See ibid.

308 See *Thole*, in: Säcker, Berlin Commentary on energy law, t. 1, p. 1288 f., para. 190.

309 See *Thole*, in: Säcker, Berlin Commentary on energy law, t. 1, p. 1288 f., para. 190.

310 See ibid.

Federal Network Agency itself can also take action against infringements in an abuse proceeding under sec. 30 or a supervisory proceeding under sec. 65 of the EnWG.[311] Moreover, the predefining powers of the Federal Network Agency have a special relevance for access to gas networks.[312]

---

311 See ibid.

312 Sec. 50 of the GasNZV. See *Thole*, in: Säcker, Berlin Commentary on energy law, t. 1, p. 1288 f., para. 190.

B. Regulation of access to gas networks in Russia in a comparative perspective

I. Overview of the gas industry of Russia

1. Historical development

Before discussing the current structure of the gas industry of Russia it is worthwhile to describe its technical characteristics as well as historical evolution of the sector.

The fundament of the technical infrastructure of the modern gas industry of Russia is the Unified Gas Supply System (hereinafter also UGSS), which consists of the high pressure trunk pipelines and several gas reserves with the unique characteristics.[313] The history of the UGSS dates back to 1946 when the first trunk pipeline Saratov-Moscow was built in the USSR.[314] In 1990 the length of the trunk pipelines of the UGSS in Soviet area exceeded 220,000 km.[315]

The substantial changes in the gas industry of Russia started from 1989 when the USSR Gas Industry Ministry was restructured into Gazprom State Gas Concern.[316] The Presidential Decree of 01.06.1992 on ensuring the operation of the Unified Gas Supply System[317] laid down that the UGSS is exclusively owned by the Russian Federation (hereinafter RF).[318] The State Committee for the Management of State Property of Russia would act as a representative of the owner in relation to the assets of the UGSS. According to the Decree, the Committee should entrust Gazprom State Gas Concern with the responsibility of the economic management of the UGSS and thereby transfer the named assets to the group with the right of full economic governance.

The next step of the reform was the Presidential Decree of 14.08.1992 on peculiarities of transformation of state undertakings, associations and

---

313 *Mechetny*, Legal regulation of gas supply in Russia, p. 15.

314 *Mechetny*, Legal regulation of gas supply in Russia, p. 11.

315 Ibid.

316 See the history of JSC Gazprom available at: http://www.gazprom.com/about/history/chronicle/1989-1995, last accessed on 16.11.2017.

317 Decree N 538 of 01.06.1992 of the President of the RF on ensuring the operation of the Unified Gas Supply System [Ukaz Prezidenta RF Ob obespechenii deatelnosti Edinoy sistemi gazosnabzhenia strani], published in 'Journal of Congress of People's Deputies and Supreme Soviet of the RF' of 11.06.1992, N 23, p. 1271.

318 According to Art. 1 para. 2 of the Constitution of Russia of 12.12.1993 [Konstitutsiya Rossiiskoy Federatsii ot 12.12.1993], as amended on 30.12.2008, 05.02.2014 and 21.07.2014, published in SZ of 04.08.2014, N 31, p. 4398, the names 'Russia' and 'Russian Federation' shall be equal.

organisations of fuel and energy complex into joint stock companies[319], which established that the transformation of the state undertakings, associations and organisations of fuel and energy complex into joint stock companies and their privatisation should not be implemented according to the general rule[320] but should follow the special orders from the President.

This was succeeded by the Presidential Decree of 05.11.1992 on the transformation of Gazprom State Gas Concern into Russian Joint Stock Company Gazprom[321], which founded Russian Joint Stock Company Gazprom (hereinafter also RJSC Gazprom). According to this Decree, a number of gas production, gas transmission and other undertakings, as well as associations and institutes were transformed into subsidiary joint stock companies of RJSC Gazprom. The Decree established that the charter capital of RJSC Gazprom should be formed from a) 100% of the capital of the undertakings, which consisted of the assets of the UGSS constituting federal property, b) controlling block of shares (not less than 51%) of the reorganised subsidiary joint stock companies and c) all shares and assets of Gazprom State Gas Concern, privatisation of which was not forbidden. In addition, pursuant to the Decree, all rights and obligations of Gazprom State Gas Concern were transferred to RJSC Gazprom, including the rights to use subsoil, mineral and natural resources, as well as the rights and obligations derived from the contracts entered into by Gazprom State Gas Concern. According to

319 Decree N 922 of 14.08.1992 of the President of the RF on peculiarities of transformation of state undertakings, associations and organisations of fuel and energy complex into joint stock companies [Ukaz Prezidenta RF Ob osobennostyakh preobrazovaniya gosudarstvennikh predpiyatiy, obyedineniy, organizaciy toplivno-energeticheskogo kompleksa v aktsionernie obshchestva], published in 'Collection of acts of the President and the Government of the RF' of 31.08.1992, N 9, p. 591.

320 The general rule is incorporated in the Decree N 721 of 01.07.1992 of the President of the RF on organisational measures of transforming state undertakings and voluntary associations of state undertakings into joint stock companies [Ukaz Prezidenta RF Ob organizatsionnikh merakh po preobrazovaniyu gosudarstvennikh predpriyatiy, dobrovolnikh obyedineniy gosudarstvennikh predpriyatiy v aktsionernie obshchestva], published in 'Collection of acts of the President and the Government of the RF' of 06.07.1992, N 1, p. 3, last amended on 31.12.1992.

321 Decree N 1333 of 05.11.1992 of the President of the RF on the transformation of Gazprom State Gas Concern into Russian Joint Stock Company Gazprom [Ukaz Prezidenta RF O preobrazovanii gosudarstvennogo gazovogo koncerna 'Gazprom' v Rossiyskoe aktsionernoe obshchestvo 'Gazprom'], published in 'Collection of acts of the President and the Government of the RF' of 09.11.1992, N 19, p. 1607, last amended on 12.05.1997.

the Decree, the undertakings Yakutgazprom[322] and Norilskgazprom, which were previously parts of Gazprom State Gas Concern, were transformed into independent joint stock companies.

The reorganisation process of the natural gas industry of Russia was completed with the Presidential Decree of 08.12.1992 on the transformation into joint stock companies and privatisation of undertakings, associations and organisations of the gas industry of Russia[323]. As of 31.03.1993 all undertakings and other entities of gas industry in Russia had been transformed into joint stock companies.[324]

The first Articles of Association of RJSC Gazprom were approved by the Ordinance of 17.02.1993 of the Council of Ministers of Russia.[325] The General Shareholders Meeting in June 1998 reorganised the Russian Joint Stock Company Gazprom into the Open Joint Stock Company Gazprom (hereinafter JSC Gazprom).[326] In this way JSC Gazprom became the owner of the UGSS.[327] In June 2015 the company was subject to another reorganisation into the Public Joint Stock Company Gazprom.[328]

---

322 In 2010 JSC Yakutgazprom was reorganised into JSC YATEC (Yakutsk Fuel and Energy Company). See the history of YATEC, available at: http://www.yatec.ru/company/history, last accessed on 16.11.2017.

323 Decree N 1559 of 08.12.1992 of the President of the RF on the transformation into joint stock companies and privatisation of undertakings, associations and organisations of the gas industry of RF [Ukaz Prezidenta RF O preobrazovanii v aktsionernie obshchestva i privatizatsii gosudarstvennix predpriyatiy, obyedineniy i organizaciy gazovogo khozyaistva RF], published in 'Collection of acts of the President and the Government of the RF' of 21.12.1992, N 25, p. 2224, last amended on 12.05.1997.

324 See *Gerke/Gudkov/Lakhno*, in: Säcker, Handbook of German-Russian energy law, p. 250.

325 Regulation of the Government of the RF N 138 of 17.02.1993 On the establishment of the Russian Joint Stock Company Gazprom [Postanovlenie Soveta Ministrov _ Pravitelstva RF Ob uchrejdenii Rossiyskogo aktsionernogo obshchestva Gazprom], published in 'Collection of acts of the President and the Government of the RF' of 01.03.1993, N 9, p. 738, last amended on 28.12.2005.

326 See the history of JSC Gazprom, available at: http://www.gazprom.com/about/history/chronicle/1998, last accessed on 16.11.2017.

327 See *Gerke/Gudkov/Lakhno*, in: Säcker, Handbook of German-Russian energy law, p. 250.

328 Abridged corporate name of the Company in English language is 'PJSC Gazprom'. See Art. 2.1. sent. 3 of the Articles of Association of JSC Gazprom approved on 26 June 2015, available at: http://www.gazprom.com/f/posts/74/562608/gazprom-articles-2015-06-26-en.pdf, last accessed on 16.11.2017. However, since none of the legal acts

According to Art. 5.1. of the Articles of Association of JSC Gazprom, the share capital of JSC Gazprom is 118,367,564,500 Russian roubles, divided into 23,673,512,900 ordinary registered shares with the par value of 5 Russian roubles each. As of 31.12.2016 the state owns a 50.23% controlling stake in the equity capital of the company.[329]

2. Current structure

The general technical characteristics of the gas industry of Russia is that gas is transported mostly in a non-liquid form exclusively through the pipelines and thus its tradability is limited.[330] In addition, the gas sector of Russia has a geographical disadvantage due to the fact that the majority of the most profitable markets are located far away from the production areas, which renders the pipeline business quite uncompetitive.[331]

The modern gas market of Russia is characterised by the dominant position of the state-controlled JSC Gazprom in all segments of the gas value chain: upstream, midstream and downstream.[332] JSC Gazprom is the major vertically integrated gas company in the world acting on all levels of the gas industry: from exploration, production, transmission, exhaustion and storage of gas to its supply to consumers.[333]

The Federal Law of 31.03.1999 on gas supply in Russia[334] (hereinafter Law on Gas Supply) is the main legislative act regulating the gas industry of Russia. All other acts prescribing different detailed rules for various issues concerning the gas industry rely on the principles and definitions provided for by this Law.

According to Art. 5 sent. 2 of the Law on Gas Supply, the federal gas supply system is one of the federal power systems of Russia, which are under the jurisdiction of the state as per Art. 71 lit. 'i' of the Constitution of Russia. The federal

concerning the company has adjusted the wording, the term 'JSC Gazprom' will be used to refer to the company in the past as well as nowadays.

329 See the shareholders' list of JSC Gazprom as of 31.12.2016, available at: http://www.gazprom.com/investors/stock, last accessed on 16.11.2017.

330 See *Gerke/Gudkov/Lakhno*, in: Säcker, Handbook of German-Russian energy law, p. 249.

331 See *Belyi*, Trends of Russia's Gas Sector Regulation, p. 1.

332 See *Seliverstov/Gudkov*, in: Roggenkamp/Barrera-Hernandez/Zillman/Del Guayo, Energy networks and the law, p. 399.

333 See ibid.

334 Federal Law on gas supply in the RF [Federalniy zakon O gazosnabzhenii v RF] N 69 of 31.03.1999, published in SZ of 05.04.1999, N 14, p. 1667, last amended on 26.07.2017.

gas supply system consists of the following gas supply systems in the territory of Russia: UGSS, Regional Gas Supply Systems (hereinafter RGSS), Gas Distribution Systems (hereinafter also GDS) and independent undertakings. Irrespective of the type of ownership and the legal form, all owners of the undertakings belonging to the federal gas supply system are subject to uniform legal principles of market design and pricing policy and uniform requirements of energy, industrial and ecological security as per Art. 5 para. 2 of the Law on Gas Supply.

Before starting to describe the so-called gas supply systems of Russia in detail, it is worthwhile to cast a glance at the definition of 'gas' in the Law on Gas Supply, and herewith the scopes of the Law as well as other regulations concerning the gas industry of Russia, to which the definitions of the Law equally apply. According to Art. 2 of the Law, 'gas' means natural gas, petroleum (associated) gas, stripped dry gas, gas from gas condensate fields extracted and gathered by gas- and oil-producing undertakings, and gas produced by gas- and oil-processing undertakings. Hence, unlike Germany, in Russia the rules concerning gas industry do not cover biogas, liquid gas, hydrogen, as well as synthetically produced methane.[335] In relation to liquid gas the Federal Anti-monopoly Service (hereinafter also FAS) states its analytical report[336] that liquefied petroleum gases are not covered by the analysis of the gas market since they constitute independent products having own peculiarities of transporting possibilities and consumption, related to significant technological differences of utilisation as compared to natural gas.

With regard to the requirements on the EU level, only the common rules for the transmission, distribution, supply and storage of natural gas are mandatory to be transposed by the Member States. However, the Gas Directive 2009 recommends to the Member States to take concrete measures to assist the wider use of biogas and gas from biomass and to grant non-discriminatory access to the gas system also to the producers of these gases, provided that such access is compatible with the relevant technical rules and safety standards.[337] Moreover, the rules established by the Gas Directive 2009 for natural gas, including LNG, also apply in a non-discriminatory way to biogas and gas from biomass or other types of gas in so far as such gases can technically and safely be injected into, and transported through, the natural gas system.[338]

335 Cf. sec. 3, 19a of the EnWG.

336 See FAS, Analytical report on the results of the analysis of the competitive situation on the wholesale market of natural gas in 2011-2014, p. 6.

337 See Recital 26 of the Gas Directive 2009.

338 Art. 1 para. 2 of the Gas Directive 2009.

a) Unified Gas Supply System (UGSS)

As mentioned, the UGSS is the fundament of the technical infrastructure of the gas industry of Russia and consists of the high pressure trunk pipelines, several gas reserves, as well as other facilities and assets throughout the whole gas value chain 'from well to burner'.[339]

aa) Rules applying to the UGSS and to its owner

According to Art. 6 of the Law on Gas Supply, the UGSS is the most essential gas supply system in Russia and its activities are regulated by the state. The Law defines it as a property and industrial complex, consisting of technologically, organisationally and economically interconnected and centrally managed production and other facilities for production, transmission, storage and supply of gas, owned by an undertaking, established according to the civil law and having acquired the named facilities either through privatisation procedure or on other legal grounds, laid down in the laws of Russia.

The functioning of the UGSS is based on the principle of its indivisibility. According to Art. 14 para. 1 of the Law on Gas Supply, for the purpose of reliability of gas supply as well as secure and sustainable operation of the facilities of the UGSS related to the general technological regime of production, transmission and supply of gas, division of the UGSS is not allowed. However, the Law does not specify which type of division is impermissible and therefore it is not sufficiently clear whether it is forbidden to divide the UGSS operationally, legally, or in terms of ownership rights. Although the legal content of this principle is not defined, its political aim appears to be conservation of the existing vertically integrated structure of the gas market and prevention of the full ownership unbundling.[340] Therefore, it may be assumed that the legislator aimed at prohibiting division of the UGSS in terms of ownership rights as well as legally, whereas the operational unbundling would not necessarily threaten the vertical structure of the incumbent.

Further to the inadmissibility of division, there is a limitation with regard to the liquidation of the undertaking owning the UGSS (i.e. JSC Gazprom) too.

339 See *Seliverstov/Gudkov*, in: Roggenkamp/Barrera-Hernandez/Zillman/Del Guayo, Energy networks and the law, p. 400. See also Transmission activities of JSC Gazprom, available at: http://www.gazprom.com/about/production/transportation, last accessed on 16.11.2017.

340 See *Seliverstov/Gudkov*, in: Roggenkamp/Barrera-Hernandez/Zillman/Del Guayo, Energy networks and the law, p. 399.

Namely, as per Art. 14 sent. 2 of the Law on Gas Supply, the liquidation is only permitted on the basis of a federal law.

JSC Gazprom is not only the current owner but also the only operator of the UGSS. The competences of the owner of the UGSS, as defined in Art. 13 of the Law on Gas Supply, include among others exploitation of the facilities of the UGSS (para. 2), uninterruptible dispatching control of the operation of the facilities of the UGSS as well as the connection points of the UGSS to other facilities (para. 3), and management of the operation of the UGSS (para. 4). In addition, JSC Gazprom is also entitled to centrally manage all facilities connected to the UGSS irrespective of who owns them, as per Art. 14 para. 2 of the Law on Gas Supply.

In spite of certain liberalisation of the stock market of JSC Gazprom in 2005, the restraints concerning the ownership of the company owning and controlling the UGSS still remained.[341] Namely, Art. 15 of the Law on Gas Supply requires that at least 50% plus one share of the total amount of ordinary shares of the undertaking owning the UGSS, i.e. JSC Gazprom, has to remain in ownership of the state, or the joint stock companies with more than 50% of the state's shareholding. Art. 15 also lays down that sale or other means of alienation of these equity shares may only be implemented on the basis of a federal law. Other shares are traded freely and are available for both domestic and foreign investors.[342]

bb) Subsidiaries of JSC Gazprom according to their activities

JSC Gazprom, on the basis of its own 'self-reformation' policy in 2007–2009, separated different types of activities within its group of companies and charged different subsidiaries with different business tasks.[343] On the upstream level, the gas fields are being developed by Exploration and Production subsidiaries. The majority of gas in Russia[344] is currently produced from a few giant and supergiant

341 See *Mechetny*, Legal regulation of gas supply in Russia, p. 16.

342 See *Seliverstov/Gudkov*, in: Roggenkamp/Barrera-Hernandez/Zillman/Del Guayo, Energy networks and the law, p. 399.

343 See *Seliverstov/Gudkov*, in: Roggenkamp/Barrera-Hernandez/Zillman/Del Guayo, Energy networks and the law, p. 402. See also *Karpova*, in: Säcker, Handbook of German-Russian energy law, p. 426.

344 As of 31.12.2016 JSC Gazprom controlled 71.7% of natural gas reserves of Russia and had a share of 65.6% in gas production of Russia. See JSC Gazprom, Gazprom in figures 2012–2016, Factbook, p. 4, available at: http://www.gazprom.com/f/posts/44/307258/gazprom-in-figures-2012-2016-en.pdf, last accessed on 16.11.2017.

gas fields in Western Siberia, which were put into operation in the Soviet times and are parts of the UGSS.[345] On the midstream level the objects are processing plants, transmission networks and storage facilities.[346] The core part of the UGSS is a unique Gas Transmission System (hereinafter also GTS-UGSS)[347]: a network of gas trunk pipelines of high pressure, managed by 17 subsidiaries of JSC Gazprom.[348] There are currently 25 underground storages in Russia all of them governed by a specialised subsidiary storage operator JSC Gazprom UGS.[349] JSC Gazprom also owns and operates several processing plants through its subsidiary JSC Gazprom Pererabotka.[350] In 2009 JSC Gazprom started operating the first LNG plant in Russia, the production of which is destined for the supplies abroad.[351] The UGSS is controlled by JSC Gazprom's Central Operations and Dispatch Department (hereinafter CODD), which maintains round-the-clock control of the complex engineering system comprised of gas production, processing, transmission and underground storage facilities.[352] On the downstream level gas is supplied through 53 regional gas supply companies consolidated into a specialised subsidiary JSC Gazprom Mezhregiongaz delivering gas to 69 federal subjects of Russia.[353] In almost all federal subjects that are covered by the UGSS these regional supply companies undertake purchase and sales of gas of JSC Gazprom and its subsidiaries, as well as of independent producers.[354]

345 *Seliverstov/Gudkov*, in: Roggenkamp/Barrera-Hernandez/Zillman/Del Guayo, Energy networks and the law, p. 400.

346 *Seliverstov/Gudkov*, in: Roggenkamp/Barrera-Hernandez/Zillman/Del Guayo, Energy networks and the law, p. 400.

347 Gazotransportnaya sistema Edinoy Sistemi Gazosnabzheniya Rossii.

348 *Gavrilina/Gudkov/Lakhno*, in: Säcker, Handbook of German-Russian energy law, p. 185.

349 UGS stands for Underground Gas Storage. See company information of JSC Gazprom UGS, available at: http://www.gazprom.com/about/subsidiaries/list-items/gazprom-ugs, last accessed on 16.11.2017.

350 See "O Kompanii" [About the company] information on JSC Gazprom Pererabotka, available at: http://pererabotka.gazprom.ru/about, last accessed on 16.11.2017.

351 See processing activities of JSC Gazprom under: http://www.gazprom.com/about/production/processing, last accessed on 16.11.2017.

352 See Central Operations and Dispatch Department of JSC Gazprom, available at: http://www.gazprom.com/about/production/transportation, last accessed on 16.11.2017. For more details concerning the functions of the CODD see *Gerke/Lakhno*, in: Säcker, Handbook of German-Russian energy law, p. 208 f.

353 See "O kompanii Gazprom Mezhregiongaz" [About Company Gazprom Mezhregiongaz], available at: http://mrg.gazprom.ru, last accessed on 16.11.2017.

354 *Gerke/Gudkov/Lakhno*, in: Säcker, Handbook of German-Russian energy law, p. 258.

In addition, they also purchase gas on the Electronic Trading Platform of JSC Mezhregiongaz on behalf of customers.[355]

cc) Gas Transmission System of Russia and Gas Transmission System of the Unified Gas Supply System

The GTS-UGSS constitutes the world's biggest gas transmission network and consists of the major part of gas trunk pipelines of Russia with the length of 171,400 km as of 31.12.2016.[356] Gas trunk pipelines of high pressure or gas trunk-lines are pipelines designed for gas transport on long distances from production areas to consumption points.[357] The GTS-UGSS is owned and operated by JSC Gazprom through its subsidiaries and departments. Apart from the GTS-UGSS, however, there are also some regional gas trunk-lines, which are parts of the RGSS. Hence, the notion of 'gas transmission system' of the EU and Germany does not equal to the notion of 'Gas Transmission System of the UGSS'.

For clarification it has to be mentioned that the legislator of Russia uses one term *transportirovka* when referring to the notions of transmission i.e. transportation of gas through high pressure pipelines not including supply, and transportation i.e. physical transport of gas. For instance, Art. 2 of the Law on Gas Supply as well as chapter 2 pt. 3 of the rules on gas supply in Russia[358] (hereinafter Rules on Gas Supply), uses the term *gazotransportnaya organizatsiya* to describe a gas transmission undertaking, i.e. as an undertaking transporting gas and having the gas trunk pipelines, compressor stations and other industrial facilities at its disposal on the right of ownership or other legal grounds. The same article of the Rules on Gas Supply uses the term *gazotransportnaya sistema*, which logically has to match with 'transmission system', to refer to gas transportation system, i.e. a system of pipelines connecting gas producers with gas consumers, including gas trunk-lines, discharge pipes and gas distribution networks owned by transmission and distribution undertakings, as well as by customers; the term *transportirovka* is accordingly used to describe transport of

355 Ibid.

356 See JSC Gazprom, Gazprom in figures 2012-2016, Factbook, p. 4, available at: http://www.gazprom.com/f/posts/44/307258/gazprom-in-figures-2012-2016-en.pdf, last accessed on 16.11.2017.

357 See the Definition of Gas trunk-lines by JSC Gazprom, available at: http://www.gazprominfo.com/terms/gas-main, last accessed on 16.11.2017.

358 Regulation of the Government of the RF on the approval of Rules on gas supply in the RF [Postanovlenie Pravitelstva RF Ob utverzhdenii Pravil postavki gaza v RF] N 162 of 05.02.1998, published in SZ of 09.02.1998, N 6, p. 770, last amended on 04.02.2017.

gas through transportation system i.e. including distribution networks. Hence, the definitions used by the legislation of Russia are not consistent. Moreover, there is no term in the legislation of Russia, which would match exactly to the notion of 'transmission' of the EU law, i.e. transport of gas through high pressure pipelines, with a view to its delivery to customers but not including supply.

Therefore, according to the definitions discussed, JSC Gazprom cannot be considered as the only gas transmission undertaking of Russia in the sense of the notion of the EU and Germany since not all high pressure gas pipelines are under the control of JSC Gazprom. For that reason the term 'GTS-UGSS' will be used when referring to the transmission network of JSC Gazprom.

To the complexity of the division between the transmission and distribution based on the levels of pressure of the pipelines, it has to be mentioned that the result is not in all occasions straightforward and for that reason the EU legislator limited the definition of 'transmission' in Art. 2 para. 3 of the Gas Directive 2009 to "mainly […] high pressure pipelines".

b) Regional Gas Supply Systems (RGSS)

Apart from the UGSS there are several RGSS in Russia. The definition of RGSS stipulated in Art. 7 para. 1 of the Law on Gas Supply does not differ from the definition of the UGSS of Art. 6. The only difference is the functional and technical independence of RGSS from the UGSS.[359] Further, the law lays down that RGSS are the fundament of the gas supply systems of the federal subjects of Russia and their activities are supervised by the competent state authorities. However, the role of RGSS is not as significant as that of the UGSS.[360] For example, in the Republic of Sakha (Yakutia) the state-owned JSC Sakhatransneftegaz owns and operates the system of regional high pressure trunk pipelines with the length of 2,503 km as well as supplies natural gas produced by its subsidiary.[361] JSC Norilskgazprom and JSC Taimirgaz produce and supply gas, as well as own and operate the system of regional high pressure trunk pipelines with the total length of 1,077 km in two federal subjects of Russia, Krasnoyarsk Krai and Yamalo-Nenets Autonomous Okrug.[362] Further, there are RGSS independent from the

---

359 See also *Perchik*, Pipeline law, p. 18.

360 See *Seliverstov/Gudkov*, in: Roggenkamp/Barrera-Hernandez/Zillman/Del Guayo, Energy networks and the law, p. 400.

361 See "O Kompanii" [About the company], information on JSC Sakhatransneftegaz, available at: http://aostng.ru/about/company/, last accessed on 16.11.2017.

362 See "Kompaniya segodnya" [The company today], information on JSC Norilskgazprom, available at: http://www.ngaz.ru/company/about, last accessed on 16.11.2017.

UGSS in Sakhalin Oblast and Kamchatka Krai.[363] According to the FAS,[364] the following RGSS exist in the territory of Russia as of 31.12.2014: Norilsk system with high pressure pipelines with length over 1000 km; Yakutia system - 466 km; Chukotka system - 103 km; Sakhalin-Khabarovsk system - 556 km; trans-sakhalin system - 800 km.

c) Gas Distribution Systems (GDS)

After the transmission through high pressure trunk pipelines gas is distributed through middle and low pressure pipelines, the so-called distribution networks with the total length of over 700,000 km.[365] Gas distribution network is a technological complex of GDS, consisting of external pipelines from a source to a gas consumer service line as well as facilities and engineering devices for them.[366]

aa) Rules applying to GDS

According to Art. 7 para. 2 of the Law on Gas Supply, GDS constitutes a property and industrial complex, consisting of organisationally and economically interconnected facilities for transportation and delivery of gas directly to the consumers in the territories of federal subjects of Russia. GDS are independent from the UGSS and RGSS and is owned by an undertaking, established according to the civil law and having acquired the named facilities either through privatisation procedure or on other legal grounds, laid down in the laws of Russia and in the laws of the respective federal subject of Russia. According to pt. 2 of the rules on gas consumption and provision of services of gas supply in Russia[367] (hereinafter Rules on Gas Consumption), a Gas Distribution Undertaking

---

363 *Gavrilina/Gudkov/Lakhno*, in: Säcker, Handbook of German-Russian energy law, p. 185.

364 See FAS, Analytical report on the results of the analysis of the competitive situation on the wholesale market of natural gas in 2011–2014, p. 6.

365 The total length of the distribution pipelines operated by undertakings of JSC Gazprom group constituted 746,300 km in late 2015, cf. http://www.gazprom.com/about/marketing/russia, last accessed on 16.11.2017.

366 See the definition of gas distribution networks by JSC Gazprom, available at: http://www.gazprominfo.com/terms/gas-distribution, last accessed on 16.11.2017.

367 Regulation of the Government of the RF on the approval of Rules on gas consumption and provision of services of gas supply in the RF [Postanovlenie Pravitelstva RF Ob utverzhdenii Pravil polzovaniya gazom i predostavleniya uslug po gazosnabzheniyu v RF] N 317 of 17.05.2002, published in SZ of 20.05.2002, N 20, p. 1870, last amended on 19.06.2017.

(hereinafter also GDU) is a specialised undertaking, exploiting GDS and providing services related to the delivery of gas to the consumers. As per the Rules on Gas Consumption, a GDU can be either the owner of GDS or an undertaking, which concluded a contract with the owner of GDS on its exploitation.[368]

bb) Reformation of GDS

As a result of privatisation in the 1990s, in the territories of the federal subjects of Russia about 700 GDUs arose.[369] Originally, JSC Gazprom did not have any role in gas distribution since the GDUs had emerged from municipal authorities.[370] However, many GDUs were driven into insolvency or merged with neighbours into regional companies, and JSC Gazprom – to which their substantial debts were owed – exchanged this debt for equity and took over significant number of GDUs.[371] As a result, single GDUs were established in several federal subjects of Russia.[372]

Currently there are around 310 GDUs in Russia and the number of GDUs within a federal subject differs from 1 to 33 (e.g. Krasnodar Krai).[373] More than 250 GDUs controlled by JSC Gazprom and operating distribution networks with

---

368 Art. 7 of the Law on Gas Supply also defines an undertaking owning GDS (but not necessarily a GDU) as a specialised entity, which exploits and develops gas networks and their facilities in the relevant territory as well as provides services related to the delivery of gas to the consumers and their support.

369 See *Gerke/Gudkov/Lakhno*, in: Säcker, Handbook of German-Russian energy law, p. 259. See also IEA, Russia Energy Survey 2002, p. 119.

370 See *Stern*, The future of Russian gas and Gazprom, p. 38.

371 See ibid. *Gerke*, *Gudkov* and *Lakhno* consider that a big number of state-regulated GDUs did not allow achieving effective management and security of gas supply simultaneously. In addition, operation of some distribution systems was not profitable due to low sales volume, which in turn prevented their economic and technical development. Thus, the reduction of the number of GDUs was justified by the need of uniform policy in the field of gas distribution and implementation of gasification programs of the federal subjects. In addition, this approach would facilitate the transition to the uniform tariffs within a region, provided that the tariffs of the merged GDUs are lower than those of the non-consolidated ones. See *Gerke/Gudkov/Lakhno*, in: Säcker, Handbook of German-Russian energy law, p. 258 ff.

372 See *Gerke/Gudkov/Lakhno*, in: Säcker, Handbook of German-Russian energy law, p. 259.

373 See *Gerke/Gudkov/Lakhno*, in: Säcker, Handbook of German-Russian energy law, p. 258.

the total length of 650,900 km are consolidated under the umbrella of a specialised subsidiary of JSC Gazprom Mezhregiongaz JSC Gazprom Gazoraspredelenie.[374]

d) Independent undertakings

According to the definition stipulated in Art. 2 of the Law on Gas Supply, independent undertakings are producers and suppliers of gas, which are independent from the owners of the gas supply systems (the UGSS and RGSS) and GDS. The gas produced by independent undertakings covers approximately 35% of gas demand in Russia.[375] The major independent gas producers are JSC Novatek and state-owned JSC NK Rosneft, as well as PJSC Lukoil, JSC NK RusNeft, PJSC Sibneftegaz, PJSC ANK Bashneft and others.[376]

The independent undertakings may sell their gas under the terms of a direct contract with the owner of the UGSS, through their representations, through independent traders, or on the Electronic Trading Platform.[377] However, the volumes of the gas sold at the Electronic Trading Platform are quite limited.[378] At the same time, independent undertakings have a significant competitive advantage: gas produced by them is not subject to state price regulation pursuant to Art. 21 of the Law on Gas Supply[379] and therefore, may be sold at free price on the domestic market.[380] However, they depend on access to the

374 See "O Kompanii" [About the company], information on JSC Gazprom Gazoraspredelenie, available at: http://gazoraspredelenie.gazprom.ru, last accessed on 16.11.2017. The distribution network's under JSC Gazprom Gazoraspredelenie's control constitutes over 80% of the total length of the national distribution networks. See *Böhme*, EU-Russia Energy Relations, p. 65.

375 As of 31.12.2016 JSC Gazprom produced 65.6% of gas produced in Russia. See JSC Gazprom, Gazprom in figures 2012–2016, Factbook, p. 4, available at: http://www.gazprom.com/f/posts/44/307258/gazprom-in-figures-2012-2016-en.pdf, last accessed on 16.11.2017. See also *Karpova*, in: Säcker, Handbook of German-Russian energy law, p. 424.

376 See FAS, Analytical report on the results of the analysis of the competitive situation on the wholesale market of natural gas in 2011–2014, p. 6.

377 *Gerke/Gudkov/Lakhno*, in: Säcker, Handbook of German-Russian energy law, p. 261 f.

378 *Belyi*, Trends of Russia's Gas Sector Regulation, p. 4.

379 See also *Karpova*, in: Säcker, Handbook of German-Russian energy law, p. 423 f.

380 *Seliverstov/Gudkov*, in: Roggenkamp/Barrera-Hernandez/Zillman/Del Guayo, Energy networks and the law, p. 400. However, the competitive prices offered by independent suppliers are usually higher than the regulated prices of JSC Gazprom's subsidiaries. See also *Mechetny*, Legal regulation of gas supply in Russia, p. 17 f.

GTS-UGSS owned by JSC Gazprom and to local GDS in order to be able to supply their gas.[381]

Hence, gas produced by JSC Gazprom or its affiliates is supplied at regulated prices on the domestic market. Any additional gas over the volumes of these supplies is acquired at market prices either from independent undertakings or from JSC Gazprom, as well as other trading companies, which resell the gas of non-Gazprom producers.[382]

It has to mentioned that chapter 1 pt. 2 of the Governmental Regulation of 29.12.2000 on state regulation of prices for gas, tariffs for services of its transportation and charges for technical connection of gas-powered equipment to gas distribution networks[383] (hereinafter Regulation on Prices for gas, Tariffs for transportation services and Fees for connection of gas-powered equipment) additionally introduces the term 'independent transportation undertakings' and defines them as undertakings providing services of gas transportation through the pipelines belonging to them on the right of ownership or on other legal ground and being independent from the owners of the gas supply systems (the UGSS and RGSS) and GDS. Moreover, chapter 2 pt. 4 lit. 'c' of the Regulation also refers to the independent undertakings operating pipelines, tariffs for the transportation services of which underlie the state regulation.

e) Unbundling

Before referring to the rules on access to gas networks, it is important to describe the requirements of unbundling in relation to gas industry in the legislation of Russia. Unlike the EU and Germany, where unbundling of transmission and distribution activities from vertically integrated undertakings is considered to be a prerequisite of a non-discriminatory and transparent access to networks,

---

381 *Seliverstov/Gudkov*, in: Roggenkamp/Barrera-Hernandez/Zillman/Del Guayo, Energy networks and the law, p. 400.

382 See Russian gas market, available at: http://www.gazprom.com/about/marketing/russia, last accessed on 16.11.2017. See also *Ahrend/Tompson*, Russia's Gas Sector, p. 8.

383 Regulation of the Government of the RF on state regulation of prices for gas, tariffs for services of its transportation and charges for technical connection of gas-powered equipment to gas distribution networks in the territory of the RF. [Postanovlenie Praviteslstva RF O gosudarstvennom regulirovaniy tsen na gaz, tarifov na uslugi ego transportirovke i plati za tekhnologicheskoe prisoedinenie gazoispolzuyushchego oborudovania k gazoraspredelitelnim setyam na teritorii RF] N 1021 of 29.12.2000, published in SZ of 08.01.2001, N 2, p. 175, last amended on 17.05.2016.

the legislation of Russia does not attach particular importance to this issue and requires from the so-called natural monopolies only unbundling of accounts on general terms, with no specific regulation for the gas industry.

aa) Unbundling of accounts

Pursuant to Art. 3 of the Federal Law of 17.08.1995 on natural monopolies[384] (hereinafter Law on Natural Monopolies), a natural monopoly is a state of the market of commodities, in which demand is more efficiently satisfied when due to technological peculiarities of the production there is no competition (due to substantial reduction of the production costs per unit of commodity as a result of increasing output). In addition, the commodities manufactured by natural monopolies cannot be substituted with other commodities in the market, thus causing the demand in the given commodity market to be less responsive to changes in price compared to the demand for other types of commodities. Natural monopolies (undertakings) are accordingly commercial entities engaged in the production (sales) of commodities under the conditions of natural monopoly.[385]

The Law on Natural Monopolies further lists the types of activities, which constitute natural monopolies and fall under the scope of this law, inter alia, activity of transport of gas through pipelines, in Art. 4 para. 1. Therefore, gas transmission as well as distribution undertakings constitute natural monopolies. As per Art. 8 para. 4 of the Law on Natural Monopolies, natural monopolies are obliged to keep separate accounts according to the types of activities. These activities are natural gas production, services of natural gas transport through pipelines, natural gas storage and natural gas supply (sales), as defined by Art. 2 of the Regulation on Prices for gas, Tariffs for transportation services and Fees for connection of gas-powered equipment.

The requirement of unbundling of accounts plays a significant role for establishing gas prices and tariffs for the transportation services for independent undertakings by the competent authority since the accounts separated according to production, transmission and supply activities, as required by the Law on Natural Monopolies as well as the Regulation on Prices for gas, Tariffs

384 Federal Law on natural monopolies [Federalniy zakon O estestvennikh monopoliyakh] N 147-FZ of 17.08.1995, published in SZ of 21.08.1995, N 34, p. 3426, last amended on 29.07.2017.

385 See also *Falter*, Russia's natural monopoly, p. 26 ff.

for transportation services and Fees for connection of gas-powered equipment, serve as the basis for the relevant calculations.[386]

bb) De facto legal unbundling

The Presidential Decree of 28.04.1997 on fundamental provisions of the structural reform in the sectors of natural monopolies[387] (hereinafter Decree on Structural Reforms) laid down that as the third stage of the reform of the gas industry in 1999-2000 the structural entities within RJSC Gazprom implementing gas transmission had to be separated from those undertaking gas production. However, no further details regarding the level of separation had been provided, thus this plan did not mean a pure legal unbundling. Moreover, no other legal act has been issued until now that would implement the intention proclaimed by the Decree.

Even though not required by the laws, JSC Gazprom, as mentioned, on the basis of its own 'self-reformation' policy in 2007–2009, separated different types of activities within its group of companies and implemented legal unbundling through charging different subsidiaries with different business tasks.[388] The transmission system GTS-UGSS is managed by 17 subsidiaries of JSC Gazprom, who are active exclusively as transmission operators.[389] All undertakings that are parts of the UGSS, including those that are legally separated, are controlled by JSC Gazprom's CODD.[390] However, the de facto legal unbundling did not concern only separation of transmission from other activities of JSC Gazprom, but many other activities too, including storage and processing. Thus, the ground of the implemented unbundling is not the separation of the activities as it is accepted

386 See *Karpova*, in: Säcker, Handbook of German-Russian energy law, p. 425 f.

387 Decree of the President of the RF on fundamental provisions of the structural reform in the sectors of natural monopolies [Ukaz Prezidenta RF Ob osnovnikh polozheniyakh strukturnoy reformi v sferakh estestvennikh monopoliy] N 426 of 28.04.1997, published in SZ of 05.05.1997, N 18, p. 2132, last amended on 23.07.2001.

388 See *Seliverstov/Gudkov*, in: Roggenkamp/Barrera-Hernandez/Zillman/Del Guayo, Energy networks and the law, p. 402. See also *Karpova*, in: Säcker, Handbook of German-Russian energy law, p. 426. See above part B.I.2.a)bb).

389 *Gavrilina/Gudkov/Lakhno*, in: Säcker, Handbook of German-Russian energy law, p. 185.

390 See Central Operations and Dispatch Department of JSC Gazprom, available at: http://www.gazprom.com/about/production/transportation, last accessed on 16.11.2017. For more details concerning the functions of the CODD see *Gerke/Lakhno*, in: Säcker, Handbook of German-Russian energy law, p. 208 f.

in the EU doctrine with the aim of creating more equal, non-discriminatory and transparent access to gas networks; Rather the purpose of such reformation constitutes merely an entrepreneurial interest to achieve a clearer organisation and improved management of the complex business with many different directions by means of a more overseeable structure.

Even though the state-owned JSC Gazprom has implemented de facto legal unbundling within its organisation according to types of activities, it cannot be perceived as legal unbundling in the whole gas industry as such. Firstly, there is no legal act that would render it impossible for the unbundled structural entities to undertake the activities of any other legally separated areas. Secondly, even though JSC Gazprom undertakes the vast majority of the activities that are crucial for introducing competition in the sector, i.e. transport of gas through high pressure pipelines, it still does not operate all such pipelines, as pointed out above.

The de facto legal unbundling within JSC Gazprom also concerned the GDUs, even though the vast majority of the sector is supplied by the dominant player.[391] By as early as 2004 all deliveries of JSC Gazprom were sold to customers directly by the regional gas supply companies with GDUs acting only as transporters charging a service payment.[392]

However, the experiences in the Member States of the EU have shown that the aim of non-discriminatory and transparent access to networks cannot be achieved only through legal unbundling, where the legally separated undertaking further stays integrated in the umbrella undertaking.[393] For securing the independence of the network operating undertaking it is necessary to implement a functional unbundling, also referred to as management-unbundling.[394] Accordingly, already at the time when the legal unbundling was introduced by the Gas Directive 2003, it had been accompanied with the requirements for functional unbundling.

In the first half of the 2000s, ideas were broadly discussed in Russia to support structural measures aimed at unbundling of vertically integrated gas undertakings in order to definitely eliminate possibilities and incentives for such

391 See also EBRD energy sector assessment 2010, p. 234.

392 *Stern*, The future of Russian gas and Gazprom, p. 39.

393 *Säcker/Schönborn*, in: Säcker, Berlin Commentary on energy law, t. 1, p. 545, para. 2.

394 Ibid.

undertakings to discriminate against third parties.[395] Among others there was a radical proposal of full ownership unbundling which would prohibit combination of competitive with natural monopoly types of activity within one entity or group of entities.[396] However, these ideas had never gained broad support and instead the principle of indivisibility of the UGSS proclaimed by the Law on Gas Supply was further promoted.[397]

395 See *Seliverstov/Gudkov*, in: Roggenkamp/Barrera-Hernandez/Zillman/Del Guayo, Energy networks and the law, p. 402.

396 See ibid.

397 See ibid.

II. Rules of access to gas networks

For the independent undertakings, which are not related to the vertically integrated undertakings owning transmission networks, regional gas supply systems or distribution networks, non-discriminatory access to the network is the most important prerequisite for their market entry and fulfilment of their supply contracts, and thus for competition on the gas supply markets. According to chapter 3 pt. 7 of the Rules on Gas Supply, customers or suppliers of gas are entitled to have their gas transported through the gas transmission network of JSC Gazprom as well as the distribution networks in compliance with the relevant regulations of the Government of Russia. The corresponding obligation of owners of networks is laid down by the Law on Natural Monopolies and the Law on Gas Supply.

The Law on Natural Monopolies prescribes special obligations for natural monopolies in Art. 8, i.e., inter alia, for gas transmission and distribution undertakings. According to Art. 8 para. 1 of the Law, natural monopolies are not entitled to refuse to conclude a contract with consumers on the production (sales) of the goods, which are subject to regulation pursuant to the present law, in case the natural monopoly has a possibility to produce (sell) such goods. Thereby, services of the gas transmission and distribution undertakings may also be considered as 'goods' for the purposes of this provision.[398] Further, Art. 8 para. 3 of the Law on Natural Monopolies requires from the natural monopolies to provide non-discriminatory access to the markets and/or offer goods and services, which are subject to regulation, in compliance with the anti-monopoly legislation of Russia. The term 'anti-monopoly legislation' is defined by Art. 2 and Art. 3 of the Federal Law of 26.07.2006 on protection of competition[399] (hereinafter Law on Competition) as consisting of the Law on Competition and other federal laws regulating the relations connected with the protection of competition. As it can be derived from Art. 2 of the Law, these relations may also be regulated by the Regulations of the Government of Russia and the normative acts of the Federal Anti-monopoly Service, however, they do not constitute parts of the anti-monopoly legislation of Russia.

---

398 See also *Varlamova*, Competition Law of Russia, p. 438 and *Perchik*, Pipeline law, p. 36.

399 Federal Law on protection of competition [Federalniy zakon O zashchite konkurentsii] N 135-FZ of 26.07.2006, published in RG of 27.07.2006, N 162, last amended on 29.07.2017.

The Law on Natural Monopolies provides for the basic principles of the activities of all natural monopolies, which are then further detailed in the laws and legal acts regulating the respective industries.[400] Accordingly, the Law on Gas Supply, derived from Art. 8 para. 1 of the Law on Natural Monopolies, introduces the principle of non-discriminatory third party access to the gas networks and obliges the owners of gas transmission and distribution networks by Art. 27 para. 1 sent. 1 to provide such access to any undertaking operating in the territory of Russia to the spare capacities in their transmission and distribution networks in the manner established by the Government of Russia. As per Art. 27 para. 1 sent. 2 of the Law, the quality of the gas intended for the supply has to comply with the requirements which are approved in the manner provided by the Government of Russia. Thus, the provision of the Law on Gas Supply on TPA transferred and adjusted Art. 8 para. 1 of the Law on Natural Monopolies to gas industry, whereas 'consumers' correspond to 'undertaking operating in the territory of Russia', 'goods' match with services of owners of gas transmission and distribution networks; a 'possibility to produce (sell) such goods' coincides with the existence of 'spare capacities in their transmission and distribution networks'.

As part of the reforms in the sectors of natural monopolies, inter alia, in the gas industry in Russia back in 1997, which started by the adoption of the Decree on Structural Reforms and aimed at creating competition and increasing efficiency of the activities of the natural monopolies, the respective legal act, the Governmental Regulation of 14.07.1997 establishing conditions of access to the transmission system of JSC Gazprom (hereinafter Regulation on access to the GTS-UGSS)[401] was developed and approved as foreseen by the Decree. With regard to conditions of access to distribution networks, the Governmental Regulation on the approval of the provisions on ensuring access of undertakings to local distribution networks (hereinafter Provisions on access to distribution networks) was adopted on 24.11.1998.[402]

---

400 See also *Varlamova*, Competition Law of Russia, p. 439.

401 Regulation of the Government of the RF on ensuring access of independent undertakings to the gas transmission system of JSC Gazprom [Postanovlenie Pravitelstva RF Ob obespechenii dostupa nezavisimikh organizaciy k gazoratransportnoy sisteme otkritogo aktsionernogo obshchestva Gazprom] N 858 of 14.07.1997, published in SZ of 21.07.1997, N 29, p. 3525, last amended on 19.06.2014.

402 Regulation of the Government of the RF on the approval of provisions on ensuring access of undertakings to local distribution networks [Postanovlenie Pravitelstva RF Ob utverzhdenii Polozheniya ob obespechenii dostupa organizatsiy k mestnim gazoraspredelitelnim setyam] N 1370 of 24.11.1998, published in SZ of 30.11.1998, N 48, p. 5937, last amended on 08.08.2013.

The aim of access to the networks is transportation of gas, as per chapter 3 pt. 7 of the Rules on Gas Supply, thus usage of networks of third parties for the purpose of gas transport constitutes the contents of the TPA right. The legal basis for claiming access to networks of transmission and distribution undertakings is the existence of a gas supply contract on the delivery to a consumer as well as the presence of sufficient gas volumes.[403] The dogmatic difference between the TPA right under the legislations of Germany and Russia is that in the first case access to gas network constitutes a statutory obligation, whereas in the second case is represents an obligation to conclude a contract for gas transportation.

On the basis of Art. 5 of the Law on Natural Monopolies, for the regulation and the control of the activities of the natural monopolies, inter alia, transport of gas through pipelines, federal bodies of executive power are formed. Chapters 2 and 3 of the Regulation on Prices for gas, Tariffs for transportation services and Fees for connection of gas-powered equipment further prescribe the prices and tariffs underlying the state regulation in the territory of Russia, as it will be discussed in detail below.

It has to be mentioned that the legislation of Russia on the TPA to gas networks concerns only the access for the purpose of supply within Russia. According to Art. 3 para. 1 of the Law on Gas Export of 18.07.2006,[404] the undertaking that is the owner of the UGSS as well as its 100% subsidiaries are awarded with the exclusive right of export of gas.

1. Access to the Gas Transmission System of JSC Gazprom

Access rights of independent undertakings to the gas transmission network of JSC Gazprom is regulated by the Law on Natural Monopolies, the Law on Gas Supply, the Regulation on access to the GTS-UGSS and the Rules on Gas Supply.

In the following, the scope of the Regulation on access to the GTS-UGSS and the procedure for gaining access to the GTS-UGSS set out by the Regulation presented. In particular, the Regulation has an important position among the legal acts regulating the relationships connected with the access to the GTS-UGSS since it defines the term 'spare capacity of gas transmission system' and

403 *Perchik*, Pipeline law, p. 54.

404 Federal law N 117-FZ of 18.07.2006 on gas export [Federalniy zakon Ob eksporte gaza], published in SZ of 24.07.2006, N 30, p. 3293, last amended on 30.11.2013.

outlines prerequisites and stages of conclusion of contracts for gas transportation through the GTS-UGSS.[405]

a) Scope of regulating access to the GTS-UGSS

TPA to the existing transmission networks in the legislation of Russia refers to the right of access of the independent undertakings to the gas transmission networks owned by JSC Gazprom. Thus, the relationships between JSC Gazprom and its subsidiaries or otherwise associated undertakings concerning the access to the GTS-UGSS are not regulated.

In addition, as mentioned, not all high pressure transmission pipelines in the territory of Russia are parts of the UGSS, i.e. owned by JSC Gazprom, but some of them also constitute integral elements of RGSS on regional levels or are beyond any gas supply system of Russia, i.e. constitute neither the UGSS nor RGSS nor GDS. Yet, the title[406] as well as the contents of the Regulation on access to the GTS-UGSS, establishing conditions of the access to the transmission network, only refer to the access to the gas transmission network owned by JSC Gazprom, i.e. GTS-UGSS. What is more, there is no legislative act in Russia, which would prescribe rules for access to other high pressure pipelines than those owned by JSC Gazprom.[407] The approach concerning the division between the levels, which serves as a basis for origination of rights and obligations in Russia differs from that of the EU and Germany. The definition of the transmission part of the gas industry in Russia is not made only according to the function of the pipelines but also based on the ownership status. Hence, the Regulation on access to the GTS-UGSS regulates access issues to those high pressure pipelines used for gas transportation over long distances that are owned by JSC Gazprom. For ease of comparative assessment, 'gas transmission undertakings' mentioned further in the paper will imply the undertakings of the system of JSC Gazprom providing gas transportation services through the GTS-UGSS.

This legislative gap leads to the practical problems for the enforcement of rights of the persons who are in need of accessing a high pressure pipeline

---

405 *Seliverstov/Gudkov*, in: Roggenkamp/Barrera-Hernandez/Zillman/Del Guayo, Energy networks and the law, p. 401.

406 'Ensuring access of independent undertakings to the gas transmission system of JSC Gazprom' [Obespechenie dostupa nezavisimikh organizaciy k gazoratransportnoy sisteme otkritogo aktsionernogo obshchestva Gazprom].

407 See also *Seliverstov/Gudkov*, in: Roggenkamp/Barrera-Hernandez/Zillman/Del Guayo, Energy networks and the law, p. 402.

that is not part of the UGSS and is not owned by JSC Gazprom. In the case Sakhalin-2,[408] the owner of the pipeline Sakhalin-2, Sakhalin Energy Investment Company Ltd., access to which was indispensable for the access seeker in order to transport gas to its own LNG facility for further processing, denied to allow transportation of gas claiming among other reasons that the operation of the pipeline was not subject to any legal act and therefore, its owner was free to use it according to its own will. However, the Court, starting out from Art. 27 of the Law on Gas Supply that obliges the owners of gas supply systems to grant non-discriminatory access to spare capacities of their networks, came to the conclusion that the pipeline, which was destined to be used for transporting gas but at that moment was still part of an ongoing project, underlay the Regulation on access to the GTS-UGSS by way of analogy. The absence of a legal act regulating the specific case should not mean that the relationship is not regulated at all, as per statement of the Court.

b) The holder of the third party access right to the Gas Transmission System of JSC Gazprom and the obliged party

As stipulated in chapter 3 pt. 4 of the Regulation on access to the GTS-UGSS, for the purpose of transporting gas, any undertaking operating in the territory of Russia is entitled to non-discriminatory access to the GTS-UGSS of JSC Gazprom. Accordingly, the party obliged to grant non-discriminatory access to the GTS-UGSS is an undertaking of the system of JSC Gazprom operating respective section of the GTS-UGSS, i.e. JSC Gazprom itself, its subsidiaries and dependent companies, as well as any other undertakings controlled by JSC Gazprom, as defined by the Regulation.

Based on the wording of chapter 3 pt. 4 of the Regulation on access to the GTS-UGSS, not only producers or suppliers, but also any other undertakings, e.g. customers acting in the territory of Russia may claim the TPA.[409] In addition, chapter 3 pt. 7 of the Rules on Gas Supply also refers to the right of customers or suppliers to have their gas transported through the networks.

Even though the aforementioned provision of the Regulation on access to the GTS-UGSS as well as the general rule on granting access to gas networks

---

408 Judgment of the Commercial Court of Far Eastern District N F03-3922/2015 of 15.09.2015 [Postanovleniye Arbitrazhnogo Suda Dalnevostochnogo Okruga] (hereinafter Sakhalin-2).

409 See also *Seliverstov/Gudkov*, in: Roggenkamp/Barrera-Hernandez/Zillman/Del Guayo, Energy networks and the law, p. 401.

stipulated in Art. 27 of the Law on Gas Supply refer to the entitlement of 'any undertaking', all further rules and conditions established by the Regulation on access to the GTS-UGSS cover the procedure concerning independent undertakings, so only such undertakings may be considered as persons holding TPA right. Therefore, the reference to 'any independent undertaking' would contribute to increased specificity and more precise expression of the rule.

aa) *Notion of independent undertakings*

Chapter 1 of the Regulation on access to the GTS-UGSS defines independent undertakings as undertakings, which are not part of the system of JSC Gazprom and lists in brackets independent producers, suppliers and customers of gas. The Regulation also defines 'undertakings of the system of JSC Gazprom' as JSC Gazprom itself, its subsidiaries and dependent companies[410], as well as any other undertakings controlled by JSC Gazprom. In contrast to this definition of independent undertakings, Art. 2 of the Law on Gas Supply limits the notion to the producers and suppliers of gas. In any event, the definition of the Law does not refer to the independence from the system of JSC Gazprom, but from any gas supply system (the UGSS, RGSS and GDS). Hence, unlike the Law on Gas Supply, for the purposes of the Regulation on access to the GTS-UGSS an independent undertaking will also be an undertaking owning RGSS or GDS, unless it constitutes a part of the system of JSC Gazprom.

Even though none of the two definitions offer criteria for determining independence, it can be concluded that for the purposes of the Regulation on access to the GTS-UGSS an undertaking may only then be considered independent, when it is not controlled, i.e. when the decisions of its management bodies are not decisively influenced by the undertakings of JSC Gazprom's system.[411]

A critical point, however, is the existing difference between definitions of the same notion in two legal acts, the Law on Gas Supply on the one hand, and the Regulation on access to the GTS-UGSS on the other hand, both of them regulating the relations within the same sector.

---

410 According to former Art. 106 of the Civil Code of Russia, a company could be recognised as 'dependent' if another company possessed over 20% of its shares. However, the provision has been repealed as of 01.09.2014.

411 See also *Gerke/Gudkov/Lakhno*, in: Säcker, Handbook of German-Russian energy law, p. 569.

bb) *Nationality of the holders of the third party access right to the GTS-UGSS*

The Decree on Structural Reforms laid down that the reforms of the gas industry were, inter alia, aimed at granting non-discriminatory access to spare capacities of the networks to 'Russian independent producers'.[412] However, the Regulation on access to the GTS-UGSS did not continue with the differentiation according to the nationality and entitled undertakings 'in the territory of Russia' with the right of non-discriminatory access to the GTS-UGSS of JSC Gazprom. Art. 27 of the Law on Gas Supply also stuck to the territorial principle and referred to granting TPA right to the undertakings 'operating in the territory of Russia'[413]. Therefore, it can be concluded that undertakings, which carry out their activities in the territory of Russia, irrespective of their nationality, may be subject to the right of access to the GTS-UGSS.

To sum up, the undertakings of the system of JSC Gazprom, i.e. any undertakings controlled by JSC Gazprom, as defined by the Regulation on the access to the GTS-UGSS, and operating respective sections of high pressure gas pipelines are the obliged parties of the mandatory TPA to the GTS-UGSS. All other undertakings operating in the territory of Russia as producers, suppliers or customers of gas are entitled to non-discriminatory access to the transmission network of JSC Gazprom.

cc) *Discrimination already by the definition of regulated relationships*

Even though the TPA right is described as 'a right of any undertaking to non-discriminatory access' in chapter 3 pt. 4 of the Regulation on access to the GTS-UGSS, as observed throughout the Regulation as well as stated by chapter 2 pt. 2, the present Regulation defines conditions and order of access of independent undertakings in the territory of Russia to the GTS-UGSS for the supply of gas to consumers in Russia. Thus, the equal treatment of independent undertakings, gas suppliers, producers or customers on the one hand, and the subsidiaries of or undertakings otherwise related to JSC Gazprom also acting as suppliers, producers or customers on the other hand, is upfront excluded by the fact, that the relationships regarding application of access and conditions are not covered by the same legal act. As a result, unlike the EnWG of Germany, where both forms of discrimination, vertical, i.e. unequal treatment of external network

412 *Nezavisimie Rossiyskie proizvoditeli.*

413 *Osushchestvlyayushchie deatelnost na teritorii RF.*

users against the ones affiliated with the network operator, as well as horizontal, i.e. unequal treatment of an extern network user against other extern network users are prohibited,[414] for the legislator of Russia only prohibition of the latter form of discrimination is relevant.

What is more, the relationships between JSC Gazprom and its subsidiaries or otherwise associated undertakings concerning the access to the GTS-UGSS are not regulated at all, meaning that JSC Gazprom is absolutely free to grant to the 'dependent undertakings' access under any conditions including charging any fee for transportation services; whereas the independent undertakings have to stick to the procedure prescribed by the Regulation on access to the GTS-UGSS.

In practice, the formal grounds of refusal of access based on the Regulation on access to the GTS-UGSS are often used by JSC Gazprom to discriminate between market players and to eliminate competition in the upstream or downstream markets, as will be discussed further below.[415]

c) Prerequisites of access to the Gas Transmission System of JSC Gazprom

According to chapter 3 pt. 5 of the Regulation on access to the GTS-UGSS, JSC Gazprom grants access to its transmission network to independent undertakings on the basis of contracts concluded between these undertakings and JSC Gazprom or its gas transmission undertakings on the behalf of JSC Gazprom, if the following requirements are met:

a) There is spare capacity in the transmission network from the connection point to the extraction point in the period of gas supply requested by the supplier;
b) The quality and features of the supplied gas comply with the standards and technical requirements of the system of JSC Gazprom as well as with other normative-technical documents;
c) The suppliers have the pipelines leading to the network and the customers, the discharge pipes with data collection and quality control points at their disposal for the start date of gas supply requested by the supplier.

The definition of spare capacity has decisive importance in these legal relations since access has to be granted only to such capacities.[416] Chapter 1 of the Regulation

414 See *Säcker/Boesche*, in: Säcker, Berlin Commentary on energy law, t. 1, p. 1243 f., para. 40 f.
415 See below part B.III.2.d)bb)(3).
416 See *Gudkov*, Gas transportation in Russia, NiG, 4/2009, p. 48.

on access to the GTS-UGSS defines 'spare capacity of the GTS-UGSS' as technically possible capacity of the network for receipt and transport of gas except for those volumes of gas transport, which are needed i) for undertakings of the system of JSC Gazprom and independent undertakings under existing contracts at that certain moment and ii) for compulsory gas supplies by undertakings of the system of JSC Gazprom in accordance with the decisions of the President and the Government of Russia, i.e. for state needs.[417] Hence, if e.g. technically possible capacity of the transmission network constitutes 10 billion m^3, 5 billion m^3 are booked for existing contracts and 2 billion m^3 are reserved for compulsory supplies, 3 billion m^3 will be considered to be spare capacity, to which the independent undertakings may claim their TPA right.[418]

With regard to the quality of the supplied gas, Art. 27 sent. 2 of the Law on Gas Supply also prescribes that the quality of the gas intended for the supply has to comply with the requirements which are approved in the manner provided by the Government of Russia.

d) Contractual arrangement of gas transportation through the GTS-UGSS

Pursuant to chapter 3 pt. 8 of the Rules on Gas Supply, the conditions and order of gas transmission through the GTS-UGSS are stipulated in contracts for gas transportation through the GTS-UGSS. Due to the conceptual differences between the approaches in the legislations under examination in terms of the division between transmission and distribution levels presented above,[419] and also since the Russian equivalent for both transmission and distribution contracts coincide with each other (*dogovor transportirovki gaza*), the reference will be made to 'contract for gas transportation through the GTS-UGSS' instead of mentioning 'gas transmission contract'.

The contracts for gas transportation through the GTS-UGSS are formed between JSC Gazprom or its gas transmission undertakings on the behalf of JSC Gazprom on the one hand, and the independent producers, suppliers, or customers on the other hand. In terms of duration, there are three types of contracts as defined by chapter 1 of the Regulation on access to the GTS-UGSS: short-term contracts with a duration not exceeding 1 year; middle-term

417 See *Gerke/Gudkov/Lakhno*, in: Säcker, Handbook of German-Russian energy law, p. 577.

418 See ibid.

419 See above part B.II.1.a).

contracts from 1 to 5 years; and long-term contracts with a duration of more than 5 years.

The independent undertakings wishing to gain access to the GTS-UGSS have to follow the procedure and stages defined by the Regulation on access to the GTS-UGSS as well as the Rules on Gas Supply.

aa) Application for access to the GTS-UGSS

First of all, independent undertakings seeking access to the GTS-UGSS have to submit an application to JSC Gazprom in a form approved by the commission of the Government of Russia for the issues of the use of oil and gas high pressure pipelines on a submission of JSC Gazprom. The application has to contain the following mandatory data as per chapter 3 pt. 6 of the Regulation on access to the GTS-UGSS:

1) Information about the supplier;
2) Sources of the gas and their characteristics;
3) Start and end date of the gas supply;
4) Volumes of the gas supplies for every quarter of the first year and for every year for the whole period of middle- and long-term contracts; for every month for the whole period of short-term contracts;
5) Conditions of the gas supplies (firm and interruptible);
6) Quality characteristics and parameters of the supplied gas;
7) Connection point of the pipelines leading to the GTS-UGSS;
8) Point of the gas delivery to the customer;
9) Confirmation of willingness to accept gas in declared volumes by the GDUs and the customers in the period of the gas supply;
10) Documents certifying the right of ownership on the gas or the existence of contractual obligations on gas sales (purchase).

The requirements concerning the contents of the application have to be uniform for all applicants. Refusal to accept the application containing all mandatory data is not allowed.

Applications for the conclusion of short-term contracts have to be submitted not later than 1 month and not earlier than 3 months before the start date of the supply; in the case of middle-term contracts not later than 3 months and not earlier than 1 year before the first year of the gas supply; for long-term contracts not later than 6 months and not earlier than 3 years before the first year of the gas supply.

The applications of independent undertakings for access to the GTS-UGSS are handled by the CODD; it delivers opinions about the technical possibility of transporting gas through the GTS-UGSS.[420] However, the CODD does not constitute an independent legal person and is not independently responsible to other participants of the gas market.[421] According to chapter 4 pt. 19 of the Rules on Gas Supply, the CODD is a department of JSC Gazprom.

bb) Decisions on applications for access to the GTS-UGSS

According to chapter 3 pt. 11 and 12 of the Regulation on access to the GTS-UGSS, JSC Gazprom has to decide within 15 days on the applications for short-term contracts, within 2 months for middle-term contracts and within 3 months for long-term contracts from the day of receipt of the application. As a result of examining an application, JSC Gazprom will make one of the following decisions: a) agree to conclude a contract, either in full or partial compliance with the terms requested in the application; or b) refuses to conclude a contract and give reasons for its decision (reasoned refusal). The applicant is informed within 3 days about the decision made on the application.

(1) Consent to conclude contract for gas transportation through the GTS-UGSS

JSC Gazprom has to make a decision on a full or partial approval of an application for access to the GTS-UGSS depending on the spare capacities available in the network and considering the priorities of granting access set out by the Regulation on access to the GTS-UGSS.

Chapter 3 pt. 9 of the Regulation on access to the GTS-UGSS regulates the cases when the volumes of gas transmission requested by independent undertakings and the volumes of transmission planned by JSC Gazprom for a certain period exceed the spare capacity of the transmission network. On such occasion, the commission of the government of Russia for the issues of the use of oil and gas trunk pipelines for access to the GTS-UGSS[422] can make a decision entitling an independent undertaking to use the existing technical possibility of the transmission network, not exceeding the volumes of spare capacities in

---

420 *Gerke/Gudkov/Lakhno*, in: Säcker, Handbook of German-Russian energy law, p. 572 f.

421 *Varlamova*, Competition Law of Russia, p. 442.

422 Note that commission of the government of Russia for the issues of the use of oil and gas trunk pipelines for access to the GTS-UGSS has been abolished by the Regulation N 215 of the Government of the RF of 16.04.2004.

the requested period. The decision has to consider technological reserves of the network in compliance with the applicable standards. Therefore, if there is not as much spare capacity in the network as requested by an independent undertaking, it may still be granted access to the volumes that are available in the system in that period.

Art. 27 sent. 3 of the Law on Gas Supply lays down that in the first place access to the networks has to be granted to the suppliers of stripped dry gas gained after processing associated petroleum gas. Associated petroleum gas is produced in the process of oil production. In order to prevent its burn and thus increase of CO_2 emissions, this gas may be processed into stripped dry gas, which has characteristics similar to those of natural gas and can be used for the same purposes as natural gas.[423]

According to chapter 3 pt. 10 of the Regulation on access to the GTS-UGSS, in cases of lack of spare capacity in the transmission network, necessary for approving all applications, the priority has to be given in the first place to the suppliers for communal and household needs of the population and to the suppliers of stripped dry gas, which is gained after processing associated petroleum gas.[424] The undertakings, which purchase and sell natural gas on the organised auctions, are in the second place. The suppliers planning supplies for a longer period as compared to other applicants are following on the third place. All other applications of independent undertakings are handled in compliance with the anti-monopoly legislation and are granted access either proportionally according to the requested volumes of the transmission or based on an auction in the manner established by the Government of Russia.

Interestingly, the provision concerning the order in which applications of independent undertakings are approved, beyond the ones to be approved as a priority, only considers the option of granting access proportionally according to the requested volumes ceteris paribus.[425] The possibility of a tender as well as the reference to 'all other applications' appeared in the provision after the amendment in 2001. Moreover, according to the current version of the provision, the principle of proportionality does not necessarily apply in the case of equal conditions. In fact, for those applicants not enjoying priority access rights

423 See information about associated petroleum gas by JSC Gazprom, available at: http://www.gazprominfo.com/articles/associated-gas, last accessed on 16.11.2017.

424 JSC Gazprom operates a number of processing plants. See http://www.gazprom.com/about/production/processing, last accessed on 16.11.2017.

425 See also *Grigoryev*, The Russian gas industry, ELJ 28:125, p. 131 ff.

the principle of first-come-first-served applies, based on which applications are approved according to the date of their receipt.[426]

It should also be mentioned that the provision concerning the priority access right of the suppliers of stripped dry gas, which has been added to the Regulation by the amending Governmental Regulation N 566 of 19.06.2014, lacks clarity in the positioning of the suppliers of stripped dry gas towards the suppliers for communal and household needs of the population. According to chapter 3 pt. 10 sent. 2 of the Regulation on access to the GTS-UGSS, both customers of gas transmission undertakings enjoy equal priority access rights to the GTS-UGSS. This uncertainty leaves space for different interpretations of the provision, therefore it is recommended to clarify the priorities unambiguously.

(2) Reasoned refusal to conclude a contract for gas transportation through the GTS-UGSS

JSC Gazprom may refuse to conclude a contract for gas transportation through the GTS-UGSS but has to give reasons for this decision.[427] Unlike the law of the EU and Germany, the Regulation on access to the GTS-UGSS as well as other acts of the legislation of Russia do not define what arguments are eligible for justifying a refusal, i.e. what the possible grounds of refusal are. Yet, it can be presumed that if the prerequisites of access to the transmission network stipulated in chapter 3 pt. 4 of the Regulation on access to the GTS-UGSS are not fulfilled, the application can be rejected. Therefore, lack of capacity, lack of connection, as well as insufficient quality of gas can serve as a reason for a refusal. However, in practice gas transmission undertakings also refer to non-compliance with other provisions of the Regulation on access to the GTS-UGSS by independent undertakings in order to give reasons for their refusal. Moreover, the Regulation on access to the GTS-UGSS also does not prescribe that the ground of refusal of access has to be contained in the Regulation itself.

Therefore, it is preferable that possible grounds for refusal of access are clearly stipulated in the Regulation on access to the GTS-UGSS, as is the case in sec. 20 para. 2 sent. 1 of the EnWG of Germany, according to which the network operators may refuse the access only if they substantiate that on operational or other grounds granting access is not possible or not reasonable, taking into account the objectives of sec. 1 of the EnWG.

---

426 *Varlamova*, Competition Law of Russia, p. 444.

427 Reasoned refusal to conclude a contract (*Reshenie o motivirovannom otkaze ot zaklyiucheniya dogovora*).

cc) Arrangement of contracts for gas transportation through the GTS-UGSS

After deciding on a full or partial approval of an application, JSC Gazprom submits an offer to conclude a contract to the applicant, the supplier or the customer, as regulated by chapter 3 pt. 10 of the Rules on Gas Supply. The offer has to be submitted together with the permission of access to the transmission network, issued in the manner established by the Government of Russia. The party which received an offer, i.e. the independent undertaking, has to consent on the conclusion of the contract within 30 days from the moment of receipt of the offer, unless a different term has been set in the offer itself. In the case of a dissent with the offered conditions, the party which received the offer has to submit a report of disagreement to the offering party i.e. JSC Gazprom. If the independent undertaking does not receive any feedback within 30 days after sending the report of disagreement, it may refer the matter to the court. Apart from that, it may terminate the existing contract for gas transportation with JSC Gazprom after the expiry of its duration (e.g. the customer may stop extracting gas), i.e. the independent undertaking does not have to stick to the conditions of the new offer. If the independent undertaking continues to fulfil the existing contract (e.g. the customer continues extracting gas) after the expiry of the mentioned 30 days or after the expiry of the duration of the contract, this action is considered as a consent to the conclusion of the contract for gas transportation through the GTS-UGSS with the conditions offered by JSC Gazprom.

Apart from this procedure, the deadlines set out in chapter 3 pt. 13 of the Regulation on access to the GTS-UGSS have to be considered too. Namely, contracts for gas transportation through the GTS-UGSS have to be concluded within a certain period after the date of the decision on the approval: within 1 month for short-term contracts, within 2 months for middle-term contracts, and within 3 months for long-term contracts.

e) Conditions of gas transportation through the GTS-UGSS

Contracts for gas transportation through the GTS-UGSS contain provisions on volumes, transmission routes, tariffs, and other conditions as agreed by the parties and in accordance with the legislation. JSC Gazprom adopts the form of the contract in compliance with the conditions of transport of gas laid down in the Regulation on access to the GTS-UGSS as well as other legislative acts of Russia.

The Regulation on access to the GTS-UGSS prescribes conditions of transport of gas in terms of duties of the parties, early termination of contracts for gas transportation through the GTS-UGSS, expenses of connection to the network and charges for the transportation services.

aa) Duties of independent undertakings

According to chapter 4 pt. 18 of the Regulation on access to the GTS-UGSS, the independent undertakings making use of the transmission network of JSC Gazprom have the following duties:

1) To ensure the level of preparedness of gas for transportation in accordance with applicable standards and technical conditions, as well as data collection at the points of delivery and receipt of gas;[428]
2) To present operative information about technological regimes of their facilities of gas industry and gas pipelines to JSC Gazprom within the prescribed time;
3) To inform JSC Gazprom about accidents, extraordinary situations, planned preventive maintenance, and other works on their facilities, as well as about possible alterations of the volumes of gas input into the transmission network as compared to the volumes stipulated in the contract;
4) To agree with JSC Gazprom on the schedules of restoring the regime of gas supplies up to the level laid down by the contract;
5) To comply with the norms and requirements of pipeline maintenance and security of gas transportation;
6) To grant unrestricted access to the authorised representatives of JSC Gazprom for controlling data collection of volumes and quality of gas;
7) To ensure a constant and stable radio or telephone connection between dispatching units of the supplier and JSC Gazprom.

bb) Duties of JSC Gazprom

According to chapter 4 pt. 20 of the Regulation on access to the GTS-UGSS, the undertakings of the system of JSC Gazprom[429] have the following duties:

---

428 The duty of data collection itself may also be fulfilled by the gas transmission undertaking on behalf of the independent undertaking as per Art. 5 pt. 22 of the Rules on Gas Supply.

429 See the definition of 'undertaking of the system of JSC Gazprom' above in part B.II.1.b) aa).

1) To provide information about the availability of spare capacities in the transmission network and about their plans concerning the employment of the transmission network in certain periods of time on certain sites, as well as about applications received for access to these sites (to the extent of the mandatory data required for an application, stipulated under chapter 3 pt. 6 numbers 1, 3 to 5 and 7 to 10 of the Regulation on access to the GTS-UGSS[430]) and dates of their receipt;
2) To provide information upon request of independent undertakings about the availability of spare capacities in the transmission networks in certain periods of time on certain sites, as well as about applications received for access to these sites (to the extent of the mandatory data required for an application, stipulated under chapter 3 pt. 6 numbers 1, 3 to 5 and 7 to 10 of the Regulation on access to the GTS-UGSS[431]);
3) To provide gas transportation services to independent undertakings in a non-discriminatory manner in compliance with the Regulation on access to the GTS-UGSS;
4) To inform gas suppliers and customers timely about alterations of work regimes, accidents and extraordinary situations in the transmission network, as well as failures of the data collection system of gas;
5) To inform gas suppliers and customers in good time about planned maintenance and preventive works, influencing the fulfilment of gas suppliers' obligations and work regimes of gas customers;
6) To grant unrestricted access to the authorised representatives of suppliers and customers of gas for controlling data collection of volumes and quality of gas.

Apart from these duties, a contract for gas transportation through the GTS-UGSS may also determine that the gas transmission undertaking has to fulfil the duty of data collection at the points of delivery and receipt of gas on behalf of the supplier (customer), as per chapter 5 pt. 22 of the Rules on Gas Supply.

In order to organise the process of gas transport, the owner of the pipelines, which is in most cases JSC Gazprom itself, in its turn concludes with the undertakings of the system of JSC Gazprom exploiting respective sections of the GTS-UGSS either maintenance contracts or lease agreements.[432]

430 See above part B.II.1.d)aa).

431 See ibid.

432 *Korepanov*, Contracts for gas transportation through high pressure pipelines, p. 207 f.

cc) *Early termination of contracts for gas transportation through the GTS-UGSS*

According to chapter 4 pt. 19 of the Regulation on access to the GTS-UGSS, a contract may be terminated before it is due to expire in the following cases:

1) If the supplier culpably fails to deliver gas to the transmission network in the volumes and terms stipulated in the contract; in this case a new contract with modified conditions may be concluded;
2) If the supplier does not pay for gas transportation services in the manner and within the time limits prescribed by the contract;
3) If an independent undertaking culpably fails to fulfil any of those obligations stipulated in chapter 4 pt. 18 of the Regulation on access to the GTS-UGSS.[433]

dd) *Expenses of connection to the network*

According to chapter 4 pt. 16 of the Regulation on access to the GTS-UGSS, all expenses related to the connection of facilities of independent undertakings to the existing transmission network have to be borne by the independent undertakings, unless a different term has been set either in the contract or in the legislation of Russia. However, unlike the law of the EU and Germany, the legislation of Russia defines neither the methodology for the calculation nor sets tariffs for such connection services for independent undertakings.[434] Accordingly, it is up to the agreement between the contracting parties to arrange the amount of expenses related to the connection to the network.

Usually, a contract for the connection to the GTS-UGSS between an independent undertaking and JSC Gazprom is concluded separately from the contract

433 See above part B.II.1.e)aa).

434 However, the legislation of Russia regulates charges for the connection of gas-powered equipment to distribution networks in Art. 23.2 of the Law on Gas Supply and by the Regulation on Prices for gas, Tariffs for transportation services and Fees for connection of gas-powered equipment, as well as charges for the connection of objects of capital construction to distribution networks (see Regulation of the Government of RF N 1314 of 30.12.2013 on the approval of the Rules on connection (technical connection) of objects of capital construction to distribution networks, as well as amending and repealing several acts of the Government of RF [Postanovlenie Pravitelstva RF Ob utverzhdenii Pravil podklyucheniya (tekhnicheskovo prisoedeneniya) obyektov kapitalnovo stroitelstva k setyam gazoraspredeleniya, a takzhe ob izmenenii i priznanii utrativshimi silu nekotorikh aktov Pravitelstva RF], published in SZ of 13.01.2014, N 2 (part I), p. 137), last amended on 15.04.2014.

for gas transportation. Technical conditions for the connection to the network are issued by the gas transmission undertakings as per chapter 3 pt. 4 sent. 2 of the Rules on Gas Supply.

ee) Charges for transportation services through high pressure gas networks

Independent undertakings have to pay for the transportation services provided by JSC Gazprom. It has to be noted, that according to chapter 2 pt. 5 of the Regulation on Prices for gas, Tariffs for transportation services and Fees for connection of gas-powered equipment, however, state regulation of tariffs for the transportation services applies transitionally only to independent undertakings, until uniform tariffs for all suppliers will be introduced.

According to Art. 8 of the Law on Gas Supply, the federal bodies of executive power have the authority to define the principles for the formation of prices for gas and tariffs for services of gas transportation through transmission and distribution networks. Thus, the Regulation on Prices for gas, Tariffs for transportation services and Fees for connection of gas-powered equipment concerns only principles and does not set prices or tariffs as such.[435] Art. 21 of the Law on Gas Supply also defines that the provision of services of gas transportation is considered as a natural monopoly by the Law and is therefore regulated. According to chapter 2 pt. 4 of the Regulation on Prices for gas, Tariffs for transportation services and Fees for connection of gas-powered equipment, only the tariffs for independent undertakings for transportation services through high pressure pipelines are subject to state regulation. Thus, the charges to be paid for transportation services by undertakings of the system of JSC Gazprom to other undertakings of the group operating the GTS-UGSS are not regulated.

As per chapter 4 pt. 17 of the Regulation on access to the GTS-UGSS, the payment has to be made in compliance with the tariffs approved by the Federal Energy Commission (hereinafter also FEC). However, the FEC has been reorganised into the Federal Tariff Service in 2004, which has been subsequently abolished in 2015 and the FAS became its legal successor. Accordingly, the provisions of the Federal Anti-monopoly Service approved by the Regulation of the Government of Russia on 30.06.2004[436] (hereinafter Provisions of the FAS)

---

435 *Karpova*, in: Säcker, Handbook of German-Russian energy law, p. 423.

436 Regulation of the Government of RF on the approval of the provisions of the Federal Anti-monopoly Service [Postanovleniye Pravitelstva RF Ob utverzhdenii Polozheniya o Federalnoy antimonopolnoy sluzhbe] N 331 of 30.06.2004, published in RG of 31.07.2004, N 162, amendments of 17.10.2016 effective from 01.01.2017, last amended on 01.07.2016.

lay down in chapter 2 pt. 5.3.21.16 that the Federal Anti-monopoly Service has the competence of approving the tariffs for the transport of gas through pipelines. This inaccuracy will also be addressed in more detail below when discussing the competent authority for the enforcement of TPA rights in the gas sector. Further, the FAS is also in charge of setting out the rules for applying prices (tariffs) for the goods (works, services) of natural monopolies, pursuant to chapter 2 pt. 5.2.9(25) of the Provisions of the FAS.

According to chapter 4 pt. 11 of the Regulation on Prices for gas, Tariffs for transportation services and Fees for connection of gas-powered equipment, the tariffs for the transportation services should be calculated considering that they have to a) compensate economically reasonable expenses related to the transport of gas, of the undertakings, activities of which are regulated (i.e. transmission and distribution undertakings) b) include a reasonable return rate for the undertakings, activities of which are regulated, c) enable satisfaction of solvent demand on gas, reach an economic balance between the interests of suppliers and customers, d) take account of all taxes and other obligatory fees as set by the legislation of Russia, e) take account of differences between various groups of customers and regions in relation to the actual value of transportation services and gas supply (sales) for these groups or regions, f) facilitate competition within the gas sector as well as between different sectors (substitute fuels).

According to Art. 23.1 of the Law on Gas Supply, a competent federal body of executive power controls (supervises) the processes of fixing and applying regulated tariffs (as well as prices) in the field of gas supply. According to pt. 4 of the Governmental Regulation of 27.06.2013 on state control (supervision) in the field of regulated state prices (tariffs)[437] (hereinafter Regulation on State Control of Regulated Prices and Tariffs), the Federal Anti-monopoly Service and the bodies of executive power in the field of state regulation of prices (tariffs) of federal subjects of Russia are entitled to undertake such control. According to pt. 6 lit. 'b' of the aforementioned Regulation, these bodies check whether the organs of executive power of federal subjects as well as legal entities of the gas industry comply with the legislation of Russia in terms of correctness and economic reasonableness of expenses and other data, which are considered while

437 Regulation of the Government of the RF on state control (supervision) in the field of regulated state prices (tariffs), as well as amending and repealing several acts of the Government of the RF [Postanovlenie Pravitelstva RF O Gosudarstvennom kontrole (nadzore) v oblasti reguliruemikh gosudarstvom tsen (tarifov), a takzhe izmenenii i priznanii utrativshimi silu nekotorikh aktov Pravitelstva RF] N 543 of 27.06.2013, published in SZ of 08.07.2013, N 27, p. 3602, last amended on 05.02.2016.

fixing the tariffs (and prices) in the gas industry, economic reasonableness of factual expenses and correctness of application of tariffs by the legal entities.

Even though the tariffs for gas transport through pipelines are approved by the FAS, the conditions of payments (terms, form etc.) are defined by the contract for gas transportation through GTS-UGSS as per chapter 6 pt. 31 of the Rules on Gas Supply.

f) Grounds of refusal of access to the GTS-UGSS invoked in practice

As mentioned above, the grounds of refusal of access to the GTS-UGSS are not directly foreseen by the legislation. Thus, it may be presumed that as grounds for refusal of access may serve the prerequisites of access to the network prescribed in chapter 3 pt. 5 of the Regulation – lack of spare capacity in the transmission network from the connection point to the extraction point in the period of gas supply requested by the supplier; insufficient quality and features of the supplied gas; lack of connection, i.e. pipelines leading to the network and the customers, the discharge pipes with data collection and quality control points for the start date of gas supply requested by the supplier.

However, the fact that on the one hand, the Regulation of access to the GTS-UGSS contains many other requirements in relation to applying and granting access to the GTS-UGSS, and on the other hand, there are no statutory grounds of refusal of access foreseen by any legal act in Russia, lead to a situation where the monopolist transmission network operator is free to invoke non-fulfilment of any unsubstantial mandatory requirement of the Regulation on access to the GTS-UGSS as a ground for refusal of access and therewith ban the independent undertaking from the market of gas supply. In the vast majority of cases where actions have been brought against refusals of access to the GTS-UGSS, JSC Gazprom has relied exactly on non-fulfilment of such requirements and did not give an economic or technological explanation of the impossibility or unreasonableness of granting access.

The Regulation on access to the GTS-UGSS also does not prescribe that the ground of refusal of access has to be contained in the Regulation itself. However, in the case Gazprom vs. FAS (Real-Gaz)[438], the FAS as well as the courts, while arguing the inadmissibility of the grounds invoked by JSC Gazprom for

438 Judgment of the Federal Commercial Court of Moscow District N A40-69840/12-79-654 of 27.02.2013 [Postanovleniye Federalnogo Arbitrazhnogo Suda Moskovskogo Okruga] (hereinafter Gazprom vs. FAS (Real-Gaz)).

substantiating its refusal, stated that these grounds were not foreseen by the Regulation on access to the GTS-UGSS.[439]

In the following, examples of grounds of refusal of access invoked in practice will be presented based on the cases before the FAS and the courts of Russia.

aa) Lack of capacity

The existence of spare capacity in the gas transmission network is one of the prerequisites of access to the GTS-UGSS as per chapter 3 pt. 5 para. 2. According to the definition contained in chapter 1 of the Regulation on access to the GTS-UGSS, spare capacity is technically possible capacity of the network for receipt and transport of gas except for those volumes of gas transport, which are needed for undertakings of the system of JSC Gazprom and independent undertakings under existing contracts at that certain moment and for compulsory gas supplies by undertakings of the system of JSC Gazprom in accordance with the decisions of the President and the Government of Russia. Therefore, lack of capacity should be one of the main reasons for refusing access to the GTS-UGSS. However, the case law of Russia in this regard is very limited, not least because of the fact that there is no other mechanism for examining whether there is spare capacity in the gas network other than the information provided by CODD, i.e. JSC Gazprom itself.

In the case Gazprom vs. FAS (Real-Gaz), even though JSC Gazprom had not declared lack of capacity as a reason of refusal of access initially, the natural monopoly has later relied on the fact that there were no capacities in the transmission network from the connection point to the extraction point in the period of gas supply requested by the supplier, i.e. LLC Real-Gaz. However, this fact has not been confirmed in the course of the further investigation and thus the refusal of JSC Gazprom has been declared unsubstantiated. The assumption of the FAS and the courts concerning the existence of spare capacity in the network relied on the fact that JSC Gazprom granted full access to the same section for transportation through the same route to another undertaking, after the natural monopoly had refused to conclude a contract with LLC Real-Gaz.

In the case Sakhalin-2, the access seeker, JSC NK Rosneft applied to Sakhalin Energy Investment Ltd, the owner of the gas pipeline Sakhalin-2, for granting access in order to transport up to 8 billion m^3 gas. The owner of Sakhalin-2 denied giving access to the pipeline invoking the existing lack of sufficient capacity in the network, among other reasoning for refusal. In the course of

439 See Gazprom vs. FAS (Real-Gaz), p. 2.

the investigation it has been ascertained that indeed there were no capacities of 8 billion m^3 in the pipeline since the overall capacity of the pipeline constituted 18.2 billion m^3 and some 16 billion m^3 were being used and/or contracted. However, the Appellate Court considered that the obliged party – the owner of the pipeline had to grant access to JSC NK Rosneft to the existing capacities of the network, irrespective of the requested volumes, referring to chapter 3 pt. 9 of the Regulation on access to the GTS-UGSS.[440] According to this provision, when the volumes of gas transmission requested by independent undertakings and the volumes of transmission planned by JSC Gazprom for a certain time period exceed the spare capacity of the transmission network, the independent undertakings are entitled to use the existing technical possibility of the transmission network, considering the technological reserves in compliance with the applicable standards, and not exceeding the volumes of spare capacity in the requested period. Moreover, the Appellate Court also pointed to the fact that the access seeker had requested network capacity of up to 8 billion m^3 without stating the lowest volume acceptable.[441]

bb) Lack of connection

In the case Gazprom vs. FAS (Real-Gaz), along with the lack of capacity, JSC Gazprom also mentioned the lack of connection as a reason for not granting access to LLC Real-Gaz. Namely, the natural monopoly stated that it could not guarantee the delivery of gas until the gas network of the town Mihailovka where the customer of LLC Real-Gaz should be supplied. However, the Appellate Court did not accept this reasoning since the contrary has been proven in the course of the investigation.

Like in the case of lack of capacity, the Appellate Court did not have any independent verifiable technical information at its disposal from which it could derive the conclusion. While determining the existence of the connection to the gas network of the town Mihailovka the Court had to rely on the fact that JSC Gazprom has been granting access to another undertaking for the same route and for supplying the same customer.

---

440 In this case, even though the pipeline was not part of the GTS-UGSS, the Appellate Court applied the Regulation on access to the GTS-UGSS by way of analogy. See more details above in part B.II.1.a).

441 See Sakhalin-2, p. 13 f.

cc) Non-compliance with the requirements of the Regulation on access to the GTS-UGSS

As observed above, the Regulation on access to the GTS-UGSS prescribes a number of mandatory requirements for the application and order of access to the GTS-UGSS. The majority of the cases of refusal of access to the GTS-UGSS are substantiated by JSC Gazprom with non-compliance with the requirements prescribed by the Regulation.

In the case FAS vs. Gazprom (NGK/SibEvroGaz)[442], the Appellate Court accepted the non-compliance with the term of submission of application stipulated in chapter 3 pt. 8 of the Regulation on access to the GTS-UGSS by the access seeker as a substantiated ground for refusal of access. The applicants in this case, NGK (JSC National Gas Company) and LLC SibEvroGaz referred to JSC Gazprom with an application on granting access to the GTS-UGSS for a short-term contract not at least 1 month earlier as required by the Regulation, but only a week before the requested start date of the supply. JSC Gazprom refused access on this ground and the courts also confirmed its eligibility since a delayed submission of the application made it impossible for JSC Gazprom to agree on the directions of the gas transportation, amend the transport routes and instruct its gas transmission undertakings in a timely manner.[443] A breach of the term of submitting an application prescribed in chapter 3 pt. 8 of the Regulation on access to the GTS-UGSS has also been claimed as a ground for refusal of access by JSC Gazprom in the case Trans Nafta[444] before FAS. However, the parties have reached a consensus, for which reason the case was dismissed by the FAS.

In the case Gazprom vs. FAS (Tatarstan)[445], the Appellate Court considered the incomplete provision of mandatory data prescribed in chapter 3 pt. 6 of the Regulation on access to the GTS-UGSS as a sufficient ground for JSC Gazprom to refuse access. In this case the access seeker JSC Trans Nafta submitted an application for access with the purpose of supplying two customers in the

442 See Judgment of the 9th Commercial Appellate Court of 17.04.2006 case N 09AP-16028/05-AK [Postanovleniye devyatogo Arbitrazhnogo Suda] (hereinafter FAS vs. Gazprom (NGK/SibEvroGaz)).

443 See FAS vs. Gazprom (NGK/SibEvroGaz), p. 5.

444 Decision of the Federal Anti-monopoly Service in relation to JSC Gazprom and LLC Novosibirskgaz, case N1 10/21-08 of 13.05.2008 [Resheniye Federalnoy Antimonopolnoy Sluzhbi Rossii] (hereinafter Trans Nafta), p. 2.

445 See Judgment of the Federal Commercial Court of Moscow District of 29.10.2009 N KA-A40/11185-09 case N A40-83706/08-2-160 [Postanovleniye Federalnogo Arbitrazhnogo Suda Moskovskogo Okruga] (hereinafter Gazprom vs. FAS (Tatarstan)).

Republic of Tatarstan. JSC Gazprom refused access for the reason that JSC Trans Nafta did not clarify in its application the exact data concerning each supply. The Appellate Court agreed with JSC Gazprom and stated that the access seeker did not follow the requirement of chapter 3 pt. 6 n. 8 and 9 of the Regulation on access to the GTS-UGSS. According to these provisions applications on access to the GTS-UGSS of independent undertakings have to contain information about the point of the gas delivery to the customer and a confirmation of willingness to accept gas in declared volumes by the GDUs and the customers in the period of the gas supply. The Court explained that the access seeker should have provided the point of the delivery of gas for each and every customer. Even though the Regulation on access to the GTS-UGSS does not contain such a provision, the Court concluded that the volumes of gas to be supplied also had to be confirmed separately for each customer by the access seeker. Moreover, the Court had revealed in the course of the investigation that gas needed to be delivered to both of these two customers through different pipelines and different gas distribution stations and the access seeker did not submit any documents confirming the willingness of the GDUs and the customers to accept gas in the period of gas supply.[446] However, the Court did not substantiate why the breach of these formal requirements would have led to a technical or economic hindrance for JSC Gazprom and would therefore be a sufficient ground for denying access to the GTS-UGSS. The Court's analysis therefore differs from the case FAS vs. Gazprom (NGK/SibEvroGaz) where the Court elaborated on the obstacles a breach of the Regulation on access to the GTS-UGSS (delayed application) would cause for the operation of JSC Gazprom as a network operator.[447]

dd) Supply of customers through other sources

The reference to the transmission network operator with the application for access to the network and provision of all the mandatory data about the supply and the customer presupposes the fact that the gas supplier and the customer have already agreed on a gas supply contract. However, in some cases JSC Gazprom has refused access to the GTS-UGSS and substantiated its refusal by stating that the demand of the gas customer, for the gas supply to which the access to the network was requested, is already covered. This was the case in Gazprom vs. FAS (Real-Gaz), where as one of the reasons of the refusal of access JSC Gazprom stated that the demand of the customer had been covered by other

446 See Gazprom vs. FAS (Tatarstan), p. 2.
447 See FAS vs. Gazprom (NGK/SibEvroGaz), p. 5.

suppliers and there had been no need for supply.[448] The Court did not accept this reasoning as an eligible refusal ground. However, the Court did not elaborate on the principle point that the coverage of gas demand of suppliers could not be deemed as a ground for refusal of access. Instead, the Court examined whether the statement of JSC Gazprom constituted the truth and ascertained that at the moment of refusing of access to the GTS-UGSS the customer did have demand on supply of gas and could have been supplied by LLC Real-Gaz if the latter was granted access to the network.[449]

Also, in the case Gazprom vs. FAS (Transgaz)[450], JSC Gazprom refused access to the GTS-UGSS and referred to the oversupply of the market and coverage of the demand of the customer by gas supply undertakings of the system of JSC Gazprom.[451]

Similarly, in the case Trans Nafta, as one of the reasons of refusal of access, JSC Gazprom claimed that the gas supply contract between the customer and JSC Trans Nafta was void since the customer had an obligation to purchase gas from an undertaking of the system of JSC Gazprom as a condition for receiving a permission for using gas as fuel.[452] However, as mentioned, this case was dismissed and the FAS did not analyse the principal eligibility of this ground of refusal.

g) Summary

To summarise, there are several bulk issues where the regulation of access to the gas transmission network of JSC Gazprom is incomplete and ambiguous.

First of all, the undertakings of JSC Gazprom and the independent undertakings do not have equal access rights to the GTS-UGSS, which is in principle the main hindrance of introducing competition to the gas sector.[453] This means that the legislation of Russia is in itself discriminatory towards the different market players of the gas supply market. An independent gas supplier on the one hand, is placed at a competitively disadvantageous position as

448 See Gazprom vs. FAS (Real-Gaz), p. 2.

449 See Gazprom vs. FAS (Real-Gaz), p. 3 f.

450 Judgement of the 9th Commercial Appellate Court on examination of lawfulness and reasonableness of the decisions of commercial courts not entered into force, case N 09AP-8871/2007-AK [Postanovleniye devyatogo Arbitrazhnogo Apelyatsionnogo Suda po proverke zakonnosti I obosnovannosti reshenii arbitrazhnikh sudov, ne vstupivshikh v zakonnuyu silu] (hereinafter Gazprom vs. FAS (Transgaz)).

451 See Gazprom vs. FAS (Transgaz), p. 2.

452 See Trans Nafta, p. 2 f.

453 See also *Smirnova*, Anti-monopoly regulation of gas markets, slide 8.

compared to a supplier which is a subsidiary of JSC Gazprom on the other hand, since different rules are applied to them for entering the gas supply market.

Secondly, the reference of the Regulation on access to the GTS-UGSS to the entitlement of 'any undertaking' with the right of access to the GTS-UGSS is not precise enough since all further rules and conditions established by the Regulation cover the procedure concerning granting access to independent undertakings only. Considering that chapter 3 pt. 7 of the Rules on Gas Supply refers to the right of 'customers or suppliers', it seems that the purpose of the legislator was to emphasise that both customers as well as suppliers may claim access to the GTS-UGSS. Thus, reference to the right of 'any independent undertaking' would serve as the best option for precisely expressing the sense of the provision.

Thirdly, the legislation of Russia does not provide for a consistent definition of an independent undertaking. There are namely two versions of explaining this term, by the Law on Gas Supply and by the Regulation on access to the GTS-UGSS, the first one focusing on the independence from any gas supply system, as the main characteristic of the notion, and the latter putting emphasis on the independence from JSC Gazprom. However, the exact meaning of the term 'independence' is not clear in either of the two definitions, nor can clarification be obtained from other acts of the legislation of Russia.

Fourthly, the rules of priority access to the GTS-UGSS are laid down in two legal acts, the Law on Gas Supply and the Regulation on access to the GTS-UGSS, however, the provisions are not in-line with each other. The first one only refers to the priority right of the suppliers of stripped dry gas gained after processing associated petroleum gas, whereas the latter provides for a list of places of gas suppliers to be granted with priority access rights, however putting the two types of gas suppliers, the suppliers for communal and household needs of the population and the suppliers of stripped dry gas both in the first place so that it is impossible to make a conclusion based on this provision which one of the suppliers would in fact be granted a priority access right in the case of lack of capacity. Moreover, apart from the difference that the provisions of the EU and Germany do not lay down priority rights for any undertaking except for the suppliers of biogas, the legislative acts of Russia do not prescribe precise conditions of the application of the proportionality principle of capacity allocation as well as auctioning; this sharply contrasts the legislation of Germany, where the rules of auctioning as well as secondary capacity allocation are detailed as part of the congestion management rules in the GasNZV. Further, the Regulation on access to the GTS-UGSS contains a rule concerning the possibility of preferential treatment of independent undertakings towards JSC Gazprom in terms of access to spare capacities in the GTS-UGSS based on a decision of the commission of the government of Russia for the issues of the use of oil and gas trunk pipelines for access to the GTS-UGSS, however no more details of such possibility are set out (e.g. the application procedure for such a right, grounds for granting access etc.). What is more, this commission ceased to exist in 2004 and the Regulation on access to the GTS-UGSS has not been updated accordingly in this respect, even though several amendments have been implemented since then.

Fifthly, the Regulation on access to the GTS-UGSS connects the possibility of receiving priority access with the duration of the planned gas supply according to the principle "the longer the better" whereas in the doctrine followed in the EU and Germany, long-term gas supply contracts are generally seen rather as an obstacle to effective competition in the long-run.[454]

Sixthly, the Regulation on access to the GTS-UGSS attributes the function of approving tariffs for the transportation services still to the FEC, which has been out of date for more than 10 years now. The competent authority has already been changed twice since then: firstly, the FEC had been reorganised into the Federal Tariff Service (hereinafter also FTS), which had been abolished afterwards. No amendment has been introduced into the Regulation in this respect though.

Lastly, even though the Regulation on access to the GTS-UGSS obliges JSC Gazprom to substantiate its refusal to conclude a contract, it does not prescribe possible legitimate grounds for such refusal, unlike the energy law of Germany, which lays down that refusal of access is only admissible in case when – on operational or other grounds – granting access is not possible or not reasonable. As a result, JSC Gazprom is free to invoke a number of issues, including those not even contained in the Regulation on access to the GTS-UGSS, as a ground for refusal of access and in many cases succeeds too. Moreover, there is no mechanism for the protection included in the legislation of Russia, like the provision of the EnWG of Germany obliging the network operator to immediately notify the regulatory authority in the case of refusing access to its network and thus allowing the regulatory authority to address the potential cases of abusive refusal independently, even if the party concerned has not informed the authority and has not filed the corresponding application.

454 Cf. e.g. recitals 37 and 42 of the Gas Directive 2009.

In 2006 the Federal Anti-monopoly Service proposed a draft of a new act replacing the existing Regulation on access to the GTS-UGSS with a declared aim to increase the efficiency of the TPA, which is still under discussion.[455]

2. Access to gas distribution networks

a) Scope of regulating access to distribution networks

TPA to gas distribution networks in Russia is regulated by the Law on Natural Monopolies, the Law on Gas Supply, the Provisions on access to distribution networks, and the Rules on Gas Supply.

The local gas distribution networks, access to which is regulated, comprises the system of pipelines and equipment for supplying customers with gas within a territorial unit as per chapter 2 pt. 3 of the Provisions on access to distribution networks. However, like the case of GTS-UGSS, not all pipelines supplying customers are considered to be distribution networks and thus, not all are covered by the Provisions on access to distribution networks. For instance, a pipeline leading to JSC "Belaya berezka" belongs to the company itself, constituting neither part of the distribution network nor the GTS-UGSS and thus not falling within the scope of the regulations for access to the network. However, a part of the population and some commercial organisations cannot be supplied with gas otherwise than through this pipeline. Thus, there is no legal basis for ensuring access to this pipeline in case a part of the population decides to conclude a gas supply contract with another supplier.[456]

b) The holder of the third party access right to local distribution networks and the obliged party

Pursuant to chapter 1 pt. 1 sent. 2 of the Provisions on access to distribution networks, any undertaking in the territory of Russia is entitled to have non-discriminatory access to the local distribution networks for transporting gas to customers. The parties which are obliged to grant non-discriminatory access to distribution networks are accordingly the local GDUs, which operate the networks. According to chapter 2 pt. 3 of the Rules on Gas Supply gas distribution undertakings are specialised undertakings of republics, territories, regions, cities, inter-regions and villages, developing and exploiting gas supply systems of

455 *Seliverstov/Gudkov*, in: Roggenkamp/Barrera-Hernandez/Zillman/Del Guayo, Energy networks and the law, p. 402.

456 See *Larin*, Pipeline transport is in need of regulation.

these territories, ensuring gas supply, as well as providing services of gas transportation through their networks. From this definition it could be concluded that the GDUs are the owners of the networks. However, according to another definition of GDU stipulated in the Rules on Gas Consumption, a GDU can be either the owner of GDS (including network) or an undertaking, which concluded a contract with the owner of GDS on its exploitation.

Based on the wording of chapter 1 pt. 1 sent. 2 of the Provisions on access to distribution networks, not only suppliers, but also any other customers acting in the territory of Russia may claim the TPA to the distribution networks. In addition, chapter 3 pt. 7 of the Rules on Gas Supply also refers to the right of customers or suppliers to have their gas transported through the networks. Further, 'supplier' is defined in Art. 2 of the Law on Gas Supply as owner of gas or a person authorised by owner of gas, supplying gas to consumers on the basis of contracts. It also has to be mentioned that 'consumer' for the purposes of the Law on Gas Supply means both a person acquiring gas for his own domestic needs as well as for his own industrial or other household needs.

The Provisions on access to distribution networks do not differentiate according to nationality and entitle undertakings 'in the territory of Russia' with the right of non-discriminatory access to distribution networks. Art. 27 of the Law on Gas Supply also refers to granting TPA right to the undertakings 'operating in the territory of Russia'. Thus, the undertakings, carrying out their activities in the territory of Russia, irrespective of their nationality, may be subject to the right of access to distribution networks under certain circumstances.

Unlike the Regulation on access to the GTS-UGSS, the Provisions on access to distribution networks do not differentiate between the undertakings according to their relation towards the undertaking providing transportation services. If in the first case only the undertakings not belonging to the system of JSC Gazprom hold the TPA right and thus are obliged to apply for access to the GTS-UGSS, in the case of seeking access to distribution networks, all suppliers and customers, i.e. also those associated with the GDU, have to apply for access as prescribed by the Provisions on access to distribution networks presented below.

c) Prerequisites of access to distribution networks

Access to local distribution networks will be granted only if the following requirements laid down in chapter 3 pt. 4 of the Provisions on access to distribution networks are met:

a) There is spare capacity in the local distribution networks (from connection point to extraction point) in the requested period of transport of gas;

b) There are pipelines and discharge pipes leading to gas customers with data collection and quality control points prepared for the start date of gas supply;
c) The quality and features of the supplied gas comply with the requirements of normative-technical documents (also stipulated in Art. 27 sent. 2 of the Law on Gas Supply).

The definition of spare capacity has decisive importance in these legal relations since access has to be granted only to such capacities.[457] Chapter 2 pt. 3 of the Provisions on access to distribution networks defines 'spare capacity of local distribution networks' as technically possible capacity of the network for receipt and transport of gas except for the volumes of gas transport, which are needed for the implementation of existing contracts in that certain time period.

d) Contractual arrangement of gas transportation through distribution networks

As per chapter 1 pt. 2 of the Provisions on access to distribution networks, gas transport through the local distribution networks is implemented on the basis of a contract between a GDU and a gas supplier or customer, concluded in accordance with the Provisions on access to distribution networks and the legislation of Russia (contract for gas transportation through distribution networks[458]).

The undertakings wishing to gain access to local distribution networks have to follow the procedure and stages defined by the Provisions on access to distribution networks as well as the Rules on Gas Supply.

aa) Application for access to local distribution networks

First of all, the suppliers or customers seeking access to local distribution networks have to submit to the GDU a copy of the gas supply contract and an application containing the following mandatory data as per chapter 3 pt. 5 of the Provisions on access to distribution networks:

1) Information about the gas supplier and customer;

---

457 See *Gudkov*, Gas transportation in Russia, NiG, 4/2009, p. 48.

458 As mentioned above, since the Russian equivalent for this contract coincides with the one for the transmission (*dogovor transportirovki gaza*), reference will be made to 'contract for gas transportation through distribution networks' instead of mentioning 'gas distribution contract'.

2) Volumes and terms of gas transportation (including the regime and periodicity), as well as the suggested order of calculations;
3) The start and end date of the gas transportation;
4) Volumes of the gas transportation for every month of the first year and for every year for the following period;
5) The name of the producer of gas, quality and parameters of the supplied gas (to be presented in the case of transporting gas of local producers);
6) The connection point of the pipelines leading to the local distribution network;
7) The point of gas extraction or transfer for its further transportation through the networks of other undertakings;
8) The confirmation of willingness to accept gas in declared volumes by the GDUs and the customers in the period of gas transportation.

Refusal to accept the application containing all mandatory data is not allowed. However, unlike in the case of an application to access the GTS-UGSS, the Provisions on access to distribution networks do not specify explicitly that requirements concerning the contents of the application have to be uniform for all applicants.

Pursuant to chapter 3 pt. 5 of the Provisions on access to distribution networks, applications for the conclusion of contracts with a duration up to 1 year have to be submitted not later than 1 month and not earlier than 3 months before the start date of transportation; in the case of a contract with a duration from 1 to 5 years not later than 3 months and not earlier than 1 year before the first year of the gas transportation; for contracts with a duration of more than 5 years not later than 6 months and not earlier than 3 years before the first year of the gas transportation.

bb) Decisions on applications for access to local distribution networks

According to chapter 3 pt. 8 of the Provisions on access to distribution networks, the GDU has to decide within 15 days on applications for contracts with a duration up to 1 year, and within 3 months on applications for contracts with a duration of more than 1 year from the moment of their registration, unless the parties have agreed on a different term. As a result of examining an application, the GDU will make one of the following decisions: a) agree to conclude a contract, either in full or partial compliance with the application; b) refuse to conclude a contract and give reasons for its decision. The applicant is informed within 3 days about the decision made on the application.

(1) Consent to conclude contract for gas transportation through distribution networks

GDUs may approve applications for access to the local distribution networks fully or partially according to available spare capacities in the network and considering the priorities of granting access set out by the Provisions on access to distribution networks.

Art. 27 sent. 3 of the Law on Gas Supply lays down that in the first place access to the networks has to be granted to the suppliers of stripped dry gas, which is gained after processing associated petroleum gas.[459] Unlike the Regulation on access to the GTS-UGSS, the Provisions on access to distribution networks have not adopted this rule in the priorities.

Chapter 3 pt. 7 of the Provisions on access to distribution networks states that in cases of lack of spare capacity of the local distribution network, necessary for approving all applications, the priority has to be given to the applications of those undertakings, which ensure communal and household needs of the population at the location of the distribution network. Among suppliers of gas for different purposes, the priority is given to the applicants planning transportation for a longer period as compared to other applicants. If the conditions are equal, applications for access to the local distribution network are approved proportionally according to the requested volumes of gas transportation.

Unlike the Regulation on access to the GTS-UGSS, which prescribes the possibility of an auction for the applications beyond the ones to be handled as priorities, the Provisions on access to distribution networks do not foresee such an option. In addition, the Regulation on access to the GTS-UGSS stipulates the possibility of a proportional approval of applications only after granting access to the applicants having priority over the others, whereas according to the Provisions on access to distribution networks the principle of proportionality applies also to the applications having priority in the case of equal conditions. Accordingly, if two suppliers of communal and household needs of the population at the location of the distribution network ceteris paribus apply for access to the distribution networks, in the case of lack of sufficient capacity for the approval of both applications each supplier will be granted access proportionally to the requested volume of transportation. The same conclusion cannot be derived from the Regulation on access to the GTS-UGSS though.

459 See above part B.II.1.d)bb)(1).

(2) Reasoned refusal to conclude contract for gas transportation through distribution networks

GDUs may refuse to conclude a contract for gas transportation through distribution networks and have to state reasons for this decision.[460] The Provisions on access to distribution networks as well as other acts of the legislation of Russia do not define what arguments are eligible for justifying a refusal. Yet, it can be presumed that if the prerequisites of access to distribution networks as well as the other requirements of the Provisions on access to distribution networks are not fulfilled, the application can be rejected. Thus, lack of capacity, lack of connection, as well as insufficient quality of gas can serve as a reason for refusal. However, in practice GDUs often refer to other grounds in order to give reasons for their refusal.[461] Moreover, the Provisions on access to distribution networks also do not prescribe that the ground of refusal of access has to be contained in the Provisions themselves.

Therefore, it is preferable that possible grounds for refusal of access are clearly stipulated in the Regulation on access to the GTS-UGSS, as is the case in sec. 20 para. 2 sent. 1 of the EnWG of Germany, according to which the network operators may refuse access only if they substantiate that – on operational or other grounds – granting access is not possible or not reasonable, taking into account the objectives of sec. 1 of the EnWG.

cc) Arrangement of contracts for gas transportation through distribution networks

After deciding on full or partial approval of an application, the GDU submits an offer to conclude a contract to the applicant, the supplier or the customer, as regulated by chapter 3 pt. 10 of the Rules on Gas Supply. A draft contract has to be delivered within 10 days after the date of the decision on the approval as per chapter 3 pt. 8 of the Provisions on access to distribution networks, unless the parties have agreed on a different term. According to the Rules on Gas Supply, the offer has to be submitted together with the permission of access to the distribution network, issued in the manner established by the Government of Russia. The party, which received the offer, has to consent on the conclusion

---

460 Reasoned refusal to conclude a contract (*Reshenie o motivirovannom otkaze ot zaklyiucheniya dogovora*).

461 For example, the existence of a gas supply contract between a gas distribution undertaking and a gas supplier in Astrakhan case (N A06-2960-8/03) to be discussed in detail below.

of the contract within 30 days from the moment of receipt of the offer, unless a different term has been set in the offer itself. In the case of dissent with the offered conditions the party, which received the offer, has to submit a report of disagreement to the offering party, i.e. the GDU. If the supplier or the customer does not receive any feedback within 30 days after sending the report of disagreement, it may refer the matter to the court. Apart from that, it may terminate the existing contract for gas transportation with the GDU after the expiry of its duration (e.g. the customer may stop extracting gas), i.e. the applicant does not have to stick to the conditions of the new offer. If the undertaking continues to fulfil the existing contract (e.g. the customer continues extracting gas) after the expiry of the mentioned 30 days or after the expiry of the duration of the contract, this action is considered as a consent on the conclusion of the contract for gas transportation through distribution networks with the conditions offered by the GDU.

Apart from this procedure, the deadline set out in chapter 3 pt. 9 of the Provisions on access to distribution networks have to be considered too. Namely, a contract for gas transportation through distribution networks has to be concluded within 1 month after the date of receipt of a draft contract by the applicant.

Essential conditions of contracts for gas transportation through distribution networks are gas volumes and the terms of gas transportation (including the regime and periodicity), tariffs and order of calculations. Contracts have to comply with the legislation of Russia, especially the Provisions on access to distribution networks as well as the Rules on Gas Supply.

e) Conditions of gas distribution

The Provisions on access to distribution networks lay down conditions of gas distribution in terms of duties of the parties, expenses of connection to the network and charges for the transportation services.

aa) Duties of suppliers and customers

According to chapter 4 pt. 13 of the Provisions on access to distribution networks, gas suppliers and customers or gas transportation undertakings on their behalf, making use of local distribution networks, have the following duties:

1) To ensure the preparedness of gas for transportation in accordance with the requirements of applicable normative-technical documents as well as data collection at the points of delivery and receipt of gas;[462]

462 The duty of data collection itself may also be fulfilled by the GDU on behalf of the supplier or customer as per Art. 5 pt. 22 of the Rules on Gas Supply.

2) To present operative information to the GDU within the prescribed time about technological regimes of a gas pipeline or a system of gas pipelines leading to the GDU;
3) To inform the GDU about accidents on their facilities, ongoing and capital repair works, and possible alterations of the volumes of gas input into the local distribution network as compared to the volumes stipulated in the contract;
4) To agree with the GDU on the schedules of restoring the regime of gas supplies up to the parameters laid down by the contract;
5) To comply with the norms and requirements of pipeline maintenance and security of the gas distribution network during gas transportation;
6) To grant unrestricted access to the points of control and data collection of gas volumes and quality to the authorised representatives of the GDU;
7) To ensure a constant and stable radio or telephone connection between dispatching units of the supplier and customer, and the GDU.

bb) Duties of Gas Distribution Undertakings

According to chapter 4 pt. 14 of the Provisions on access to distribution networks, the GDUs have the following duties:

1) To provide information upon request of suppliers and customers of gas about the availability of spare capacities in the local distribution networks in certain periods of time on certain sites of the network as well as information about applications received for access to these sites;
2) To inform gas suppliers and customers timely about alterations of work regimes, accidents in the local distribution networks, failures of the data collection system of gas, repair and preventive works, influencing the fulfilment of duties concerning transportation of gas;
3) To grant unrestricted access to the authorised representatives of suppliers and customers of gas for controlling data collection of volumes and quality of gas.

Apart from these duties, contracts for gas transportation through distribution networks may also determine that the GDU has to fulfil the duty of data collection at the points of delivery and receipt of gas on behalf of the supplier (customer), as per chapter 5 pt. 22 of the Rules on Gas Supply.

cc) Right of connection to the network and expenses

According to chapter 4 pt. 11 sent. 1 of the Provisions on access to distribution networks, suppliers and customers of gas are entitled to the connection of pipelines and discharge pipes to the local distribution network in case there are free capacities in their respective sites.

Pursuant to chapter 4 pt. 11 sent. 2, as a matter of principal, all expenses related to the connection of pipelines and discharge pipes of suppliers and customers to the local distribution network have to be borne by the supplier and the customer as a rule. However, unlike the law of the EU and Germany the legislation of Russia defines neither the methodology for the calculation nor sets tariffs for the connection services for suppliers and customers. Art. 23.2 of the Law on Gas Supply as well as the Regulation on Prices for gas, Tariffs for transportation services and Fees for connection of gas-powered equipment regulate the payment for the connection of gas-powered equipment[463] to distribution networks but not the payment for the connection of the pipelines and discharge pipes of suppliers and customers.[464] Accordingly, it is up to the agreement between the parties to specify the amount of expenses related to the connection to networks.

Usually, a contract for the connection to distribution networks between a supplier or a customer and the GDU is concluded separately from the contract for gas transportation. Technical conditions for the connection to the network are issued by GDUs as per chapter 3 pt. 4 sent. 2 of the Rules on Gas Supply. The detailed technical rules for connections are prescribed by the Regulation of 13.02.2006 approving rules for defining and granting technical conditions for the connection of capital construction objects to engineering-technical networks as well as rules for the connection of capital construction objects to engineering-technical networks.[465]

463 According to chapter 1 pt. 2 of the Regulation on Prices for gas, Tariffs for transportation services and Fees for connection of gas-powered equipment, gas-powered equipment are boilers, kilns, industrial stoves, technological lines, waste-heat boilers, power generators and other installations, which employ gas as fuel for heat production for purposes of centralized and autonomous heating, for power generation, for supply of hot-water, for food preparation, for technological processes of various industries, as well as other devices, appliances, aggregates, technological equipment and facilities, employing gas as feedstock.

464 The legislation of Russia also regulates charges for the connection of objects of capital construction to distribution networks (see fn. N 435 on p. 75).

465 Regulation N 83 of 13.02.2006 approving rules for defining and granting technical conditions of connection of capital construction objects to engineering-technical

dd) Charges for transportation services through distribution networks

Suppliers and customers have to pay for the transportation services provided by the GDUs. According to Art. 8 of the Law on Gas Supply, the Government of Russia has the authority to define the methodology and principles for the calculation of prices for gas and tariffs for services of gas transportation through transmission and distribution networks. Thus, the Regulation on Prices for gas, Tariffs for transportation services and Fees for connection of gas-powered equipment concerns only principles and does not set prices or tariffs as such.[466] Art. 21 of the Law on Gas Supply also determines that the provision of services of gas transportation is considered as a natural monopoly by the Law and is therefore regulated. According to chapter 2 pt. 4 of the Regulation on Prices for gas, Tariffs for transportation services and Fees for connection of gas-powered equipment, the tariffs for the transportation services through local distribution networks are subject to state regulation.

Further, the Law on Gas Supply stipulates a rule concerning the regulation of tariffs for services of GDUs exclusively, not covering tariffs for the transportation services through high pressure pipelines. Namely, Art. 23 lays down that the federal organ of executive power in the area of regulating tariffs approves the tariffs for the transportation services of GDUs with a duration of not less than 3 and not more than 5 years. These tariffs may be differentiated considering economic and social conditions of gas supply in various parts of the territory of Russia.

As per chapter 4 pt. 10 of the Provisions on access to distribution networks, payments by independent undertakings under contracts for gas transportation through distribution networks have to be made in compliance with the tariffs approved by the FEC. However, the FEC has been reorganised into the Federal Tariff Service in 2004, which has been subsequently abolished in 2015 and the FAS became its legal successor. Accordingly, the Provisions of the FAS lay down in chapter 2 pt. 5.3.21.16 that the Federal Anti-monopoly Service has the competence of approving the tariffs for the transport of gas through pipelines. This inaccuracy will also be addressed in more detail below when discussing the competent authority for the enforcement of the TPA right in gas sector. Further, the

networks as well as rules for the connection of capital construction objects to engineering-technical networks [Postanovlenie Ob utverzhdenii pravil opredeleniya I predostavleniya tekhnicheskikh uslovii podklucheniya obiekta kapitalnogo stroitelstva k setyam inzhenerno-tekhnicheskogo obespecheniya i pravil podklucheniya obiekta kapitalnogo stroitelstva k setyam inzhenerno-tekhnicheskogo obespecheniya].

466 *Karpova*, in: Säcker, Handbook of German-Russian energy law, p. 423.

FAS is also in charge of setting the rules for applying prices (tariffs) for the goods (works, services) of natural monopolies, pursuant to chapter 2 pt. 5.2.9(25) of the Provisions of the FAS.

The legislation on access to transmission networks could be criticised because it does not deal with the relationship between the entities of JSC Gazprom and only regulates the issues between independent undertakings and JSC Gazprom. The Provisions on access to distribution networks do cover the relationships related to access to the networks between all undertakings irrespective of their relation to JSC Gazprom, but still introduce a rule which differentiates between suppliers and customers according to their owners when it comes to the charges for transportation services through distribution networks. Unlike the Regulation on access to the GTS-UGSS, which does not make any further differentiation as to charges for transportation services, chapter 4 pt. 10 of the Provisions on access to distribution networks requires only the payments by independent undertakings (and not by all other customers of the GDU) to comply with the approved tariffs. It has to be mentioned, that the initial version of this provision did not refer to independent undertakings, but stipulated a uniform rule. After the amendment on 28.07.2000 the provision has been changed to its current redaction.

As a result of this ruling, undertakings of the system of JSC Gazprom, i.e. non-independent undertakings, requesting access to distribution networks, may receive unequal treatment in terms of lower or higher charges for transportation services through distribution networks. Moreover, GDUs may have high incentives to grant advantages to suppliers or customers, in cases where both sides of the contract for gas transportation are undertakings related to JSC Gazprom (e.g. the supplier is JSC Mezhregiongaz and the GDU is a subsidiary of JSC Gazoraspredelenie). In practice, when a subsidiary of JSC Mezhregiongaz supplies gas through the distribution network of a subsidiary of JSC Gazoraspredelenie (both undertakings of the system of JSC Gazprom) they conclude a tripartite contract for gas supply and transportation with an end-customer. According to such contracts end-customers are obliged to pay charges for transportation services to GDUs calculated in compliance with regulated tariffs.

Despite this provision, however, the Regulation on Prices for gas, Tariffs for transportation services and Fees for connection of gas-powered equipment, which defines the prices, tariffs and fees underlying the state regulation in chapter 2 pt. 4 lit 'd' as well as in chapter 3 pt. 7 lit. 'd', refers, inter alia, to the 'regulation of tariffs for the transportation services through distribution networks' as a uniform term, and not to 'tariffs for independent undertakings' as it does in the case of tariffs for the transportation services through high pressure pipelines under chapter 2 pt. 4 lit. 'b' and chapter 3 pt. 7 lit. 'b'. Thus, there is no justification for the regulation in chapter 4 pt. 10 of the Provisions on access to distribution networks whereas the tariff is uniform for all customers of GDUs based on the Regulation on Prices for gas, Tariffs for transportation services and Fees for connection of gas-powered equipment.

According to chapter 4 pt. 11 of the Regulation on Prices for gas, Tariffs for transportation services and Fees for connection of gas-powered equipment, tariffs for the transportation services should be calculated considering that they have to a) compensate economically reasonable expenses related to the transport of gas, of the undertakings, activities of which are regulated (i.e. transmission and distribution undertakings) b) include a reasonable return rate for the undertakings, activities of which are regulated, c) enable satisfaction of solvent gas demand, reach an economic balance between the interests of suppliers and customers, d) take account of all taxes and other obligatory fees as set by the legislation of Russia, e) take account of differences between various groups of customers and regions in relation to the actual value of transportation services and gas supply (sales) for these groups or regions, f) facilitate competition within the gas sector as well as between different sectors (e.g. substitute fuels). In addition, according to chapter 4 pt. 15(4) of the Regulation on Prices for gas, Tariffs for transportation services and Fees for connection of gas-powered equipment, expenses related to the exploitation of capacities employed for storage and regasification of liquefied natural gas, which are technologically connected to distribution networks, are also considered while fixing the tariffs for the transportation services through distribution networks.

According to Art. 23.1 of the Law on Gas Supply, a competent federal body of executive power controls (supervises) the processes of fixing and applying regulated tariffs (as well as prices) in the field of gas supply. According to pt. 4 of the Regulation on State Control of Regulated Prices and Tariffs, the Federal Anti-monopoly Service and the bodies of executive power in the field of state regulation of prices (tariffs) of federal subjects of Russia are entitled to undertake such control. According to pt. 6 lit. 'b' of the aforementioned Regulation, these bodies check whether the organs of executive power of federal subjects as well as legal entities of the gas industry comply with the legislation of Russia in terms of correctness and economic reasonableness of expenses and other data, which are considered while fixing the tariffs (and prices) in the gas industry, economic reasonableness of factual expenses and correctness of application of tariffs by the legal entities.

Even though the tariffs for gas transport through pipelines are approved by the FAS, the payment conditions (terms, form etc.) are defined by contracts for gas transportation through distribution networks as per chapter 6 pt. 31 of the Rules on Gas Supply.

According to chapter 4 pt. 12 of the Provisions on access to distribution networks, contracts for gas transportation through distribution networks may also include a special condition about the limitation of offsetting payments for transportation services on account of repayment of debts of the GDUs towards the gas suppliers.

f) Summary

To summarise, there are several bulk issues where the regulation of access to local distribution networks of Russia is incomplete and ambiguous.

First of all, the definition of a GDU is not consistent throughout different legal acts of Russia in terms of their relationship towards gas distribution networks.

Secondly, the requirement of the Law on Gas Supply regarding the priority access rights to networks of suppliers of stripped gas has not been reflected in the Provisions on access to distribution networks.

Thirdly, there is a contradiction between the Provisions on access to distribution networks and the Regulation on Prices for gas, Tariffs for transportation services and Fees for connection of gas-powered equipment regarding the regulated tariffs for access to distribution networks. The first legal act lays down that the payments by independent undertakings have to be made in compliance with approved tariffs whereas the second act stipulates that tariffs for the transportation services through distribution services underlie state regulation, without specifying whether the undertakings are independent or not.

Fourthly, the Provisions on access to distribution networks connect the possibility of receiving a priority access right of access with the duration of the planned gas supply according to the principle "the longer the better" whereas in the doctrine followed in the EU and Germany, long-term gas supply contracts are generally seen rather as an obstacle to effective competition in the long-run.

Fifthly, the Provisions on access to distribution networks still attribute the function of approving tariffs for the transportation services to the FEC, which has lost its competency more than 10 years ago. The competent authority has been changed already twice since then: first, the FEC was reorganised into the FTS, which was later abolished. No amendment has been introduced into the Provisions on access to distribution networks in this respect though.

Lastly, even though the Provisions on access to distribution networks oblige the GDU to substantiate its refusal to conclude a contract, they do not prescribe possible legitimate grounds for such refusal, unlike the energy law of Germany, which lays down that refusal of access is only admissible in case where on operational or other grounds granting access is not possible or not reasonable. Moreover, there is no mechanism for the protection included in the legislation of Russia like the provision of the EnWG of Germany obliging the network operator to immediately notify the regulatory authority in the case of refusing access to its network and thus allowing the regulatory authority to address the potential cases of abusive refusal independently, even if the party concerned has not informed the authority and has not filed the corresponding application.

In 2013, the Federal Anti-monopoly Service proposed a draft of a new act replacing the Provisions on access to distribution networks with an aim to increase the efficiency of the TPA to distribution networks. This draft has not yet been adopted.[467]

3. Requirements of information disclosure

Information disclosure by gas transmission and distribution undertakings is one of the most important safeguards for the implementation of non-discriminatory access to networks. This in turn determines the existence of competition on gas markets as well as market transparency. The provision of transparent and non-discriminatory access to the infrastructure was also declared as one of the milestones on the way of the development of domestic energy markets in Russia.[468] In the following, the requirements of information disclosure in relation to gas transmission and distribution undertakings as well as the types of information subject to free access under the legislation of Russia will be presented.

a) Obligation of information disclosure

General rules on disclosure of information concerning the regulated activities of natural monopolies are provided for by the Law on Natural Monopolies. Sector-specific detailed rules of disclosure of information concerning the regulated activities of gas transmission and distribution undertakings are set out in the Regulation on standards of information disclosure by natural monopolies

467 See the draft regulation under: http://fas.gov.ru/documents/documentdetails.html?id=684, last accessed on 16.11.2017.

468 See p. 39 and 82 of the Energy strategy of Russia for the period up to 2030 approved by Decree N 1715-r of the Government of RF of 13.11.2009 [Rasporyazhenie Pravitelstva RF Ob Energeticheskoy strategii Rossii na period do 2030 goda], published in SZ of 30.11.2009, N 48, p. 5836.

providing services of gas transportation through pipelines of 29.10.2010[469] (hereinafter Regulation on information disclosure).

Under Art. 8 para. 5 of the Law on Natural Monopolies, natural monopolies are obliged to grant free access to the information concerning their activities, which are regulated pursuant to the present law. Free access to the information shall be provided through publishing it in the media, including the internet, and on the basis of written requests of consumers. In addition, pursuant to Art. 8.1 of the Law, natural monopolies have to comply with certain standards of information disclosure, inter alia, accessibility of disclosed information to the general public, transparency of the activities regarding the production of regulated goods (as well as provision of services, performance of works), and publicity of the conditions of sales of regulated goods (as well as services, works).

The Regulation on information disclosure further specifies the meaning of 'information disclosure' as granting the general public access to the information about regulated activities of natural monopolies regardless of the purpose of obtaining this information.[470] Natural monopolies, i.e., inter alia, gas transmission and distribution undertakings have to disclose information through (1) publishing it on their official websites or any other official website on the internet; (2) publishing it in the official print media distributed in the respective territory of the federal subject of Russia where the undertakings provide the regulated services of transportation; (3) providing information upon written (including electronical) requests of consumers of transportation services free of charge.[471] The order in which information must be provided by gas transmission and distribution undertakings to consumers is also regulated in further detail.[472]

The Regulation on information disclosure prescribes that any change in the disclosed information is subject to the publication through the same sources where the initial information was published within the predefined deadlines as per chapter 1 pt. 8 of the Regulation.

---

469 Regulation of the Government of the RF on the approval of standards of information disclosure by natural monopolies providing services of gas transportation through pipelines [Postanovleniye Pravitelstva RF Ob utverzhdenii standartov raskritiya informatsii subyektami estestvennikh monopoliy, okazivayushimi uslugi po transportirovke gaza po truboprovodam] N 872 of 29.10.2010, published in SZ of 08.11.2010, N 45, p. 5855, last amended on 30.12.2013.

470 Chapter 1 pt. 2 of the Regulation on information disclosure.

471 Chapter 1 pt. 3 of the Regulation on information disclosure.

472 Chapter 1 pt. 5 of the Regulation on information disclosure.

b) Types of information subject to disclosure

Art. 8 para. 5 of the Law on Natural Monopolies lists the types of information which are subject to free access. According to this list, free access has to be provided, inter alia, to the following types of information about:

- the prices (tariffs) for regulated goods (works, services) of natural monopolies;
- the existence (or lack) of the technical possibility of access to the regulated goods (works, services) of natural monopolies and the progress of processing of applications for the technical connection to the infrastructure of natural monopolies;
- the conditions of supply of regulated goods (works, services) by natural monopolies and the conditions of the technical connection to the infrastructure of natural monopolies.

Correspondingly, the Regulation on information disclosure also lists the types of information to be disclosed by gas transmission and distribution undertakings. The list of information subject to disclosure provided for in chapter 2 para. 11 of the Regulation on information disclosure is exhaustive. The obligation of disclosure covers, inter alia, the information about:

- tariffs of gas transportation services through pipelines, which are subject to state regulation, with a reference to the source of an official publication of the decision of the regulatory body on the establishment of relevant tariffs;
- the existence (or lack) of the technical possibility of access to the regulated services of gas transportation through pipelines;
- the registration and progress of processing of applications for access to the regulated services of gas transportation through pipelines, as well as applications for the connection to high pressure gas pipelines or distribution networks of natural monopolies;
- the conditions of the provision of regulated services of gas transportation through pipelines by natural monopolies as well as about the conditions of the connection to high pressure gas pipelines or distribution networks of natural monopolies.

The deadlines, forms, and periodicity of publishing the information[473] are set either by the FTS (e.g. for information concerning tariffs)[474] or by the Federal

473 Art. 2 and Art. 3 of the Regulation on information disclosure.

474 See Order of the FTS N 36-e of 31.01.2011 on the approval of forms, deadlines, and periodicity of information disclosure by natural monopolies providing services of gas transportation through pipelines, as well as rules of completing these forms

Anti-monopoly Service (e.g. for information concerning the technical possibility, processing of applications, and conditions of access and connection)[475]. The Regulation on information disclosure only obliges gas transmission and distribution undertakings to publish, on a quarterly basis, the information on the existence (or lack) of the technical possibility of access to the services of gas transportation for each month. Moreover, undertakings have to provide detailed information with regard to entry and exit points to/from the network if the tariffs for these undertakings also differ according to entry and exit points. Furthermore, chapter 2 pt. 15 of the Regulation on information disclosure prescribes that the information on changes of data influencing the existence or lack of technical possibility, including alterations of technical characteristics of high pressure pipelines or distribution networks, as well as weather conditions etc. have to be published, with reference to the indefinite character of the information as the case may be.

The Regulation on information disclosure also provides for more detailed rules about disclosing the conditions for the provision of regulated services of gas transportation as well as about disclosing the conditions for the connection to high pressure pipelines or distribution networks. The Regulation lists the following conditions, which have to be disclosed: substantial conditions and a standard form of a contract for gas transportation, if available; substantial conditions and a standard form of a contract for connection services to high pressure pipelines or distribution networks, if available; information on deadlines of submitting applications for the provision of gas transportation services; requirements in relation to the contents of applications as well as a list of documents required to be submitted in order to gain access to the services of gas transportation.

[Prikaz FST Ob utverzhdenii form, srokov i periodichnosti raskritiya informatsii subyektami estestvennikh monopoliy, okazivayushimi uslugi po transportirovke gaza po truboprovodam, a takzhe pravil zapolneniya ukazannikh form], published in RG of 06.04.2011, N 72.

475 See Order of the Federal Anti-monopoly Service of Russia N 231/14 of 07.04.2014 on the approval of forms, deadlines, and periodicity of information disclosure by natural monopolies providing services of gas transportation through pipelines [Prikaz Federalnoy Antimonopolnoy Sluzhbi Rossii Ob utverzhdenii form, srokov i periodichnosti raskritiya informatsii subyektami estestvennikh monopoliy, okazivayushimi uslugi po transportirovke gaza po truboprovodam], published in RG of 22.08.2014, N 190.

It has to be mentioned that the requirement of disclosure does not equal the obligation of publication, as some information may be subject to disclosure only upon request. However, at some points in the Regulation on information disclosure[476] the legislator of Russia uses the word *raskritie* meaning 'disclosure', which implies 'publication' within the meaning of the respective provisions.

c) Overseeing compliance with requirements of information disclosure

The compliance by natural monopolies with the standards of information disclosure is overseen by the executive body regulating natural monopolies. Non-compliance with the obligation of granting free access to the information regarding regulated activities as well as non-compliance with the information disclosure standards entails administrative liability. According to Art. 19.8.1. of the code of administrative offences of Russia of 30.12.2001[477] (hereinafter Code of Administrative Offences of Russia), fines from 100,000 to 500,000 Russian roubles may be imposed on those natural monopolies, which do not comply with the requirements of the Law, and their officials may be fined with 5,000 to 20,000 Russian roubles. Pursuant to chapter 2 pt. 5.3.1.21 of the Provisions of the FAS, within the scope of its powers the Federal Anti-monopoly Service fulfils the duty of supervision over the compliance with the standards of information disclosure by natural monopolies.

Apart from the obligations of natural monopolies on the provision of the information listed in the respective legal acts, on more general terms, natural monopolies are also obliged to deliver all documents, information and explanations to the executive bodies regulating natural monopolies that are needed for the fulfilment of their functions, as per Art. 13 para. 2 of the Law on Natural Monopolies. In addition, all commercial undertakings are by virtue of Art. 25 para. 1 of the Law on Competition obliged to provide information, documents, as well as explanations etc. to the FAS within the scope of the powers the latter. Correspondingly, pursuant to Art. 13 para. 1 of the Law on Natural Monopolies, employees of the executive bodies regulating the natural monopolies are entitled, within the scopes of their respective powers, to have unrestricted access to the

476 E.g. chapter 1 pt. 2, pt. 3 and chapter 2 pt. 15 of the Regulation on information disclosure.

477 Code of administrative offences of the RF [Kodeks RF Ob administrativnikh narusheniyakh] N 195-FZ of 30.12.2001, published in RG of 31.12.2001, N 256, last amended on 30.10.2017.

information on the activities of natural monopolies in the possession of these undertakings themselves or any other undertakings, as well as local authorities. Similarly, the employees of the FAS are entitled to have unrestricted access to commercial undertakings as per Art. 24 of the Law on Competition, in order to obtain information within the scope of their powers.

d) Summary

To summarise, the main criticism towards the provisions on the regulation of disclosure and publishing of information in relation to gas transportation services in Russia is the fact that the legislation of Russia does not differentiate between the terms 'obligation to publish' and 'obligation to disclose'. The duty of publishing differs significantly from the obligation to disclose since, in the first case, the undertaking is bound to make information public within a certain periodicity and in a certain way without any additional request from third parties, whereas in the case when an undertaking is obliged to disclose, it has the duty to do so only upon request of an eligible party. Moreover, the disclosure may mean that the information is shared only with the party that requested it and does not necessarily mean that the disclosed information is made public (e.g. commercial secrets disclosed by an undertaking to the regulatory authority upon its request). The ambiguity regarding the terminology is already rooted in the definition of the 'information disclosure' as well as in the ways to 'disclose' provided for in the Regulation on information disclosure since the term is defined as 'granting the general public access to the information about regulated activities of natural monopolies, regardless of the purpose of obtaining this information', which according to its contents tends more to the description of the obligation of publication. However, the possible ways of information disclosure in the Regulation on information disclosure also suggest 'providing information upon written requests of consumers of transportation services' as one of the forms of 'information disclosure'.

Even though the legislation of Russia provides for the basic requirements for transparency of information in relation to regulated activities of undertakings providing gas transportation services, the impossibility of the verification of the information provided by these undertakings renders the obligations ineffective. The legislation of Russia does not provide for any mechanism for an independent verification of the information concerning the existence of spare capacities in the pipelines. Therefore, suppliers and customers, as well as authorities have to rely on the information provided by the dispatching departments of the respective undertakings providing gas transportation services (CODD for JSC

Gazprom).[478] Moreover, the credibility of such information is weakened by the fact that no legal or further unbundling has been implemented throughout the gas industry in Russia. In the case Gazprom vs. FAS (Real-Gaz), the FAS as well as the commercial courts relied on the information derived from the existing contracts for gas transportation as well as acts of gas delivery, while assessing the technical possibility of gas transportation through the relevant section of the GTS-UGSS of JSC Gazprom. The FAS and the courts based their assumption on the technical preparedness of that section of the GTS-UGSS for the period applied for by an independent gas supplier (LLC Real-Gaz) only on the fact that JSC Gazprom had granted access to the network for gas transportation through the same route during the past several years. The assumption of the FAS and the courts concerning the existence of spare capacities in the network relied on the fact that JSC Gazprom granted full access to the same section for transportation through the same route to another undertaking, after the natural monopoly had refused to conclude a contract with LLC Real-Gaz.

This situation creates clear incentives for transmission and distribution undertakings to refuse access to their networks and reserve capacities for their own commercial interests.[479] This was what happened in the case Gazprom vs. FAS (Real-Gaz): As a result of the cancelation of the supply contract between LLC Real-Gaz and its customer, the customer was forced to conclude a contract with more stringent conditions on the application of penalties with a gas supply subsidiary of JSC Gazprom, which led to an increased financial burden on the company. Moreover, the undertaking, from which LLC Real-Gaz was going to purchase gas, was compelled to sell its gas for a lower price to JSC Gazprom in order to avoid losses due to the inevitable incineration.

As a consequence of the lack of possibilities of the verification of information as regards the existence of spare capacities in the pipelines, the information concerning the shortest available routes of gas transportation cannot be verified either. In case transmission and distribution undertakings use this opportunity to increase their profits, the viability of gas sales of independent suppliers could be threatened through adding significantly to their transportation costs.[480]

Another problem regarding transparency is connected with the issue that the legislation of Russia only regulates access of independent undertakings

478 See also *Böhme*, EU-Russia Energy Relations, p. 69.

479 Cf. IEA, Russia Energy Survey 2002, p. 122. See also *Varlamova*, Competition Law of Russia, p. 444.

480 See also *Stern*, The future of Russian gas and Gazprom, p. 181.

to the GTS-UGSS, not affecting the relations between JSC Gazprom and the undertakings of its system. Gas transmission undertakings have to disclose information concerning the tariffs set by the regulatory bodies for the services of gas transportation. However, the charges to be paid by other undertakings of the system of JSC Gazprom for transportation services of the transmission undertakings of the system of JSC Gazprom are neither regulated nor transparent.[481] Also, other conditions of the provision of transportation services by gas transmission undertakings to the undertakings of the system of JSC Gazprom remain unknown. The absence of an obligation to disclose this information creates additional incentives for JSC Gazprom, which operates at all levels of the gas value chain, to place the undertakings of its own system in a competitively advantageous position on gas supply markets through charging them with lower fees than those based on the approved tariffs for the transportation services.[482]

---

481 Cf. IEA, Russia Energy Survey 2002, p. 121.

482 See also *Stern*, The future of Russian gas and Gazprom, p. 180.

III. Enforcement of the right of access to gas networks

The discussion of the provisions on granting access to the gas networks would be incomplete without addressing the issue of possibilities for access seekers to enforce their access rights. The efficiency of the legal provisions can only be assessed comprehensively in this way. While the chapter B. II above described the legal contents of TPA rights to gas networks, this part deals with the instruments of their enforcement.

As a rule, a refusal to conclude the contract or a partial approval of the application is the subject-matter of dispute between the applicant for access to the network on the one hand, and the gas transmission or distribution undertaking on the other hand. The applicants seeking access to the networks have two options to enforce their rights: judicial and administrative.[483]

1. Judicial review

The possibility of judicial review for network access seekers in Russia is very limited since a clear dogmatic assignment of the TPA right does not exist. In Germany, the statutory right of access can be directly claimed in the court. Moreover, obligations to contract[484] are not necessarily related to any specific categorisation of contracts or to sectors but are rather derived from objective criteria. In Russia, the possibility of judicial enforcement of TPA rights is closely related to the categorisation of contracts for gas transportation through the GTS-UGSS and contracts for gas transportation through distribution networks (hereinafter jointly referred to as contracts for gas transportation) as the so-called public contracts. The reason is that the obligation to contract and therefore, the prohibition of refusal to contract, if there is a possibility of providing the respective services, characterises only the public contracts. However, the issue of whether the contracts for gas transportation constitute public contracts is controversial.

---

483 *Gerke/Gudkov/Lakhno*, in: Säcker, Handbook of German-Russian energy law, p. 573 f.

484 *Kontrahierungszwang*. See *Busche*, Private autonomy and obligation to contract, p. 124 ff., 299 ff. and 618.

In the following paragraphs, the notion of public contract in the legislation of Russia, the grounds of categorisation of contracts for gas transportation as a public contract and the relevant case law of Russia will be examined.

a) Public Contracts

A public contract, as stipulated in Art. 426 para. 1 sent. 1 of the Civil Code of Russia[485], is a contract concluded by a person performing entrepreneurial or other income-generating activity and establishing its obligations for the sale of goods, performance of works, or rendering of services, and this person, due to the nature of these activities, must exercise them with respect to everyone, who applies for it. Since by virtue of Art. 27 of the Law on Gas Supply the owners of gas transmission and distribution systems are obliged to provide non-discriminatory access to any undertaking operating in the territory of Russia to the spare capacities in the transmission and distribution networks, contracts for gas transportation constitute public contracts.[486]

Moreover, Art. 426 para. 1 sent. 1 of the Civil Code of Russia provides for a non-exhaustive list of exemplary public contracts, containing retail trade, carriage by transport for common use, communications services, energy supply, medical and hotel service. Since the supply of gas constitutes a form of energy supply, covering, inter alia, transportation of gas as per Art. 2 of the Law on Gas Supply, a contract for gas transportation may also be qualified as a public contract.

Even though specific detailed rules apply to the procedure for the conclusion of contracts for gas transportation, such contracts fall under the general regulation concerning public contracts too. Art. 426 para. 4 of the Civil Code of Russia explicitly emphasises that in the cases stipulated in the law, the Government of Russia may issue rules, which are obligatory for parties, with regard to the conclusion and performance of public contracts (model contracts, provisions etc.).

In addition, even though the legal acts regulating the contracts for gas transportation do not mention explicitly whether such contracts have a public nature, this fact may be derived by way of analogy from chapter 2 pt. 9 of the Regulation of the Government of Russia of 27.12.2004 on the Rules of non-discriminatory

485 Civil Code of the RF, Part 1, N 51-FZ 30.11.1994 [Grazhdanskiy kodeks RF, Chast 1], published in SZ of 05.12.1994, N 32, p. 3301, last amended on 26.07.2017, effective from 06.08.2017.

486 See also *Perchik*, Pipeline law, p. 103.

access to the services of electricity distribution and provision of these services[487] (hereinafter Rules on access to the services of electricity distribution), which states that an electricity distribution contract constitutes a public contract.

The Civil Code of Russia provides for rules applicable to public contracts and therewith to contracts for gas transportation. Namely, according to Art. 426 para. 1 sent. 2, the person performing entrepreneurial or other income-generating activity (i.e. the party to a public contract) does not have the right to show preference to some persons as compared with the others with respect to the conclusion of a public contract, except for those cases, permitted by the law or other legal acts. Further, according to Art. 426 para. 2 of the Civil Code of Russia, terms of the public contract, including the price of the commodities, works, and services, have to be equal for the consumers of the relevant category. Other conditions should not be determined deriving from the advantages of certain consumers or through giving them preference, unless a law or another legal act allows granting privileges to a certain category of consumers. Pursuant to Art. 426 para. 3 of the Civil Code of Russia, the person performing entrepreneurial or other income-generating activity is not allowed to refuse to conclude a public contract if there is a possibility of providing the consumer with the respective goods or services or performing the respective work for it. According to Art. 426 para. 5 of the Civil Code of Russia, the terms of a public contract which not correspond with the requirements of para. 2 and 4 of the present article are void.

---

487 Regulation of the Government of RF on the approval of Rules of non-discriminatory access to the services of electricity distribution and provision of these services, Rules of non-discriminatory access to the services of operative-dispatching control in electrical energetics and provision of these services, Rules of non-discriminatory access to the services of administrator of wholesale trade system and provision of these services and Rules of technical connection of the applications of electricity customers, objects of electricity generation and objects belonging to distribution undertakings and other persons [Postanovleniye Pravitelstva RF Ob utverzhdenii pravil nediskriminatsionnogo dostupa k uslugam po peredache elektricheskoy energii i okazaniya etikh uslug, pravil nediskriminatsionnovo dostupa k uslugam po operativno-dispecherskomy upravleniyu v elektroenergetike i okazanie etikh uslug, pravil nediskriminatsionnovo dosputa k uslugam administratora torgovoy sistemi optovovo rinka i okazanie etikh uslug i pravil tekhnologicheskovo prisoedeneniya energoprinimayushikh ustroistv potrebiteley elektricheskoy energii, obyektov po proizvodstvy elektricheskoy energii, a takzhe obyektov elektrosetevovo khozyaystva, prinadlezhashchikh setevim organizatsiyam i inim litsam] N 861 of 27.12.2004, published in SZ of 27.12.2004, N 52 (part 2), p. 5525, last amended on 28.07.2017.

Accordingly, in the case of contracts for gas transportation, a possibility, which gives rise to the obligation of a gas transmission or distribution undertaking to conclude the contract, consists of the following components: spare capacity in the pipelines from the connection to the extraction point[488]; compliance of the gas quality with the requirements of normative-technical documents[489]; and the presence of the gas pipelines and discharge pipes leading to gas customers with data collection and quality control points[490]. Only the presence of the above components together obliges gas transmission and distribution undertakings to conclude a contract for gas transportation.

Further the Civil Code of Russia prescribes the rules for an unsubstantiated refusal from the side of the party obliged to conclude the contract. Namely, as per Art. 445 para. 4 of the Civil Code of Russia, the other party is then entitled to refer to the court with a claim for compelling the obliged party to conclude a contract. In this case the contract will be deemed as concluded with the conditions stipulated in the decision of the court. The party entitled to the conclusion of a public contract may also bring an action for the disagreement in relation to certain conditions of the public contract.[491] According to Art. 446 of the Civil Code of Russia, in the case of a disagreement in relation to certain conditions of a public contract during its conclusion, the courts may define the contested terms by their decisions; however, this is only possible in relation to the terms that have been contested within 6 months of the emergence of the disagreement.

However, it is not possible to compel the commercial organisation to adjust unjustifiably high charges for services of connection to high pressure pipelines since the legislation of Russia does not foresee an obligation of the commercial

---

488 As stipulated in chapter 3 pt. 5 para. 2 of the Regulation on access to the GTS-UGSS and chapter 3 pt. 4 para. 2 of the Provisions on access to distribution networks.

489 As stipulated in chapter 3 pt. 5 para. 3 of the Regulation on access to the GTS-UGSS and chapter 3 pt. 4 para. 4 of the Provisions on access to distribution networks.

490 As stipulated in chapter 3 pt. 5 para. 4 of the Regulation on access to the GTS-UGSS and chapter 3 pt. 4 para. 3 of the Provisions on access to distribution networks.

491 Cf. para. 55 sent. 2 of Judgment of the Plenum of the Supreme Court of the RF and the Plenum of the Supreme Commercial Court of the RF of 01.07.1996 N6/8 on several issues concerning the application of part I of the Civil Code of the RF [Postanovleniye Plenuma Verkhovnovo Suda RF i Plenuma Verkhovnovo Arbitrazhnovo Suda RF O nekotorikh voprosakh, svyazannikh s primeneniyem chasti pervoy Grazhdanskogo kodeksa RF], published in RG of 13.08.1996, N 152.

undertaking to conclude a contract for the connection services to such pipelines, i.e. it does not constitute a public contract.

Moreover, according to Art. 445 para. 4 sent. 2, the party groundlessly avoiding the conclusion of the contract can be obliged to compensate the other party for the losses incurred as a result of this avoidance. Accordingly, the freedom of contract stipulated in Art. 421 of the Civil Code of Russia does not apply in these situations and the commercial organisation is limited in its freedom to choose the contracting party as well as the conditions of the public contract.[492]

In the case law, however, the issue of whether contracts for gas transportation constitute public contracts in the sense of Art. 426 para. 1 of the Civil Code of Russia is very controversial, as will be shown in the following paragraphs.

b) Astrakhan case

In the case LLC Astrakhan regional gas realisation company vs. JSC Astrakhangasservice (hereinafter Astrakhan case)[493], the disparity of opinions from different instances of the courts concerning the public character of the contract for gas transportation through distribution networks resulted in many years of court proceedings and, ultimately, a continual refusal to grant access to the distribution network. In Astrakhan case, the GDU owning the local gas distribution network (JSC Astrakhangasservice) acquired gas from the gas supplier (LLC Astrakhan regional gas realisation company) for the subsequent supply of gas to the population by virtue of a gas supply contract for the period from 31.12.2001 to 31.12.2002. The contract would renew automatically, unless one of the parties informed the other party about its will to discontinue the agreement. In due time before the expiry of the contract, the gas supplier informed the GDU about its decision not to continue supplying gas according to the existing contract after the date of its expiry. The gas supplier explained that there was no more need to make use of the services offered by the GDU in terms of collecting payments for the supplied gas from the population since the gas supplier was

492 *Sukhanov*, Civil Law, vol. III, p. 185 f.

493 Case N A06-2960-8/03 consisting of 4 decisions: Decision of the Commercial Court of Astrakhan Oblast of 11.02.2004 [Resheniye Arbitrazhnovo Suda Astrakhanskoy oblasti]; Judgment of the Appellate Court of 29.03.2004 [Postanovleniye apelyatsionnoy instantsii]; Judgment of the Federal Commercial Court of Cassation of Volga Federal District of 17.06.2004 [Postanovleniye kassatsionnoy instantsii Federalnovo Arbitrazhnovo Suda Povolozhskovo okruga]; Judgment of the Presidium of the Supreme Court of the RF of 05.04.2005 N 11857/04 [Postanovleniye Arbitrazhnovo Suda RF], published in VVAS 2005, N 7.

going to undertake this activity on its own. Thus, the gas supplier now only needed to exercise its TPA right on the distribution network owned by the GDU. Soon afterwards, the gas supplier handed over a draft contract for gas transportation to the GDU, but the latter refused to conclude it and referred to the existence of the gas supply contract. This refusal served as ground for bringing the action to the court. The court of first instance considered that the gas supply contract had been terminated and ordered the GDU to conclude the contract for gas transportation through its distribution network based on the assumption that this was a public contract and, therefore, the GDU was not entitled to refuse its conclusion.[494] The appellate court agreed with the court of first instance and considered that the commercial organisation was not allowed to refuse the conclusion of a public contract if it was able to provide the respective transportation services.[495]

However, the court of cassation annulled the judgment on the ground that the gas supplier breached the anti-monopoly legislation by abusing its dominant position in the market of gas supply in the Astrakhan Oblast.[496] The court considered that terminating the gas supply contract and therewith limiting the rights of an independent economic entity constituted an abuse of a dominant position since this activity of an undertaking holding a dominant position had as its object or effect the prevention, restriction or distortion of competition and/or the infringement of the interests of other undertakings. Moreover, the court of cassation considered that the gas supply contract between the parties had not terminated with the notice of the gas supplier since according to Art. 540 para. 3, if one of the parties to the contract places a proposal on the conclusion of a new contract before the expiry of its validity term, the relations between the parties are governed by the contract concluded earlier until the new contract is signed. However, the court did not address the character of the contract for gas transportation.

In the judgment of the Presidium of the Supreme Commercial Court of Russia from 2005, the Court of final instance in commercial disputes in Russia, while implementing a supervisory review of the decision of the court of cassation, did

494 Decision of the Commercial Court of Astrakhan Oblast of 11.02.2004 N A06-2960-8/03 [Resheniye Arbitrazhnovo Suda Astrakhanskoy oblasti].

495 Judgment of the Appellate Court of 29.03.2004 N A06-2960-8/03 [Postanovleniye apelyatsionnoy instantsii].

496 Judgment of the Federal Commercial Court of Cassation of Volga Federal District of 17.06.2004 N A06-2960-8/03 [Postanovleniye kassatsionnoy instantsii Federalnovo Arbitrazhnovo Suda Povolozhskovo okruga].

not agree with the courts of first two instances that had classified contracts for gas transportation as public contracts.[497] The Supreme Commercial Court stated that the conclusion of the court of first instance as well as the appellate court concerning the public character of the contracts for gas transportation were based on a wrong application and an incorrect interpretation of the provisions of the material law. According to the reasoning of the Supreme Commercial Court, based on the wording of Art. 426 para. 1 sent. 1 of the Civil Code of Russia, a public contract had to be concluded between a commercial organisation and a consumer.[498] The Supreme Commercial Court referred to Art. 2 of the Law on Gas Supply, which defined a gas consumer as a person acquiring gas from a supplier and using it as a fuel or raw material.[499] The Court concluded that the contract for gas transportation could not be deemed to be a public contract since the party to the contract other than the GDU was a supplier of gas and not a gas consumer in the sense of the Law on Gas Supply. The Supreme Commercial Court further strengthened its position by emphasising that the obligation of the GDU to conclude the contract is contingent upon the compliance of the other party with the requirements of the laws and other legal acts, e.g. the requirement in relation to the existence of a gas supply contract; unlike a public contract, where the commercial organisation is obliged to carry out the services due to the nature of its activity. Based on these arguments the Supreme Commercial Court did not support the position of the courts considering the contract for gas transportation to be a public contract. However, the Supreme Commercial Court did not annul the decision of the court of cassation, which rejected the claim of the gas supplier concerning the refusal to grant access to the distribution network, because the gas supplier did not follow the requirements for the conclusion of contracts for gas transportation through distribution networks.

However, while interpreting the notion of the 'consumer' and rejecting the public nature of contracts for gas transportation on that ground, the Supreme

497 See p. 2 of Judgment of the Presidium of the Supreme Court of the RF of 05.04.2005 N 11857/04 [Postanovleniye Arbitrazhnovo Suda RF], published in VVAS 2005, N 7.

498 According to the current version of Art. 426 para. 1 sent. 1 of the Civil Code of Russia, public contracts are concluded between a consumer and a person performing entrepreneurial or other income-generating activity.

499 Note that the definition of a gas consumer in Art. 2 of the Law on Gas Supply has last been revised on 05.04.2013. According to the current version of the Law, gas consumer is a person acquiring gas for his own domestic needs, as well as for own industrial or other household needs. However, the amendment made in the definition would not change the outcome of the analysis made by the Supreme Commercial Court.

Commercial Court disregarded the Law on Natural Monopolies, which gives rise to the impermissibility of the refusal to conclude a contract by a natural monopoly. According to Art. 8 para. 1 of the aforementioned Law, the natural monopolies are not entitled to refuse to conclude a contract with consumers on the production (sales) of the goods, which are subject to regulation pursuant to the present Law, in case the natural monopoly has a possibility to produce (sell) such goods. Thereby, services of gas transmission and distribution undertakings may also be considered 'goods' for the purposes of this provision.[500] In addition, Art. 3 defines 'consumers' as physical or legal persons, acquiring the goods, produced (sold) by a natural monopoly.[501] The Law on Gas Supply (on which the Supreme Commercial Court based its judgment) and other acts regulating the matter specify the originating provision, inter alia, through a more precise definition of the notions of 'possibility' as well as that of the 'consumers' of the services of natural monopolies.[502]

c) Other case law

Apart from the Astrakhan case, the positions of the Courts with regard to the public character of contracts for gas transportation also varied significantly in other cases. After having supported the contrary idea in the Astrakhan case, the Supreme Commercial Court of Russia in a more recent decision while assessing the validity of several provisions of the Rules on Gas Supply,[503] relied on the assumption that contracts for gas supply and gas transportation, regulated by the Rules on Gas Supply, are public contracts. In the course of this case, the Court took the supposition for granted and neither analysed it nor presented any arguments for its assertion.

Apart from the Supreme Commercial Court, the positions of other commercial courts of Russia also differ from each other. For instance, the Federal Commercial Court of North Caucasus Federal District in its judgment in the

---

500 See also *Varlamova*, Competition Law of Russia, p. 438 and *Perchik*, Pipeline law, p. 36.

501 See also *Korepanov*, Contracts for gas transportation through high pressure pipelines, p. 65 f.

502 See above part B.II.

503 Decision of the Supreme Commercial Court of the RF of 16.04.2012 N VAS-1113/12 on refusal to recognise paras 2, 3 and 4 of the pt. 11 and 17 of the Rules on gas supply in the RF, approved by the Regulation of the Government of the RF of 05.02.1998 N 162, as invalid [Resheniye Visshevo Arbitrazhnovo Suda RF Ob otkaze v priznanii nedeystvuyushchim abzatsev 2,3,4 punkta 11 i punkta 17 Pravil postavki gaza v RF, utv. postanovleniem Pravitelstva RF], p. 5 ff.

case Trans Nafta vs. Kaspiigazprom[504] concluded that since the owners of gas transmission and distribution systems are obliged to provide non-discriminatory access to any undertaking in the territory of Russia to the spare capacities in their networks, the contracts for gas transportation constitute public contracts;[505] whereas the Commercial Court of Penza Oblast adopted the recent attitude of the Supreme Commercial Court and relied on the fact that contracts for gas transportation are public contracts without substantiating its position.[506] On the contrary, the Federal Commercial Court of West-Siberian District based its judgment on the same reasoning concerning the non-public nature of a contract for gas transportation as the Supreme Commercial Court did in Astrakhan case.[507] In addition, in a more recent decision, the Commercial Court of Omsk Oblast based its decision in favour of plaintiff on the principle of freedom of contract stipulated in Art. 421 of the Civil Code of Russia and therewith agreed with the plaintiff's statement in support of its claim that the contract for gas transportation did not constitute a public contract.[508] However, the Court did not invoke the grounds for this assumption.

504 Judgment of the Federal Commercial Court of North Caucasus Federal District dated 20.02.2002 [Postanovleniye Federalnogo Arbitrazhnogo Suda severo-kavkazkovo okruga], case N A15-91/2001-9.

505 See Trans Nafta vs. Kaspiigazprom, p. 5.

506 Decision of the Commercial Court of Penza Oblast of 01.07.2013 N A49-1664/2013 [Resheniye Arbitrazhnogo Suda Penzenskoy Oblasti], p. 4 f.

507 Judgment of the Federal Commercial Court of West-Siberian District of 29.03.2007 case N F04-1510/2007 (32316-A81-39) [Postanovleniye Federalnogo Arbitrazhnogo Suda Zapadno-sibirskogo Okruga]. In this case the court of cassation dismissed an action brought by a gas supplier asking to annul the decisions of the courts of previous instances denying its claim to compel a gas distribution undertaking to conclude a contract for gas transportation. Like Astrakhan case, the court did so rely on the fact that the gas supplier did not follow the requirements approved by the Government of Russia for the conclusion of contracts for gas transportation through distribution networks. However, it ascertained that since the detailed rules for the conclusion of contracts for gas transportation were prescribed by the Provisions on access to distribution networks and these contracts did not have the public nature, the GDU was not obliged to conclude the contract for gas transportation.

508 Decision of the Commercial Court of Omsk Oblast of 24.07.2013 N A46-598/2013 [Resheniye Arbitrazhnovo Suda Omskoy Oblasti], p. 1, 5. The Decision has been confirmed by the Judgement of the Federal Commercial Court of West-Siberian District dated 29.04.2014 N A46-598/2013 [Postanovleniye Federalnogo Arbitrazhnogo Suda Zapadno-sibirskogo okruga]. The contested notification of the Department of the Federal Anti-monopoly Service of Omsk Oblast dated 29.10.2012 № 04/44-12 on the

As it could be observed from the presented diversity of the views, the issue of whether contracts for gas transportation have a public character has never been unambiguous and clear. The continuing struggle between the court instances, as well as divergent approaches of the courts of different regions, make the procedure for the enforcement of the infringed rights before the courts too cumbersome and therefore, commercially unworkable for the producers, suppliers and customers of gas.

For the purpose of clarifying the controversy and providing a higher degree of legal certainty, it would be preferable to stipulate in the legal acts regulating contracts for gas transportation, i.e. in the Regulation on access to the GTS-UGSS and the Provisions on access to distribution networks, that these contracts constitute public contracts, as is the case with electricity networks in chapter 2 pt. 9 of the Rules on access to the services of electricity distribution.

Further, it must be noted that in cases of claims for compelling commercial organisations to conclude a public contract, commercial organisations bear the burden of proof to demonstrate lack of possibility to supply goods, perform works, or render services.[509] For the contracts for gas transportation, it means that the transmission or distribution undertaking would have to prove before the court that it does not possess enough capacities for the fulfilment of the transportation services of the required volume of gas.

2. Administrative control

Since the natural monopolies, which infringe the TPA rights of access seekers, have dominant positions in the respective markets of gas transportation services, the access seekers may claim their rights not only under the Civil Code of Russia in the courts, but also by referring to the administrative body in charge of the control of abuses of dominant positions by such undertakings. Moreover, since

termination of the action (inaction) containing signs of violation of the anti-monopoly legislation was also partially based on the assumption that contracts for gas transportation constitutes a public contract. The notification is available at: http://omsk.fas.gov.ru/solution/9863, last accessed on 16.11.2017.

509 Cf. para. 55 sent. 1 of Judgment of the Plenum of the Supreme Court of the RF and the Plenum of the Supreme Commercial Court of the RF of 01.07.1996 N 6/8 on several issues concerning the application of part I of the Civil Code of the RF [Postanovleniye Plenuma Verkhovnovo Suda RF i Plenuma Verkhovnovo Arbitrazhnovo Suda RF O nekotorikh voprosakh, svyazannikh s primeneniyem chasti pervoy Grazhdanskovo kodeksa RF], published in RG of 13.08.1996, N 152.

the issue of the public nature of contracts for gas transportation, being the key to the success of claims of access seekers in the judicial review, remains unsettled, in practice applicants for access to the networks prefer[510] to address the administrative body.

a) Historical development

Until 2004, a specialised governmental body assumed the function of overseeing the compliance with the provisions on access to the GTS-UGSS in Russia. The commission of the government of Russia for the issues of the use of oil and gas high pressure pipelines[511] was brought into being by the Regulation on access to the GTS-UGSS in 1997 and was entitled to handle disputes between parties concerning access to the GTS-UGSS in the pre-trial order[512]. The commission was abolished in 2004 by the Governmental Regulation of 16.04.2004[513].

However, the Regulation on access to the GTS-UGSS still contains provisions authorizing the abolished commission in cases of disputes. For example, according to chapter 3 pt. 14 and 15 of the Regulation, if an independent undertaking disagrees with a reasoned refusal or a partial approval of an application by JSC Gazprom, it may refer to the commission and submit the application for access, the decision of JSC Gazprom on the application and other necessary documentation. The commission examines the materials with the participation of the representatives of JSC Gazprom and the independent undertaking within a month's period and makes a final decision. As well as disputes concerning the decision on the application, and any other disagreements between the parties

---

510 See also *Gerke/Gudkov/Lakhno*, in: Säcker, Handbook of German-Russian energy law, p. 574.

511 *Komissiya Pravitelstva Rossiyskoy Federacii po voprosam ispolzovanya system magistralnikh neftegazoprovodov i nefteproduktoprovodov.*

512 See also Trans Nafta vs. Kaspiigazprom, p. 7. The Court in this case dismissed the action based on the position that the claimant (an independent undertaking) did not have legal grounds to compel the gas transmission undertaking to the conclusion of the contract until the Commission made a final decision concerning the reasonability of the refusal of access by the transmission undertaking.

513 Regulation of the Government of the RF on arranging composition of coordinating, advisory and other bodies and groups, established by the Government of the RF [Postanovlenie Pravitelstva RF Ob uporyadochenii sostava koordinatsionnikh, soveshchatelnikh, inikh organov i grupp, obrazovannikh Pravitelstvom RF] N 215 of 16.04.2004, published in RG of 22.04.2004, N 84, last amended on 11.11.2006 (last amendments effective since 03.03.2007).

regarding the conclusion, performance and termination of the contract for gas transportation are dealt with by the commission in the pre-trial order, as per chapter 4 pt. 21 of the Regulation on access to the GTS-UGSS. These provisions have not been accordingly amended after the abolition of the commission since 2004.

In the case of the distribution networks, Art. 2 of the Regulation of 24.02.1998 approving the Provisions on access to distribution networks entitled the FEC to handle the issues concerning the access of undertakings to local distribution networks. Under Regulation of the FEC dated 19.02.1999,[514] the provisions regarding the review order of issues related to the access of undertakings to local distribution networks were approved (hereinafter Provisions on review of issues related to access to distribution networks by the FEC), which provided for detailed rules concerning the procedure of the control over the compliance with the rules on access to distribution networks. The FEC had been bought into being by the Presidential Decree on Federal Energy Commission of Russia of 29.11.1995 N 1194.[515] However, by virtue of the Decree of the President of Russia dated 09.03.2004 on the system and structure of federal executive bodies[516] (hereinafter Decree on the system and structure of federal executive bodies), the FEC was reorganised[517] and a unified regulatory body, FTS, assumed the duties and competences of the FEC. However, the function of the FEC regarding the review of the issues concerning access to distribution networks was not transferred to the FTS and was not reflected in the provisions of the FTS approved

514 Regulation of the Federal Energy Commission of RF on the approval of provisions regarding the review order of issues related to the access of undertakings to local distribution networks [Postanovleniye federalnoy energeticheskoy komissii RF Ob utverzhdenii Polozheniya o poryiadke rassmotreniya voprosov, svyiazannikh s dostupom organizatsiy k mestnim gazoraspredelitelnim setyiam] N 6/1 of 19.02.1999, published in RG of 18.05.1999, N 94, repealed by the Order of the FTS of 18.05.2011 N 111-e7.

515 Decree of the President of Russia on Federal Energy Commission of RF [Ukaz Prezidenta RF O Federalnoy Energeticheskoy Kommissiyi RF] of 29.11.1995 N 1194, published in RG of 02.12.1995, N 234.

516 Decree of the President of RF on the system and structure of federal executive bodies [Ukaz Prezidenta RF O sisteme i strukture federalnikh organov ispolnitelnoy vlasti] N 314 of 09.03.2004, published in RG of 12.03.2004, N 50, abolished on 28.09.2017.

517 See "Istoriya sozdaniya federalnogo reguliruyushchego organa v Rossii" [The history of creation of the federal regulatory body in Russia (FTS)] available at: http://www.fstrf.ru/about/activity/17, last accessed on 16.11.2017.

by the Regulation of the Government of Russia of 30.06.2004[518] (hereinafter Provisions of the FTS), which laid down the competences of the FTS and the rules on the organisation of its activities. The Order of the FTS of 18.05.2012[519] subsequently abolished the Provisions on review of issues related to access to distribution networks by the FEC.

However, the Provisions on access to distribution networks had not been adapted to the discussed institutional changes as chapter 4 pt. 14 para. 2 still contains an obligation of GDUs to provide information on the spare capacities upon request of the FEC, whereas the FTS did not obtain an equivalent power according to the Provisions of the FTS.

On 21 July 2015 the FTS was abolished by virtue of the Presidential Decree N 373 on several issues of public administration and control in the area of anti-monopoly and tariff regulation (hereinafter Decree on anti-monopoly and tariff regulation) with the purpose of enhancing public administration and control in the area of anti-monopoly and tariff regulation and the optimisation of the structure of federal organs of executive power.[520] The Decree on anti-monopoly and tariff regulation defined that the functions of the FTS should be transferred to the Federal Anti-monopoly Service and also that the latter would become the legal successor of the FTS.

Until 2004 there were specialised bodies (the commission of the government of Russia for the issues of the use of oil and gas trunk pipelines for access to the GTS-UGSS and the FEC for access to distribution networks) overseeing the compliance with the rules concerning network access. In 2004, i.e. contemporaneously with the abolition of the commission for the issues of the use of oil

518 Regulation of the Government of RF on the approval of provisions of the Federal Tariff Service [Postanovleniye Pravitelstva RF Ob utverzhdenii Polozheniya o Federalnoy sluzhbe po tarifam] N332 of 30.06.2004, published in RG of 15.07.2004, N 150, repealed by the Regulation of the Government of RF of 04.09.2015 N 941, last amended on 26.03.2015.

519 Order of Federal Tariff Service of RF on repealing several acts of the Federal energy commission of RF [Prikaz Federalnoy sluzhbi po tarifam RF O priznanii utrativshimi silu nekotorikh aktov Federalnoy energeticheskoy komissii RF] N111-e/7 of 18.05.2012, published in RG of 22.06.2012, N 141.

520 Decree of the President of RF on several issues of public administration and control in the area of anti-monopoly and tariff regulation [Ukaz Prezidenta RF O nekotorikh voprosakh gosudarstvennogo upravleniya v sfere antimonopolnogo i tarifnogo regulirovaniya] of 21.07.2015 N 373, published in SZ of 27.07.2015, N 30 p. 4571.

and gas trunk pipelines, the Federal Anti-monopoly Service was established[521] by the same Decree on the system and structure of federal executive bodies that also provided for the reorganisation of the FEC into the FTS. By virtue of the Provisions of the FAS, the FAS assumed the function of the control of the compliance with the legislation in the fields of activities of natural monopolies within the scope of its predefined powers. Moreover, after the abolition of the FTS, the FAS became its legal successor also in respect of any other functions in relation to state regulation of gas sector.

b) The competent authority

The Federal Anti-monopoly Service of Russia is a national competition authority with regulatory and executive functions.[522] The FAS is a federal institution, which reports directly to the government of Russia.[523] According to chapter 1 pt. 1 of the Provisions of the FAS, the FAS issues normative acts and monitors the compliance with the anti-monopoly legislation, the legislation in the fields of activities of natural monopolies, state regulation of prices (tariffs) on goods (services), and advertising; monitors the implementation of foreign investments in economic entities of strategic importance for national defence and national security, as well as monitors the field of state defence orders, procurement of goods, works and services for state and municipal needs and the field of purchase of goods, works and services by certain types of legal persons, as well as the harmonisation of the use of closed methods of determining the suppliers (contractors).

The Federal Anti-monopoly Service of Russia operates directly or through its territorial bodies (hereinafter jointly referred to as anti-monopoly bodies), as per chapter 1 pt. 4 of the Provisions of the FAS. Since the control of competition in Russia is under the exclusive jurisdiction of the Federation, all anti-monopoly bodies of Russia – unlike in Germany – constitute federal bodies[524] and do not represent parts of the regional governmental administrations.[525]

All anti-monopoly bodies have equal powers with the exception of the additional powers of the FAS mostly concerning its regulatory competences (adoption

521 On the predecessors of the FAS as well as their respective competences see *Sushkevich*, in: Artemyev/Sushkevich, Competition Law of Russia, p. 259 ff.

522 See also *Timofeeva*, Unbundling in der russischen Elektrizitätswirtschaft, p. 132.

523 See *Pashchenko/Rachkov*, Gas industry in Russia, WiRO 6/2006, p. 165.

524 *Timofeeva*, Unbundling in the Russian electricity industry, p. 135. See also *Timofeeva*, in: Säcker, Handbook of German-Russian energy law, p. 588.

525 See *Boute*, Russian Electricity and Energy Investment Law, p. 149.

of normative acts, approving forms etc.) as set out in Art. 23 para. 2 of the Law on Competition.[526] The division of the competences between the FAS and its territorial bodies is regulated by the provisions of territorial bodies of the Federal Anti-monopoly Service, approved by the Order of the FAS of 23.07.2015[527] (hereinafter Provisions of territorial bodies of the FAS). Territorial competences of the bodies of the FAS correspond to the territories of one or several federal subjects of Russia. According to chapter 2 pt. 6.1.3. para. 2 of the Provisions of territorial bodies of the FAS, in their respective subjects of the Federation, territorial bodies have power to control activities of natural monopolies in the field of services of gas transportation through distribution networks, but their powers do not extend to overseeing compliance with the requirements regarding granting non-discriminatory access (lit. 'e' of chapter 2 pt. 6.1.3. of the Provisions of territorial bodies of the FAS) since it remains under the competence of the Federal Anti-monopoly Service.

Generally, as compared with Germany, anti-monopoly bodies of Russia can be characterised with a higher degree of centralisation, however this feature can serve as a positive factor for ensuring consistent and impartial application of law.[528]

It has to be mentioned that, as clarified above,[529] the anti-monopoly legislation of Russia is defined by Art. 2 and Art. 3 of the Law on Competition as consisting of the Law on Competition and other federal laws regulating the relations connected with the protection of competition. As it can be derived from Art. 2 of the Law, these relations may also be regulated by the Regulations of the Government of Russia and the normative acts of the FAS, however, they do not constitute parts of the anti-monopoly legislation of Russia. With regard to legislation in the fields of activities of natural monopolies, in some cases the Provisions of the FAS[530], as well as the Provisions on territorial bodies of the FAS,[531] inaccurately refer to the 'legislation on natural monopolies'. However, the

526 See also *Sushkevich*, in: Artemyev/Sushkevich, Competition Law of Russia, p. 272.

527 Order of the FAS on the approval of the provisions of territorial bodies of the Federal Anti-monopoly Service [Prikaz FAS Rossii Ob utverzhdenii polozheniya o territorialnom organe Federalnoy Antimonopolnoy sluzhbi] N649/15 of 23.07.2015, last amended on 05.04.2017.

528 *Timofeeva*, Unbundling in the Russian electricity industry, p. 136.

529 See above part B.II.

530 E.g. chapter 2 pt. 5.3.1.1, pt. 5.3.1.4 of the Provisions of the FAS.

531 E.g. chapter 2 pt. 6.1.1, pt. 6.1.3 of the Provisions on territorial bodies of the FAS.

legislation of Russia does not provide for the definition of this term and it is unclear what the legislator means by the use of the expression.

Before its abolition, the FTS was a unified national regulatory body in Russia, which undertook, inter alia, the regulation of tariffs for the transportation services of gas transmission and distribution undertakings, but was not responsible for ensuring non-discriminatory access to the goods and services of natural monopolies, unlike under the requirement of the Gas Directive 2009[532] of the EU.[533] According to chapter 1 of the Provisions of the FTS (now repealed), the FTS constituted a federal body of executive power for the regulation of natural monopolies, which implemented the functions in relation to defining (setting) prices (tariffs) and monitoring the issues concerning the definition (setting) and application of prices (tariffs) in the fields of activities of natural monopolies. Now both functions – related to prices (tariffs) as well as to ensuring compliance with the rules concerning access to the network – are concentrated under one body, the Federal Anti-monopoly Service.

c) Powers of the authority

aa) Powers of anti-monopoly bodies regarding the control over the compliance with the legislation in the fields of natural monopolies

The powers of anti-monopoly bodies, as set out in chapter 2 pt. 5 of the Provisions of the FAS, as well as in chapter 2 pt. 6.1.3. of the Provisions of territorial bodies of the FAS, cover, inter alia, control over the actions that take place with the participation of or in respect of natural monopolies and which could result in the impairment of the interests of consumers of goods, subject to state regulation;[534] control over the compliance with the requirements concerning the granting of access to the markets of services of natural monopolies, as well as the provision of services by natural monopolies on a non-discriminatory basis;[535] control over the compliance with the requirements concerning the obligatory conclusion of contracts by natural monopolies, as required by the legislation on natural monopolies.[536] In addition, as signalled by chapter 1 para. 1 of the Provisions of

532 Art. 41 para. 10 of the Gas Directive 2009.

533 For more details concerning the division of the competences between the FTS (before its abolition) and the FAS see *Timofeeva*, in: Säcker, Handbook of German-Russian energy law, p. 592 ff.

534 Chapter 2 pt. 5.3.1.2. of the Provisions of the FAS.

535 Chapter 2 pt. 5.3.1.3. of the Provisions of the FAS.

536 Chapter 2 pt. 5.3.1.4. of the Provisions of the FAS.

the FAS, the scope of functions of the FAS concerning the control of the compliance with the legislation in the fields of activities of natural monopolies is not limited to its predefined powers.[537] On the contrary, the powers of the territorial bodies of the FAS in relation to the control over the compliance with the legislation in the fields of activities of natural monopolies, as per chapter 1 para. 1 of the Provisions of territorial bodies of the FAS, are limited to the powers which are predefined by the legislation. Thus, the territorial bodies are only entitled to exercise the powers listed regarding the control of the compliance with the legislation in the field of activities of natural monopolies, whereas the FAS is not bound to this extent.

Further, by virtue of chapter 2 pt. 5.3.2.3. of the Provisions of the FAS, as well as chapter 2 pt. 4.5.1. of the Provisions of territorial bodies of the FAS, anti-monopoly bodies are formally entitled to issue instructions in the occasions prescribed, inter alia, by the legislation in the fields of activities of natural monopolies and which are obligatory for legal and natural persons, as well as the state authorities. However, no such occasion has been defined by the legislation in the fields of activities of natural monopolies so far.

The functions of anti-monopoly bodies in relation to overseeing the compliance with the legislation in the field of activities of natural monopolies may be deemed to be complementary to their functions of the control over the compliance with the anti-monopoly legislation in terms of handling issues of network access. Indeed, there is no legal mechanism which would make the control over the compliance of the activities of natural monopolies and the protection of the infringed rights of third parties workable in relation to access issues, except for the qualification of actions of gas transmission and distribution undertakings as an abuse of a dominant position under the Law on Competition; the compliance with the requirements of the legislation in the field of activities of natural monopolies, i.e. the Law on Gas Supply, the Law on Natural Monopolies as well as other legal acts regulating access to networks, is checked only in the process of examination of an alleged abuse of a dominant position. Moreover, the Provisions of the FAS in chapter 2 pt. 5.3.10. as well as chapter 2 pt. 6.4. of the Provisions of territorial bodies of the FAS, explicitly state that the violations in relation to which

537 Chapter 1 para. 1 of the Provisions of the FAS in the version prior to the amendments of 04.09.2015 contained a limitation of the powers of the FAS in relation to the control over the compliance with the legislation in the fields of activities of natural monopolies to the powers predefined by the legislation.

the anti-monopoly bodies are entitled to initiate and examine cases, but do not refer to the legislation in the field of activities of natural monopolies.

bb) Powers of anti-monopoly body regarding the control over the compliance with the anti-monopoly legislation

In respect of performing the function of the control over the compliance with the anti-monopoly legislation, an anti-monopoly body has a number of powers prescribed to it by Art. 23 of the Law on Competition. According to para. 1 pt. 1) of this provision, an anti-monopoly body has the power to initiate and examine instances of violations of the anti-monopoly legislation.

In the course of exercising its powers, according to Art. 23 para. 1 pt. 2) of the Law on Competition and its sub-points, an anti-monopoly body is entitled to issue binding instructions for economic entities for, inter alia, the following purposes: to terminate an abuse of a dominant position and to undertake actions aimed at ensuring competition; to terminate violations of rules regarding non-discriminatory access to products; to eliminate the consequences of a violation; to restore the situation that existed prior to a violation; to fulfil economic, technical, informational or other requirements in respect of the elimination of discriminatory conditions and prevention of their emergence.

In addition, as per Art. 23 para. 1 pt. 3.2) of the Law on Competition, an anti-monopoly body is entitled to issue a notice of warning to terminate actions or omissions, specifying the violation of the anti-monopoly legislation, in the cases prescribed by the present Law. The issuance of a notice of warning by an anti-monopoly body is further regulated by Art. 39.1 of the Law on Competition.

Pursuant to Art. 23 para. 1 pt. 5) of the Law on Competition, anti-monopoly bodies may hold undertakings, state bodies, and other organisations, as well as their respective officials[538] and physical persons[539], liable for the violations of the anti-monopoly legislation.

---

538 Officials mean any manager or other employee of the company having administrative or executive powers. See *Rokhlin/Nikitina*, in: Emch, inter alia, Competition Law in the BRICS Countries, p. 86, and fn. 12.

539 "[…] commercial organisations, non-commercial organisations, their officials, officials of the federal executive authorities, of the bodies of executive authority of the constituent territories of the Russian Federation, of the local self-government bodies, and of other bodies or organisations exercising the functions of the said bodies, as well as other officials of the public extra-budgetary funds, physical persons, including individual entrepreneurs" (Art. 23 para. 5).

According to Art. 23 para. 1 pt. 10) of the Law on Competition, anti-monopoly bodies are entitled to establish the dominant position of an economic entity in the course of an examination into a violation of anti-monopoly legislation and while exercising control over economic concentration. Notably, anti-monopoly bodies are the only administrative bodies which are entitled to establish a dominant position of an economic entity, and, as a rule, the courts may only annul a decision on the establishment of a dominant position because of procedural violations by anti-monopoly bodies.[540]

According to Art. 23 para. 1 pt. 11) of the Law on Competition, anti-monopoly bodies carry out inspections relating to the compliance with the anti-monopoly legislation by undertakings, state bodies and other organisations, as well as physical persons[541], may request necessary documents, information, as well as explanations in written or verbal form, from such parties, and, in accordance with the established procedure, apply to the agencies engaged in operative investigatory activities with the request to carry out operative investigations. Further, the rules applied to the investigations are prescribed by Art. 25.1 to 25.6. of the Law on Competition.[542]

Pursuant to Art. 25 para. 1 of the Law on Competition, undertakings, state bodies and other organisations, as well as their respective officials, and physical persons,[543] are in turn obliged, upon a reasonable request and in accordance with its scope of reference, to provide the anti-monopoly bodies with documents, explanations, and information, orally or in writing (including

540 *Sushkevich*, in: Artemyev/Sushkevich, Competition Law of Russia, p. 268.

541 "[…] commercial organisations, non-commercial organisations, federal executive authorities, bodies of public authority of the subjects of the Russian Federation, bodies of local self-government, other bodies or organisations exercising the functions of the above-mentioned bodies, as well as by public extra-budgetary funds, physical persons" (Art. 23 para. 11).

542 However, the FAS function of enforcing consumers' and suppliers' rights to access the network is limited to the cases of natural monopolies and abuses of dominant positions. In all other cases consumers and producers must directly enforce their rights in the court, without benefiting from the active support of the FAS in these procedures. See *Boute*, Russian Electricity and Energy Investment Law, p. 150.

543 "Commercial organisations and non-commercial organisations (their officials), the federal executive bodies (their officials), executive bodies of the constituent territories of the Russian Federation (their officials), local self-government bodies (their officials), other agencies or organisations exercising the functions of the above bodies, as well as state extra-budget funds (their officials), physical persons, including individual entrepreneurs […]" (Art. 25 para. 1 of the Law on Competition).

information constituting commercial, professional or other legally protected secrets), including official electronic correspondence, within an established timeframe.

d) Establishment of violation of the anti-monopoly legislation

The administrative procedure for the examination of the instances of infringements of TPA rights by anti-monopoly bodies constitutes an ex post control. As mentioned, such cases are classified as an abuse of a dominant position by gas transmission or distribution undertakings under the Law on Competition.

Pursuant to Art. 39 para. 1 of the Law on Competition, the FAS initiates and examines instances of the violations of the anti-monopoly legislation, and makes decisions and issues instructions as a result of those examinations. Art. 39 para. 2 of the Law states that the grounds for the initiation and examination of a case are: an application of a legal or natural person; a referral of another state or local authority; findings by anti-monopoly bodies; information in mass media regarding the alleged violation of the anti-monopoly legislation; and results of an inspection, which revealed evidences of violations of the anti-monopoly legislation. In order to establish abuse, first of all the FAS has to ascertain whether the undertaking that is alleged to have breached competition law holds a dominant position in the relevant market.

aa) Establishment of a dominant position

Art. 5 of the Law on Competition, which provides for the definition and the criteria for the establishment of a dominant position of an economic entity, prescribes in para. 5 a presumption that the position of a natural monopoly is considered to be dominant in the market, which is in the state of a natural monopoly. Thus, the other criteria for the establishment of dominance do not apply if an undertaking constitutes a natural monopoly and the market in question is the one being in the state of a natural monopoly. This presumption can always be employed in the case of infringements of TPA rights to the gas networks by gas transmission and distribution undertakings in Russia since the undertakings providing services of gas transportation constitute natural monopolies by the law, and the market of provision of gas transportation services, access right to which is being infringed, is in the state of a natural monopoly.

The provision containing the presumption (i.e. the position of a natural monopoly is considered to be dominant in the market, which is in the state of a natural monopoly) has been criticised by *Varlamova* as inaccurate. It can be derived already from the definition of a natural monopoly, provided for in Art.

3 of the Law on Natural Monopolies, that a natural monopoly is engaged in the production (sales) of commodities under the conditions of natural monopoly, hence, there is no need to emphasise this fact again when referring to the dominant position of natural monopolies.[544] However, since market definition is an inevitable precondition for the establishment of a dominant position, the legislator has correctly highlighted in the contested provision that an undertaking – natural monopoly – should be considered to be dominant only in relation to the market, which is in the state of natural monopoly and not in relation to any upstream or downstream markets, where the undertaking may also be operating and which do not constitute natural monopolies.

In order for the presumption of dominance of natural monopolies stipulated in Art. 5 para. 5 of the Law on Competition to be applicable to gas transmission and distribution undertakings, it is necessary for these undertakings to be included in the register of natural monopolies in compliance with the Law on Natural Monopolies. Anti-monopoly bodies as well as the commercial courts rely on the inclusion of undertakings in the register of natural monopolies while when assessing any potential dominant position.[545] However, since natural monopolies are not automatically included in the respective registers, this may become an obstacle for undertakings trying to get an access to the networks of the monopolists. In order to be able to assess this hindrance, it is worthwhile outlining the procedure and the responsible public body for the management of the register of natural monopolies.

According to Art. 10 para. 2 of the Law on Natural Monopolies, the regulatory bodies of the natural monopolies have a duty to establish and manage the registers of natural monopolies. Pursuant to Art. 9 para. 1 of the same Law regulatory bodies are formed according to the activities of natural monopolies, for example, the transportation of gas through pipelines. As discussed, the authority overseeing the compliance with the legislation in the areas of activities of natural monopolies in Russia is the federal executive body FAS as per chapter 1 pt. 1 of the Provisions of the FAS. Accordingly, chapter 2 pt. 5.3.4(2). of the Provisions of the FAS stipulates that the FAS has the duty to establish and manage the register of natural monopolies which are subject to state regulation and control, for the

544 See *Varlamova*, Competition Law of Russia, p. 288.

545 See e.g. Judgment of the Federal Commercial Court of Moscow District N A40-69840/12-79-654 of 27.02.2013 [Postanovleniye Federalnogo Arbitrazhnogo Suda Moskovskogo Okruga], p. 2; Judgment of the Federal Commercial Court of Moscow District N KA-A40/7901-11 of 27.07.2011, case N A40-87139/10-130-466 [Postanovleniye Federalnogo Arbitrazhnogo Suda Moskovskogo Okruga], p. 3.

purposes of determining (establishing) prices (tariffs) and implementing control over the issues related to the determination (establishment) and application of prices (tariffs).

In 2010, when the function of establishing and managing the register of natural monopolies was still attributed to the FTS, the Administrative Regulations were approved by the Order of the FTS of 30.08.2010, repealed as of 21.06.2016[546] (hereinafter Administrative Regulations of the FTS), which laid down the detailed rules concerning the procedure for the inclusion and exclusion of the natural monopolies in the register, as well as the amendment of their data. According to pt. 6 and 7 of the Administrative Regulations of the FTS, inclusion and exclusion of a natural monopoly, as well as the amendment of data in an existing registration could be initiated by an application of the natural monopoly, upon a referral by a stakeholder, or by the FTS itself. According to pt. 16 of the Administrative Regulations of the FTS, the decision as to the inclusion or exclusion of a natural monopoly in or from the register has to be made within 6 months from the moment of registration of the application or the reference or receipt of the materials serving as ground for the decision on the own initiative of the FTS. By virtue of the Decree on anti-monopoly and tariff regulation, as discussed above,[547] the FTS has been abolished and the FAS has been named as its legal successor. However, no other regulation concerning the procedure for the inclusion and exclusion of natural monopolies, as well as the amendment of data in existing entries has been adopted by the anti-monopoly body so far.

Since the anti-monopoly bodies as well as the courts rely on the inclusion of a natural monopoly in the register in order to attribute the holding of a dominant position in the market, which is in the state of a natural monopoly, to it, it is essential for the legal protection of the holders of the TPA rights that the process is handled promptly. The legislator has established an unreasonably long period

---

546 Order of the FTS approving the administrative regulations concerning the performance by the FTS of the state function of establishing and managing the register of natural monopolies, which are subject to state regulation and control [Prikaz Federalnoy sluzhbi po tarifam Ob utverzhdenii administrativnogo reglamenta ispolneniya federalnoy sluzhboy po tarifam gosudarstvennoy funktsii po formirovaniyu i vedeniyu reestra subyektov yestestvennikh monopoliy, v otnoshenii kotorikh osushchestvlyayutsya gosudarstvennoye regulirovaniye i kontrol] N417-e of 30.08.2010, published in BNA of 20.12.2010, N 51, repealed by the Order of the FAS on repealing some orders of the FTS [Prikaz FAS Rossii O priznanii utrativshimi silu nekotorikh prikazov federalnoy sluzhbi po tarifam] N797/16 of 21.06.2016.

547 See above part B.III.2.a).

for making a decision on a formal issue given that the only criterion for the inclusion of an undertaking in the register is the field of activity of the undertaking.

Notably, neither natural monopolies nor the FAS are responsible for the registration of natural monopolies. However, the start (and the end) of their activity as a natural monopoly is connected with the inclusion (exclusion) in the register. According to chapter 1 pt. 6 of the Procedure for the review of documents provided for making decisions about introduction, alteration or termination of regulation of activities of natural monopolies approved by the Order of FTS of 13.10.2010[548], the decision of the FTS about the introduction or termination of the regulation of activities of a natural monopoly serves as a ground for the decisions about the inclusion or exclusion of the natural monopoly in or from the register, respectively. For these relationships also, no other regulation has been adopted by the FAS so far.

bb) Abuse of a dominant position

Art. 10 para. 1 of the Law on Competition prohibits the actions or omissions of an economic entity occupying a dominant position, which result or may result in the prevention, restriction or elimination of competition and/or infringement of the interests of other persons (economic entities) in the area of entrepreneurship, or of that of an indefinite number of consumers. According to para. 4 of the judgment of the Plenum of the Supreme Commercial Court N 30 of 30.06.2008[549] (hereinafter Judgment on application of the anti-monopoly legislation), for the qualification of an action (or omission) as an abuse of a dominant position the presence of any of the mentioned consequences is sufficient, namely

548 Order of the FTS on the approval of Procedure for the review of documents provided for making decisions about introduction, alteration or termination of regulation of activities of natural monopolies and a list of such documents [Prikaz Federalnoy sluzhbi po tarifam Ob utverzhdenii poryadka rassmotreniya dokumentov, predstavlyiaemikh dlya prinyatiya resheniya o vvedenii, izmenenii ili prekrashchenii regulirovaniya deatelnosti subyektov yestestvennikh monopoliy, i perechnya takikh dokumentov] N481-e of 13.10.2010, published in RG of 29.12.2010, N 295, last revised on 16.12.2014.

549 Judgment of the Plenum of the Supreme Commercial Court of the RF on several questions raised in relation to the application of the anti-monopoly legislation by the commercial courts [Postanovleniye Plenuma Visshego Arbitrazhnogo Suda RF O nekotorikh voprosakh, voznikayushchikh v svyazi s primeneniyem arbitrazhnimi sudami antimonopolnogo zakonodatelstva] N 30 of 30.06.2008, published in VVAS of August 2008, N 8, last amended 14.10.2010.

the prevention, restriction or elimination of competition or infringement of the interests of other persons.

Further, Art. 10 para. 1 of the Law on Competition lists certain types of abuses, which are per se prohibited since there is an established, irrebuttable presumption that they restrict competition.[550] In relation to the listed per se abuses the presence or threat of the occurrence of the named consequences is implied and does not have to be proved by anti-monopoly bodies.[551] It has to be noted, however, that the list is non-exhaustive and the courts as well as anti-monopoly bodies are entitled to qualify other actions or omissions of undertakings of a dominant position as an abuse too.[552]

The forms of abuses which are most often applied to the infringements of TPA rights to gas networks, i.e. imposition of onerous contract terms and refusal or evasion to deal, will be addressed as follows.

(1) Imposition of onerous contract terms

The list of per se abuses of Art. 10 para. 1 of the Law on Competition includes in pt. 3) imposition of onerous contract terms, i.e. the imposition of contract terms upon the counterparty, which are unfavourable to the latter or not related to the subject of agreement. The provision further specifies that the terms may be deemed unfavourable, if they are economically or technologically unjustified and/or are not directly foreseen by legal or judicial acts.[553] The examples of unfavourable terms provided by the Law on Competition are: requirements regarding a transfer of financial assets, other type of ownership or ownership rights, as well as consent to conclude a contract concerning the goods in which the counterparty is not interested.

The Appellate Court in the case Chelyabinskgazcom[554] interpreted the notion of 'imposition of unfavourable conditions' as the offering of such terms of contract by a dominant undertaking, which are unfavourable to the counterparty and are legitimately challenged, and their acceptance is refused or evaded by the undertaking. In this judgment the Appellate Court provided for

---

550 See *Rokhlin/Nikitina*, in: Emch, inter alia, Competition Law in the BRICS Countries, p. 82.

551 See para. 4 of the Judgement on application of the anti-monopoly legislation.

552 See ibid.

553 *Varlamova*, Competition Law of Russia, p. 299.

554 Judgment of the 18th Commercial Appellate Court N18AP-468/2013 of 26.03.2013 case N A76-17481/2012 [Postanovleniye Vosemnadtsatogo Arbitrazhnogo Suda] (hereinafter Chelyabinskgazcom).

the features specifying the violation of the anti-monopoly legislation in the form of imposition of onerous contract terms: (1) activities of undertaking of a dominant position are directed towards insisting, refusing to handle the reports of disagreements, refusing or evading to accept the offer of the counterparty at the stage of conclusion of a contract; (2) the conditions offered by the undertaking of a dominant position are unfavourable to the counterparty and economically or technically unjustified and/or are not provided for/are contradictory to the applicable legislation.

An activity of an undertaking holding a dominant position can be qualified as insistence and thus, imposition, when there is sufficient evidence to show that the counterparty attempted to alter the offered conditions (including sending reports of disagreements) but did not succeed.[555] In the case Chelyabinskgazcom, the anti-monopoly body of Chelyabinsk Oblast found, and the Commercial Courts confirmed, that the reports of disagreements sent in a number of times by JSC EnSer (party claiming network access) and the receipt of either unacceptable conditions or of no feedback from the GDU JSC Chelyabinskgazcom, sufficiently demonstrated imposition by the undertaking holding a dominant position. Further, the anti-monopoly body as well as the courts also examined and established that the conditions offered by the GDU were not only not unforeseen by the applicable legislation but even contradictory to it.

It is important to note that the party applying for the conclusion of a contract for gas transportation may invoke the provision on imposition of onerous terms in the negotiations phase before the factual conclusion of the contract. Once the contract for gas transportation is concluded, the party cannot claim the adjustment of the conditions as a remedy for the violation of the Law on Competition by the undertaking providing gas transportation services. In the case Omskgazset[556], the commercial courts found that the GDU LLC Omskgazset did not violate the anti-monopoly legislation by imposing onerous contract terms since the parties had already concluded the contract for gas transportation and there was no proof of imposition.

As a remedy for the imposition of onerous contract terms, anti-monopoly bodies may only oblige the undertaking holding a dominant position to adapt the conditions and to come to an agreement with the counterparty. However,

555 *Varlamova*, Legally ensuring the development of competition, p. 121.

556 Judgment of the Federal Commercial Court of West-Siberian District of 26.09.2013 case N A46-597/2013 [Postanovleniye Federalnogo Arbitrazhnogo Suda Zapadnosibirskogo Okruga] (hereinafter Omskgazset).

anti-monopoly bodies are not entitled to define the terms of contracts for the parties by themselves.[557] On the contrary, the courts do have the right to define the terms of a public contract by their decisions pursuant to Art. 446 of the Civil Code of Russia.[558]

(2) Refusal or evasion to deal

Further, the list of per se abuses of Art. 10 para. 1 of the Law on Competition includes in pt. 5) economically or technologically unjustified refusal or evasion to conclude a contract with certain customers when there are possibilities for the production or supply of the relevant product, or such refusal or evasion is not provided for directly by legal or judicial acts (refusal or evasion to deal).

In the case of undertakings providing gas transportation services, a 'possibility for the production or supply of the relevant product', i.e. a possibility to provide transportation services means the existence of sufficient capacity in the pipelines. Apart from lack of spare capacities, the grounds of access refusal are the provision of gas of insufficient quality and a lack of connection to the network. These grounds are stipulated as prerequisites of access to gas networks in chapter 3 pt. 5 of the Regulation on access to the GTS-UGSS as well as chapter 3 pt. 4 of the Provisions on access to distribution networks. However, since the possible grounds of refusal are not specifically defined in the legislation, non-compliance with the provisions of the Regulation on access to the GTS-UGSS as well as the Provisions on access to distribution networks other than those concerning prerequisites of access by independent undertakings, suppliers and customers may also serve as a reasonable ground for refusing access by undertakings providing gas transportation services.[559]

Based on the literal construction of the provision on refusal or evasion to deal, even if the undertaking holding a dominant position has a possibility of production or supply of the product, the ground for refusal or evasion will not be questioned on compliance with the Law on Competition, if such conduct is either (1) economically or technologically justifiable, or (2) the ground

557 See also Art. 23 para. 1 pt. 6) of the Law on Competition, listing the cases when the anti-monopoly bodies refer to a commercial court in order to implement its decisions, for which the anti-monopoly bodies do not have the powers.

558 See above part B.III.1.a). See the case Chelyabinskgazcom, p. 11.

559 Non-compliance with the requirements prescribed by the Regulation on access to the GTS-UGSS served as a reasonable ground for refusal to conclude a contract in the case FAS vs. Gazprom (NGK/SibEvroGaz) (see esp. p. 5), in the case Trans Nafta and Gazprom vs. FAS (Tatarstan).

is provided for in legal or judicial acts. Apparently, it cannot be concluded from the provision that for those undertakings, the activities of which are regulated by sector-specific rules, i.e. natural monopolies, only those grounds for refusal or evasion, stipulated in the respective rules have to be accepted. Thus, a ground for refusal or evasion, which is not provided by sector-specific rules, may still be examined on economic or technological justifiability, according to the formulation of the provision.

However, in practice the provision is applied in a different way, namely, if sector-specific legislation provides for grounds for refusal or evasion, they are not examined on 'economic or technological' justifiability anymore. In the case Gazprom vs. FAS (Real-Gaz), the reference to the fact that the gas demand of the consumer was already covered by other gas suppliers was not accepted by the FAS as well as by the commercial courts as a ground for refusal of access to the GTS-UGSS since such ground was not foreseen by the Regulation on access to the GTS-UGSS. Even though the incorrectness of this ground (the customer was not fully secured with gas supplies) was revealed in the course of examination by the FAS, the anti-monopoly body and the courts accepted this ground based only on the fact that the ground was not provided for by the Regulation on access to the GTS-UGSS.

It has to be emphasised that not only refusal, but also evasion to conclude a contract, constitutes a violation of the anti-monopoly legislation. Evasion refers to the situation when undertakings with dominant positions do not refuse to deal directly, but try to delay to conclude a contract.[560] Thus, the undertakings seeking access to gas networks may already claim their rights before receiving official refusal from gas transmission or distribution undertakings, when they observe that granting access is being delayed with the intention being to avoid concluding contract for gas transportation. Such provision reduces the risk that undertakings providing gas transportation services, referring to the fact that they do not refuse to deal, gain the time and evade granting access to their networks. However, it has to be mentioned that in the case Gazprom vs. FAS (Real-Gaz), the FAS decided (and the courts confirmed) that the activity of JSC Gazprom constituted an abuse of a dominant position in the form of evasion to conclude a contract for gas transportation, even though JSC Gazprom in fact timely handled the application and refused to conclude a contract based on unjustified grounds, as it was then ascertained. Hence, the action of JSC Gazprom in this case clearly

560 *Varlamova*, Competition Law of Russia, p. 303.

constituted refusal to deal and not an evasion; however, the different definition by the FAS and the courts did not evoke any differences in qualification.

The cases of so-called constructive refusal to deal, i.e. not formally refusing to conclude a contract but consciously offering such conditions to the counterparty which it will not be able to accept, may also be classified as an evasion to deal. However, the borderline between such abuse and the abuse through imposition of onerous contract terms may become vague. When differentiating the two, it is decisive that the latter contains the necessary attribute of imposition, i.e. insistence on concluding a contract with the unfavourable conditions by the undertaking holding a dominant position, whereas in the case of evasion the same unfavourable conditions are only offered with the purpose of receiving a refusal to conclude the contract from the counterparty.

As a remedy for the refusal or evasion to deal, anti-monopoly bodies can instruct the undertaking holding a dominant position to terminate the violation and to grant access to its network on non-discriminatory terms in accordance with the applicable legislation.[561]

(3) Creation of entry or exit barriers

Creation of entry or exit barriers, prescribed in Art. 10 para. 1 pt. 9 of the Law on Competition, often intersects with the refusal or evasion to deal and is referred to as 'creation of entry barriers through refusal to deal'.[562] Especially in the presence of a strong vertically integrated undertaking in the market, refusal to deal can be directly linked to the own interests of the incumbent to foreclose competition in upstream or downstream markets. In the following cases, even though the Court or the FAS did not always directly speak of creating entry barriers for independent undertakings, the common feature of these disputes was that JSC Gazprom at least tried to win the customers of the independent undertakings through its own gas supply undertakings while refusing the independent undertakings access to the GTS-UGSS and in this way banning them from the supply market.

In the case Gazprom vs. FAS (Real-Gaz), JSC Gazprom, through refusing access to LLC Real-Gaz for reasons which turned out to be false, created a situation where the customer was forced to purchase gas from an undertaking of the system of JSC Gazprom in order to cover its demand, and the initial supplier

561 See e.g. the contested decision and instruction of the FAS in the case Gazprom vs. FAS (Real-Gaz), which was confirmed by the courts: Decision of the FAS [Reshenie FAS Rossii] of 27.01.2012 case N 1 10/108-11.

562 *Varlamova*, Competition Law of Russia, p. 302.

of LLC Real-Gaz was forced to sell gas to the undertaking of the system of JSC Gazprom at a lower price in order to avoid losses. The FAS qualified the action of the natural monopoly (and the courts confirmed) as an abuse of a dominant position by avoiding concluding a contract for gas transportation whilst there were possibilities of transportation, and by creating entry barriers to the gas market to a third party.

In the case Gazprom vs. FAS (Tatarstan), JSC Gazprom refused to grant access to the GTS-UGSS to JSC Trans Nafta due to non-compliance with the formal requirements of the Regulation on access to the GTS-UGSS (chapter 3 pt. 8 and 9), as described above. However, the incumbent granted access to the initial gas supplier of the access seeker, LLC GazEnergoKomplex, under the condition that the latter would be supplied with gas from JSC Tatgazinvest, an undertaking of the system of JSC Gazprom. The FAS also found out that, after JSC Gazprom had refused to grant access to JSC Trans Nafta, the customer of JSC Trans Nafta, JSC "Generating Company", concluded a gas supply contract with JSC Tatgazinvest too. The FAS concluded that JSC Gazprom had been preventing JSC Trans Nafta from entering the gas supply market of the Republic Tatarstan without economic and technological reasoning and was putting JSC Trans Nafta in unequal conditions as compared to other undertakings supplying in this territory, including the undertakings of the system of JSC Gazprom. In this case, however, the Courts did not accept the arguments of the FAS and considered the breach of the requirements of the Regulation on access to the GTS-UGSS as a legitimate ground for a refusal of access by JSC Gazprom.[563]

Another example of JSC Gazprom directly declaring its advantages in the downstream market of gas supply is the case Gazprom vs. FAS (Transgaz), where JSC Gazprom refused to grant access to the GTS-UGSS and referred to the oversupply of the market and the coverage of customer demand by gas supply undertakings of the system of JSC Gazprom. The Court did not make a comment on this reasoning of the incumbent since the decision of the FAS had been declared void.

cc) Procedure of examination

The institute of notices of warning has been introduced to the anti-monopoly legislation with the amendment of the Law on Competition of 2011.[564] Pursuant

---

563 See also Press release of the FAS dated 08.09.2008.

564 See also *Rokhlin/Nikitina*, in: Emch, inter alia, Competition Law in the BRICS Countries, p. 85.

to Art. 39.1 of the Law, anti-monopoly bodies issue a notice of warning to an undertaking of a dominant position on termination of actions or omissions, having features of a violation of the anti-monopoly legislation, on elimination of the causes and conditions, facilitating such a violation and on the implementation of actions aiming at the elimination of the results of this violation. A notice of warning has to be issued as per Art. 39.1 para. 2 sent. 1 before initiating a case on an abuse of a dominant position, including the abuses prescribed by Art. 10 para. 1 pt. 3) of the Law on Competition (imposition of onerous contract terms) as well as by Art. 10 para. 1 pt. 5) (refusal or evasion to deal). Moreover, as per Art. 39.1 para. 2 sent. 2, the anti-monopoly bodies are not allowed to initiate a case without issuing a notice of warning and before the expiry of the period for the fulfilment of the requirements as defined in the notice. Further, if the undertaking holding a dominant position fulfils the requirements set out in the notice of warning, the anti-monopoly body may not initiate a case and the person that fulfilled the requirements shall not become subject to administrative liability for violation of the anti-monopoly legislation due to its elimination, as per Art. 39.1. para. 7 of the Law on Competition.

According to Art. 39 para. 3 sent. 1 of the Law on Competition, a case on the violation of the anti-monopoly legislation may be examined by the anti-monopoly body of the territory where the violation was committed or at the location (residence) of the person against whom the complaint about the anti-monopoly violation has been lodged. However, the FAS is entitled to examine any case regardless of the mentioned criteria, as per sent. 2 of the aforementioned provision.

Once a case on the violation of the anti-monopoly legislation is initiated, the anti-monopoly body establishes a commission for the examination of the case as per Art. 40 of the Law on Competition. The commission examines cases in its sessions, in which participants of the case (applicant, defendant and interested parties) are also notified to take part. The burden of proof in cases of an abuse of a dominant position lies upon the anti-monopoly body.[565] Pursuant to Art. 41 of the Law on Competition, upon the finding of an infringement of the anti-monopoly legislation in the course of the examination of a case, the commission adopts a decision ordering the undertaking to cease the violation (action or omission) as well as imposing behavioural remedies.[566] At the same time, and

565 See Art. 5 para. 4 and Art. 10 para. 2 of the Law on Competition. See also *Rokhlin/Nikitina*, in: Emch, inter alia, Competition Law in the BRICS Countries, p. 85.

566 *Rokhlin/Nikitina*, in: Emch, inter alia, Competition Law in the BRICS Countries, p. 85.

based on the decision, the commission adopts separate instructions for each person obliged to fulfil the requirements of the decision within the fixed term.

Undertakings, state bodies and other organisations, and their respective officials, as well as physical persons,[567] are obliged to fulfil decisions and instructions of the anti-monopoly bodies within the period established by these acts. In order to execute some decisions, however, the anti-monopoly bodies must refer to a commercial court, inter alia, with a claim for the obligatory conclusion of a contract as listed in Art. 23 para. 1 pt. 6) of the Law on Competition.[568]

The administrative procedure in anti-monopoly bodies may take altogether up to 9.5 months at the longest. For reviewing applications and materials anti-monopoly bodies have 1 month with the possibility of an extension of up to 3 months in certain circumstances. The process may be finished with an order on initiation of a case on the violation of the anti-monopoly legislation or with a denial to initiate a case. In the first situation, within 15 days after issuing the order, anti-monopoly bodies set a date for the examination of the case. For this purpose anti-monopoly bodies issue a determination. They have then 3 months' time, with the possibility of an extension of up to 6 months in certain circumstances from the date of the determination.[569] No formal requirements for applications and other documents for the initiation of cases as well as no state fees to be paid are seen as some of the advantages of the administrative control by anti-monopoly bodies.[570]

Pursuant to Art. 52 para. 1 sent. 1 of the Law on Competition, instructions and decisions of anti-monopoly bodies are subject to judicial review by commercial courts within 3 months after the date of adopting a decision or issuing an instruction. Instructions and decisions of a territorial anti-monopoly body may also be appealed in the collegial body of the FAS within the deadline of 1 month, as per Art. 52 para. 1 sent. 2 and para. 1.1. of the Law on Competition. Initiation of judicial proceedings by a court suspends the execution of the instruction in question, according to Art. 52 para. 2 of the Law on Competition. Hence, the

567 "Commercial organisations and non-commercial organisations (their officials), federal executive authorities of the Russian Federation (their officials), bodies of public authority of the Subjects of the Russian Federation (their officials), bodies of local self-government (their officials), other bodies or organisations exercising the functions of the above-mentioned bodies, as well as public extra-budgetary funds (their officials), physical persons [...]" (Art. 36 of the Law on Competition).

568 See also *Klein*, in: Artemyev/Sushkevich, Competition Law of Russia, p. 326 f.

569 See Art. 44 and Art. 45 of the Law on Competition.

570 *Klein*, in: Artemyev/Sushkevich, Competition Law of Russia, p. 323 f.

suspension effect is not applied to the decisions of the anti-monopoly bodies. It has to be mentioned that since everyone is guaranteed the protection of their rights in courts under the Constitution of Russia, the persons whose rights had been infringed as a result of violation of the anti-monopoly legislation, may also directly refer to judicial review[571] on this ground.

e) Sanctions

As per Art. 37 of the Law on Competition, undertakings and their officials may be held liable for breaching the Law on Competition. However, holding the persons liable does not exempt them from the duty to fulfil the decision and instruction of the anti-monopoly body or carry out other actions provided by the anti-monopoly legislation, as per Art. 37 para. 2 of the Law on Competition.

Within the framework of the administrative proceedings, according to Art. 14.31 para. 2 of the Code of Administrative Offences of Russia, for an abuse of a dominant position by a natural monopoly the anti-monopoly bodies may impose fines on undertakings of up to 1%-15% of the turnover achieved on the market where the violation occurred. Officials of the undertaking may receive fines amounting to between 20,000 and 50,000 Russian roubles or they may be disqualified for a period of up to 3 years. This provision, however, does not apply to the cases covered by Art. 9.21 of the Code of Administrative Offences of Russia, namely the infringement of the rules of non-discriminatory access and those of technical connection. Violations of the rules of non-discriminatory access, as well as the rules of technical connection, inter alia to the gas distribution networks, may lead to administrative fines amounting to between 10,000 and 40,000 Russian roubles for officials and between 100,000 and 500,000 Russian roubles for undertakings. Hence, the cases of refusal of access, i.e. an abuse of a dominant position by a natural monopoly providing gas transportation services through high pressure pipelines will be fined under Art. 14.31 para. 2 of the Code of Administrative Offences, whereas the same type of abuses committed by a GDU will be dealt through Art. 9.21 of the Code of Administrative Offences.

Pursuant to Art. 51 para. 2 of the Law on Competition, failure to fulfil the requirements set out in instructions issued by anti-monopoly bodies on the basis of decisions relating to the violation of the anti-monopoly legislation within the established period also entails administrative liability. Partial fulfilment within the established period as well as belated fulfilment of the instruction is considered to be a failure to fulfil instruction in time. Failure to meet the deadline of

571 *Klein*, in: Artemyev/Sushkevich, Competition Law of Russia, p. 317 f. and 329 f.

the instruction constitutes a violation of the anti-monopoly legislation. Art. 19.5 para. 2.1 to 2.6 of the Code of Administrative Offences of Russia prescribes fines as well as disqualification for officials of undertakings in the case of a failure to fulfil the instructions and decisions of the FAS and its territorial bodies.

In addition to an administrative fine, anti-monopoly bodies may order the recovery of the revenue gained through monopolistic activities[572] into the federal budget as per Art. 23 para. 1 lit. 'j' as well as Art. 51 para. 3 of the Law on Competition. However, the two types of sanctions may not be applied jointly as it used to be the case before the amendments of 05.10.2015 in the Law on Competition.[573] According to the appended sent. 3 of Art. 51 para. 3 of the Law on Competition, a person may not be held liable under the Code of Administrative Offences of Russia for the violation of the anti-monopoly legislation in relation to which the recovery has been ordered and executed.

Art. 178 para. 1 of the criminal code of Russia of 13.06.1996[574] (hereinafter Criminal Code of Russia) provides that the restriction of competition by means of an agreement between competitors, prohibited by the anti-monopoly legislation of Russia, constitutes a criminal offence if it has caused significant damage or loss of significant income. Such criminal offence may result in imprisonment for up to 3 years (although under aggravating circumstances the period of imprisonment may amount to six or seven years). However, before the amendments of 08.03.2015 introduced to Art. 178 para. 1 of the Criminal Code of Russia, a repeated abuse of a dominant position in the form of an unjustified refusal or evasion to conclude a contract, as well as market foreclosure, leading to the exclusion, restriction or elimination of competition, were also considered as a criminal offence under the same circumstances and the same punishment was attached to them too.

Whilst implementing measures for the termination of violations of the anti-monopoly legislation, anti-monopoly bodies are entitled to impose on persons, who committed the violation, actions aimed at the restoration of the rights of other persons, which were infringed as a result of the violation.[575] However,

572 Art. 4 para. 10) defines monopolistic activity (*monopolisticheskaya deyatelnost*) as abuse of a dominant position by an undertaking or a group, agreements or concerted practices prohibited by the anti-monopoly legislation, as well as other actions (or omissions), declared as monopolistic activities by Federal Laws.

573 *Rokhlin/Nikitina*, in: Emch, inter alia, Competition Law in the BRICS Countries, p. 86.

574 Criminal Code of the RF [Ugolovniy Kodeks RF] N 63-FZ of 13.06.1996, published in SZ of 17.06.1996, N 25, p. 2954, last amended on 26.07.2017, effective from 06.08.2017.

575 See para. 14 of the Judgment on application of the anti-monopoly legislation.

anti-monopoly bodies are not entitled to make decisions on civil matters, including the issue of compensation for damages caused by the violation.[576] This can only be done by the courts. Art. 37 para. 3 of the Law on Competitions provides that persons whose rights and interests were infringed as a result of a violation of the anti-monopoly legislation, may refer to the courts to restore their violated rights, including lost profit and compensation for property damages. Even though the aforementioned provision on private enforcement is included in the Law on Competition, the Appellate Commercial Court in the case Real-Gaz vs. Gazprom[577], relied on the respective provisions of the Civil Code of Russia when imposing the recovery of damages in the form of lost profits on JSC Gazprom for infringing the rights of LLC Real-Gaz as a result of the violation of the anti-monopoly legislation[578].

3. Control mechanism for network connection charges

In Russia services of connection to networks are offered by undertakings providing gas transportation services as a complementary service to the gas transportation. Usually, a contract for the connection to the network between a supplier or customer and an undertaking providing gas transportation services is concluded separately from the contract for gas transportation. However, in some cases, especially for transportation through distribution networks, when the supplier and the GDU are both undertakings of the system of JSC Gazprom, a tripartite contract is concluded for gas supply and transportation with an end-customer.

As presented above, both Regulations on access to the to the GTS-UGSS as well as the Provisions on access to distribution networks prescribe that all expenses related to the connection of facilities of independent undertakings (suppliers and customers) to the existing networks have to be borne by the latter (chapter 4 pt. 16 and chapter 4 pt. 11 respectively). However, unlike the law of the EU and Germany the legislation of Russia does not prescribe the principles for defining charges for the connection services for gas suppliers and customers in order to avoid excessive prices.

576 See para. 5 of the Judgment on application of the anti-monopoly legislation.

577 Judgment of the ninth Commercial Appellate Court of N 09AP-29781/2014 of 15.08.2014 case N A40-45333/13 [Postanovleniye Devyatogo Arbitrazhnogo Apellyatsionnogo Suda].

578 See case Gazprom vs. FAS (Real-Gaz).

As described, according to chapter 4 pt. 11 of the Provisions on access to distribution networks, suppliers and customers of gas are entitled to the connection of leading pipelines and discharge pipes to local distribution networks in the case of the existence of spare capacities in its corresponding sites. Therefore, a contract for gas transportation through distribution networks may be considered to be a public contract under Art. 426 para. 1 sent. 1 of the Civil Code of Russia and the obliged person is not allowed to refuse to conclude a public contract, if there is a possibility of providing the consumer with the respective goods or services or performing the respective work for it, pursuant to Art. 426 para. 3 of the Civil Code of Russia. Accordingly, upon an unsubstantiated refusal from the side of the party obliged to conclude the contract, the other party is entitled to refer to the court with a claim for compelling the obliged party to conclude the contract under Art. 445 para. 4 of the Civil Code of Russia. Moreover, terms of the public contract, including the price of the commodities, works, and services, have to be equal for the consumers of the relevant category, pursuant to Art. 426 para. 2 of the Civil Code of Russia. According to Art. 446 of the Civil Code of Russia, in the case of a disagreement in relation to certain conditions of a public contract during its conclusion, the courts may define the contested terms by their decisions, however, this is only possible in relation to the terms that have been contested within 6 months of the emergence of the disagreement.

The case is different for the provision of connection services to the GTS-UGSS since the undertakings providing gas transportation services through the GTS-UGSS do not have an obligation to provide services of connection to networks too, i.e. the transaction does not have a public nature, hence, the reference to court under Art. 445 and 446 of the Civil Code of Russia is not possible for the parties that had been refused to be connected to the GTS-UGSS without justification, or excessive charges or other unfavourable conditions have been imposed on them in return for the provision of connection services.

Apart from the possibility of judicial review for the parties seeking connection to distribution networks, there is the option of lodging an application to antimonopoly bodies because of an abuse of a dominant position by undertakings who refuse to provide connection services or impose onerous terms to parties seeking connection to distribution networks as well as the ones wishing to connect to the GTS-UGSS. However, the undertakings constituting natural monopolies on the market of the provision of gas transportation services and thus deemed to be holding a dominant position by virtue of Art. 5 para. 5 of the Law on Competition will not be automatically considered to have such a position in the markets of connection services, since this type of activity is not listed under Art. 4 para. 1 of the Law on Natural Monopolies. Hence, the anti-monopoly bodies would have to establish the dominant positions under Art. 23 para. 1 pt. 10) of the Law on Competition.

According to chapter 3 of the administrative regulations of the FAS on the establishment of a dominant position,[579] the FAS ascertains the features of the existence of a dominant position based on the analysis of the state of competition, made in compliance with the Procedure for analysing the state of competition[580]. The analysis of the state of competition includes the identification of the economic entity, formulating a definition of the time period of market analysis, formulating a preliminary definition of product and geographic markets, and an assessment of the position of the economic entity in the market. For the purpose of analysing the state of competition in the market, the FAS is entitled to request information from natural or legal persons, individual entrepreneurs, government agencies and local authorities in compliance with the legislation of Russia as per Art. 25 of the Law on Competition.

In the course of the establishment of a dominant position, the anti-monopoly bodies have to consider the rules prescribed in Art. 5 of the Law on Competition. According to para. 1 of the aforementioned provision, a dominant position is a position whereby an economic entity, a group, or groups of persons in the market of certain commodity have a decisive impact on the general conditions of commodity circulation in the relevant goods market and/or to remove other economic entities from this goods market and/or to impede access to this goods market for the other economic entities. The provision further lists the instances where the market position of an economic entity (except for financial organisations) is recognised as dominant. These instances are: 1) where the

579 Order of the FAS N 345 of 25.05.2012 on the approval of administrative regulations of the FAS on the implementation of state function regarding establishment of a dominant position of economic entities during examination of applications, materials and cases on violations of the anti-monopoly legislation and during implementing state control of economic concentrations [Prikaz FAS Rossii Ob utverzhdenii administrativnogo reglamenta FAS po ispolneniyu gosudarstvennoy funktsii po ustanovleniyu dominiruyushchego polozheniya khozyaystvuyushchego subyekta pri rassmotrenii zayavleniy, materialov, del o narushenii antimonopolnogo zakonodatelstva i pri osushchestvlenii gosudarstvennogo kontrolya za ekonomicheskoy kontsentratsiyey], published in BNA of 25.02.2013, N 8, last amended on 24.12.2015.

580 See Order of the FAS N 220 of 28.04.2010 on the approval of procedure for analyzing state of competition on the goods market [Prikaz FAS Rossii Ob utverzhdenii poryadka provedeniya analiza sostoyaniya konkurentsii na tovarnom rinke], published in BNA of 23.08.2010, N 34, last amended on 23.11.2015.

share in the certain goods market exceeds 50%, unless it is established by an anti-monopoly body that despite the excess of the aforementioned threshold the position in the market is not dominant; 2) where the share in the certain goods market is less than 50%, but an anti-monopoly body can establish the dominance of this economic entity based on the fact that the share of the entity is stable or subject to insignificant changes in the market as compared to the shares of its competitors in this market, as well as considering opportunities for access to this market for new entrants, and other criteria characterising this market. An economic entity not holding a share in the relevant market exceeding 35% may not be considered to be dominant, unless the conditions of Art. 5 para. 3 and 6 of the Law on Competition apply. The first provision refers to the collective dominance whereas the second provision recognises a position of an economic entity as dominant under Federal Law.

As a result of the analysis of the state of competition in the market, the FAS draws up an analytical report containing the conclusion on the existence of features of a dominant position. In the event of a lack of evidence for the establishment of a dominant position, the FAS may extend the deadline of the respective stage, subject the general deadlines. Only after establishing a dominant position may the anti-monopoly bodies examine whether the conduct of undertakings providing connection services constitutes an abuse of a dominant position and impose relevant remedies as described above.[581] This makes it more difficult to compel the monopolist to impose fair charges for the connection services.[582]

4. Summary

To summarise, both options of enforcing the TPA right in Russia are characterised by considerable shortcomings.

The main barrier of effective judicial review of the infringements of TPA rules is insufficiently consistent court practice with regard to qualification of contracts for gas transportation which leads to legal uncertainty in the field. In this case the Plenum of the Supreme Commercial Court of the RF may issue a judgment under Art. 13 of the Federal Law on Commercial Courts of Russia, like it had done so with regard to the anti-monopoly legislation[583], explaining the

581 See above part B.III.2.d).

582 See also *Varlamova*, Competition Law of Russia, p. 438.

583 Judgment on application of the anti-monopoly legislation.

problematic issue and introducing an approach to be adopted by the commercial courts, hence contributing to increased consistency in the area.

In relation to the administrative control of the compliance with the rules on TPA rights to gas networks in Russia, several issues need to be pointed out.

First of all, the effectiveness of the shift of competences regarding the regulation of gas networks from a specialised state body to the competition authority is questionable. Prior to the reform of 2015 abolishing the FTS, the OECD pointed out in its review of the regulatory reform of Russia[584] that the duty in relation to handling disputes between regulated monopolies and individual customers over service obligations, tariffs or contract terms unreasonably burdens the competition authority. The OECD found the remedies of the authority in such cases inefficient due to the fact that they only apply to the cases in hand. Moreover, the outcomes of the appeals are also inconsistent. The OECD suggested resolving these problems by way of a detailed and comprehensive before-the-fact definition of permissible contract terms and service obligations. In addition, independent sectoral regulators should be responsible for resolving complaints and disputes in this area. However, the FAS should continue to serve in a supervisory role by adjusting any undue restriction on competition imposed by the regulator.

Apart from the fundamental irregularities of the system of administrative control over the enforcement of the TPA right to gas networks in Russia, there are a number of more precise shortcomings of the legislation.

Firstly, according to the literal interpretation of the Law on Competition, a legitimate ground for the refusal or evasion to deal has to be either economically or technologically justifiable, or has to be provided for in legal or judicial acts. However, in practice, if the ground in question is not contained in the sector-specific legislation, the examination of the economic or technological justifiability of this ground does not take place anymore. It is more probable that the purpose of the legislator regarding this provision coincides with its interpretation by the courts and the FAS; however, it is recommendable to adapt the wording of the provision to its purpose in order to exclude its different application.

Secondly, since the legislator of Russia connected the status of a natural monopoly and the presumption of its dominant position therewith, with its inclusion in the register, this act gains an important meaning as to the legal protection of the holders of the TPA rights. Therefore, even though the introduction of the regulation in natural monopolies is followed by their registration,

584 OECD Review of Regulatory Reforms, Russia, p. 121.

the fact that neither natural monopolies nor the FAS have an explicit obligation to include these undertakings in the register constitutes a gap in the legislation and it is recommended to stipulate in the Law on Natural Monopolies that these undertakings are by the Law obliged to refer to the regulatory body for registration. Moreover, after the abolition of the act regulating the procedure of the management of the register of natural monopolies (Administrative Regulations of the FTS), no other regulation has been adopted by the FAS. In addition, due to the essential meaning of the inclusion of a natural monopoly in the register, the time period of 6 months, which was set by the Administrative Regulations of the FTS for making a decision on the inclusion, is unreasonably long since the only criterion for the inclusion of an undertaking in the register is the field of activity of the undertaking. Therefore, it is preferable to prescribe a much shorter period for handling the applications for inclusion in the register of natural monopolies by the FAS.

Thirdly, the legislation of Russia does not prescribe the principles for defining charges for the connection services for gas suppliers and customers in order to avoid excessive prices. Since the expenses of the connection are one of the most important points to be considered for gas suppliers and customers due to their high costs, leaving them out of the scope of regulation gives the transmission and distribution undertakings an opportunity to freely dictate their prices and thus impose unfavourable conditions on the other parties to the contract. The legislation of Russia is also deficient in respect of introducing an obligation to connect to the network. The undertakings providing gas transportation services through distribution networks are obliged to grant connection under certain circumstances whereas the ones providing such services through the GTS-UGSS are not, which leads to the problem that the seekers of a connection to the GTS-UGSS may not claim their rights in the courts. Another common issue in relation to both levels of networks is that the undertakings providing services of gas transportation and connecting customers and suppliers to their networks, are not considered to be inherently dominant in the relevant markets for the connection services, thereby leading to a slowdown in enforcement. For the acceleration of the procedures in the FAS and therewith achieving more effective protection of the rights of the customers of connection services, the activity of 'provision of connection services by undertakings providing gas transportation services' has to be added also to the list of natural monopolies under Art. 4 para. 1 of the Law on Natural Monopolies.

Lastly, the legislation of Russia does not provide for the definition of the term 'legislation on natural monopolies', but refers to it in many instances in the Provisions of the FAS as well as in the Provisions on territorial bodies of the FAS. Nonetheless, for the sake of legal accuracy, it is preferable to refer to 'legislation in the fields of activities of natural monopolies' as it is correctly stated in chapter 1 para. 1 of the Provisions of the FAS and chapter 1 para. 1 of the Provisions on territorial bodies of the FAS.

IV. Legal comparison

1. General comparability of regulations of access to gas networks of Russia and Germany

The general comparability of the regulation of access to gas networks in Germany and in Russia is an important precondition for the legal comparison of the individual issues since only comparable things may be reasonably compared with each other.[585] The purpose of the legal comparison is to examine the approaches to solving a problem, developed in different legal systems.[586] In order to be defined as parallel in the legal sense, the examined issues should to some extent have features in common.[587] It is important that the objects of the examination fulfil the same tasks in the respective legal systems, however, complete similarity is not required; comparability is present when an examination compares two functionally equivalent subject matters that solve the same legal problem.[588]

The preciseness of the object of the examination itself already militates in favour of the comparability of the regulation of access to gas networks in Germany and in Russia. Sets of rules in both jurisdictions regulate TPA to gas networks in the territories of the respective countries and are aimed at ensuring non-discrimination and more competition in the gas sector.

2. Comparative summary of the examined elements

Since the gas sectors of the two countries are very different due to geographical as well as historical reasons, among others, regulations of access to gas networks in Germany and in Russia have proven to be deviant in many aspects in the course of the examination. The principal differences and controversies of the legislation of Russia as compared to the legislation of Germany in relation to the material law of access to gas networks on the one hand, and regarding the enforcement of the TPA to gas networks on the other hand, is summarised below. Reference to

585 *Constantinesco*, Legal comparison, t. 2, p. 69. See also *Salaschek*, Antitrust sanctions systems, p. 269.

586 *Ebert*, Legal comparison, p. 28. See also *Salaschek*, Antitrust sanctions systems, p. 269.

587 See *Constantinesco*, Legal comparison, t. 2, p. 78. See also *Salaschek*, Antitrust sanctions systems, p. 269.

588 *Zweigert/Kötz*, Introduction to legal comparison, p. 33. See also *Salaschek*, Antitrust sanctions systems, p. 269 f.

EU law will be made where it is directly applicable or has been transposed into the energy law of Germany, to the extent that it is relevant for the comparison.

a) Comparative summary of the material law on access to gas networks

In general terms, it can be observed that the rules regulating access to distribution networks on the one hand, and the rules regulating access to the GTS-UGSS on the other hand, are not parallel whereas most of the fundamental provisions of the law of Germany as well as the EU rules regulating TPA rights to gas networks do not differentiate between distribution and transmission levels. Moreover, many provisions of the EnWG of Germany equally regulate access to gas and electricity networks, and the GasNZV prescribes uniform rules for all gas networks. According to *Larin*, comparative analysis of the Regulation on access to the GTS-UGSS and Provisions on access to distribution networks leads to the conclusion that they may well be combined into a single legal act.[589] However, the two acts differ from each other in relation to several crucial issues, without any comprehensible explanation, e.g. a different order of priority access right holders to distribution networks and to the GTS-UGSS.

Further, if in the energy law of the EU and Germany entitlement to the connection as well as charges for connection services are considered to be one of the essential ways of making non-discriminatory access technically enforceable, the legislator of Russia has an ambiguous approach to this issue. The energy law of Russia only entitles the gas customers and suppliers seeking connection to distribution networks to such rights and does not prescribe any other rules for the regulation of the matter. Moreover, there are neither grounds for refusal to connect nor the conditions for providing connection services foreseen by the legislation. This gap leads to the problem that even if access to the network is legally possible, its practical implementation remains uncertain, giving the monopolist a ground for evading the obligation of granting access through a legitimate means due to the non-existence of the relevant legal base.

The fundamental difference between the two jurisdictions is the fact that TPA to the existing transmission networks in the legislation of Russia refers to the right of access of the independent undertakings to the gas transmission networks owned by JSC Gazprom, whereas the relationships between JSC Gazprom and its subsidiaries or otherwise associated undertakings concerning the access to the GTS-UGSS are not regulated. This leads to the paradox that only the tariffs for

589 See *Larin*, Pipeline transport is in need of regulation.

independent undertakings are subject to state regulation and the undertakings of the group of JSC Gazprom may pay any price negotiated with JSC Gazprom for gas transportation services, automatically placing the independent gas suppliers at a competitively unprofitable position. Hence, the notion of non-discriminatory access means only horizontal equal treatment, and not vertical equality,[590] thereby placing independent undertakings at a competitive disadvantage in comparison to the undertakings of JSC Gazprom in the upstream and downstream markets.

The legislator of Russia, for the purposes of regulation, opted for the division of gas pipelines not according to pressure levels, like the cases in the EU and in Germany, but based on the identity of the owner of the pipelines, which has led to the gap in the regulation of access to gas networks. Most noticeably, the high pressure pipelines that do not belong to the GTS-UGSS are not subject of regulation, and the distribution pipelines that are not part of the gas distribution systems do not fall under the provisions regulating access to local distribution networks. In addition, there is a provision introducing regulation of tariffs for access to the high pressure pipelines owned by independent undertakings, however, there is no such provision regulating the access to the high pressure pipelines owned by independent undertakings.

There is no network access model as such in force which would make the arrangement of gas network access speedier for independent gas customers and suppliers, and thus contribute to the enhancement of competition, as is the case in Germany. In Russia gas suppliers have to conclude, and thus negotiate beforehand, a number of contracts for gas transportation with each operator of each part of the network through which they aim to transport gas, in order to deliver gas to their customers and thus fulfil the gas supply contracts. Moreover, the operators of gas networks do not have any obligation to cooperate with each other at any level of the supply chain in order to facilitate the arrangement of network access for the gas customers and suppliers wishing to transport gas through their networks.

Another major deviation from the EnWG of Germany are the possible grounds for refusal to grant network access are not prescribed by the legislation of Russia, neither in relation to the transmission infrastructure, nor for local distribution networks. The legal acts regulating access to the pipelines also do not define the criteria according to which a contested refusal should be measured. Even though the courts and the FAS often assume that a legitimate refusal

590 See above part A.II.2.c)aa).

ground has to be contained in the respective legal act regulating access to the network (the Regulation on access to the GTS-UGSS and the Provisions on access to distribution networks), such a provision is not included in any of these legal acts and therefore creates room for different interpretations.

The legislation of Russia concerning access to networks does not cover access issues to 'non-transportation' infrastructure, including access to LNG and storage facilities. Since LNG does not play a significant role on the supply to the domestic market,[591] leaving access to the LNG-pipelines without regulation may be acceptable transitionally. However, this cannot be the case for access to storage facilities. Currently, all underground storage facilities in Russia are owned and operated by JSC Gazprom's subsidiary, JSC Gazprom UGS.[592] Moreover, only JSC Gazprom has the right to build and operate such storages as it is the only owner and the operator of the UGSS, the division of which is forbidden by law. However, neither access nor tariffs for using storage facilities are regulated, nor does gas storage constitute a natural monopoly under the legislation of Russia.[593]

In contrast to the legislation of the EU and Germany, the regulations relating to access to gas networks in Russia do not include any mechanism for the promotion of construction of new infrastructure. On the contrary, the building of new infrastructure (e.g. underground storage facilities) is discouraged as only JSC Gazprom is entitled to construct such infrastructure. The major legislative initiative concerning the rules for creation of new and expanding the existing GTS-UGSS was a draft Federal Law on Trunk Pipeline Transport[594], presented to the State Duma back in 1999, which is still not adopted.[595] Among the basic questions connected with this topic concern financial as well as ownership issues of the new and expanded systems.[596]

591 See *Gudkov*, Gas transportation in Russia, NiG, 3/2009, p. 35.

592 UGS stands for Underground Gas Storage. See company information of JSC Gazprom UGS, available at: http://www.gazprom.com/about/subsidiaries/list-items/gazprom-ugs, last accessed on 16.11.2017.

593 See *Gudkov*, Gas transportation in Russia, NiG, 3/2009, p. 37. See also FAS, The FAS offers to deprive Gazprom of the monopoly right on gas storage, stating, inter alia, that the prices charged by JSC Gazprom UGS for gas storage to its subsidiaries are 30–35% lower than the ones applied to independent undertakings.

594 The current text of the draft Federal Law is available at: http://base.consultant.ru/cons/cgi/online.cgi?req=doc;base=PRJ;n=953, last accessed on 16.11.2017.

595 *Seliverstov/Gudkov*, in: Roggenkamp/Barrera-Hernandez/Zillman/Del Guayo, Energy networks and the law, p. 402.

596 Ibid.

Unlike the energy law of the EU and Germany, where secondary trading with capacity rights is facilitated, this does not seem to be a priority for the legislator of Russia. Even though Art. 388 to 390 of the Civil Code of Russia prescribe the conditions for and process of the cession of a claim, it is not possible to cede the claim for gas transportation towards the undertaking providing gas transportation services by the counterparties of the contract for gas transportation. Firstly, these contracts constitute public contracts, for which special rules of conclusion and implementation may be adopted by the Government of Russia pursuant to Art. 426 para. 4 of the Civil Code of Russia. Secondly, the acts regulating access to the GTS-UGSS as well as to distribution networks do not foresee a possibility of a cession of a claim. Moreover, since the process regarding an application for access is prescribed in detail and the parties seeking access to the networks have to fulfil special conditions, it can be concluded that a cession of the claims gained as a result of concluding a contract under strictly regulated procedure has to be deemed as prohibited, unless it is explicitly allowed by the legislation.

Another principle difference between the energy law of the EU and Germany on the one hand, and the legislation of Russia on access to networks on the other hand, is the lack of legal instruments in the acts of Russia that would make the declared aim of granting non-discriminatory access practically workable. The legislation of Russia is not equipped with sufficient mechanisms for guaranteeing the provision of non-discriminatory access services by gas transmission undertakings of JSC Gazprom as well as GDUs. Undertakings providing gas transportation services do have an obligation of granting non-discriminatory access to the GTS-UGSS, as also stipulated in Art. 27 of the Law on Gas Supply as well as chapter 3 pt. 4 of the Regulation on access to the GTS-UGSS and chapter 1 pt. 1 of the Provisions on access to distribution networks, considering prior access rights of certain applicants. However, there is no provision obliging the transmission and distribution undertakings to provide the access services, i.e. the transportation services, under equivalent contract terms and conditions, either using harmonised contracts or any other mechanism for guaranteeing non-discriminatory conditions for all network users; unlike the case in Germany, where, among other guarantees, each network operator has to publish model contracts and all network operators are obliged to develop common standards of contracts. Thus, the principle of non-discrimination in Russia applies to access issues one-sidedly and concerns only granting access to networks as such, but does not extend to cover the immediate provision and contractual construction of the access services.

Even though the legislation of Russia provides for the basic requirements for transparency of information in relation to regulated activities of undertakings providing gas transportation services, taking account of all standards adopted in the law of Germany as well, the impossibility of the verification of the information provided by these undertakings renders the obligations aimed at increased transparency ineffective. The legislation of Russia does not provide for any mechanism for independent verification of the information concerning the existence of spare capacities in the pipelines. Therefore, suppliers and customers, as well as authorities, have to rely on the information provided by the dispatching departments of the respective undertakings providing gas transportation services (CODD for JSC Gazprom). Moreover, the credibility of such information is weakened by the fact that no legal or further unbundling has been implemented throughout the gas industry of Russia; unlike in Germany, where stringent unbundling rules have been applied throughout the sector. In the case law too, while assessing the issue of technical possibility of gas transportation, the FAS as well as the commercial courts rely on the information derived from existing contracts for gas transportation as well as acts of gas delivery since they do not have any credible source for the verification of such information.

Moreover, the transparency requirements in the legislation of Russia are also one-sided. Since only the access of independent undertakings to the GTS-UGSS is regulated, the charges paid by other undertakings of the system of JSC Gazprom for transportation services of the transmission undertakings of the system of JSC Gazprom as well as other conditions applied to them are not covered by the transparency requirements.

b) Comparative summary of the enforcement of the right of access to gas networks

In comparison to the energy law of Germany, the enforcement possibilities of the TPA right to gas networks in Russia is deficient in many aspects.

Regarding the option of judicial review of the infringements of TPA rules, the main problem here is inconsistent court practice in relation to the qualification of contracts for gas transportation as public contracts, thereby resulting in legal uncertainty in the field. In Germany this problem does not exist partially due to the fact that the right of access to gas networks constitutes a statutory right and is not considered as an obligation to conclude a contract. Furthermore, even if TPA was considered to be a type of obligation to contract in Germany, it is still not characteristic for certain types of contracts only (i.e. public contracts in this case) and rather results from the existence of other, objective criteria (e.g. the essential facilities doctrine).

In relation to the administrative control of the compliance with the rules on TPA rights to gas networks in Russia, firstly, the approaches as to the division of the competences between anti-monopoly bodies and regulatory authorities as well as the course of the reforms adopted in Russia on the one hand, and in the EU and Germany on the other hand, are entirely contrary to each other. Under the law of the EU and Germany, national regulatory authorities are legally distinct and functionally independent from any other public or private entity, whereas in Russia anti-monopoly bodies undertake the tasks of regulatory authorities too. Moreover, in Germany the development of the division of the competences between the competition authority and sector-specific energy regulation has gradually shifted towards the regulatory bodies, in an attempt to relieve the workload of the competition authority, whereas in Russia the national regulatory body, FTS, was recently abolished at the cost of the anti-monopoly organs, who assumed all the responsibilities of the FTS. Overcharging the anti-monopoly bodies with the ex post functions of sector-specific regulation is not compatible with the competition-aimed concept of regulation due to undermining the actual tasks of the competition authorities on the one hand, and decreasing the level of independence of the body fulfilling regulatory functions on the other hand.

Lastly, unlike the law of the EU and Germany, the legislation of Russia does not prescribe the principles for defining charges for the connection services for gas suppliers and customers in order to avoid excessive prices. Since the expenses of the connection are one of the most important points to be considered for gas suppliers and customers due to their high costs, leaving them out of the scope of regulation gives the transmission and distribution undertakings an opportunity to freely dictate their prices and thus impose unfavourable conditions on the other parties to the contract. The legislation of Russia is also deficient in respect of introducing an obligation to connect to the network. The undertakings providing gas transportation services through distribution networks are obliged to grant connection under certain circumstances whereas the undertakings providing such services through the GTS-UGSS are not, which leads to the problem that the seekers of a connection to the GTS-UGSS may not claim their rights in the courts.

Conclusion

The following substantial results can be derived from the examination:

I. The regulation of access to gas networks in Russia differs from the legislation of Germany and the EU in this area in several decisive aspects.

II. The fundamental difference between the jurisdictions is the fact that the legislation of Russia regulates access to the Gas Transmission System of the Unified Gas Supply System (hereinafter GTS-UGSS) only for the undertakings which are independent from JSC Gazprom. The GTS-UGSS is the largest gas transmission network of the country, covering almost all high pressure gas pipelines of Russia. It is owned by JSC Gazprom. On the contrary, access to the GTS-UGSS is not regulated for the subsidiaries of JSC Gazprom, operating on all levels of the value chain. Moreover, in Russia, unlike the EU and Germany, vertically integrated undertakings are not even subject to the legal unbundling. Under these circumstances, the fulfilment of the ultimate purpose of the state regulation of access to gas networks, i.e. the introduction of competition in the gas sector, seems questionable. Not only can the gas transmission operator use the provisions of access to the main gas transmission network of the country to the disadvantage of third persons, but the provisions are in themselves discriminatory towards the gas suppliers that have no connection with JSC Gazprom. Non-discriminatory access to the GTS-UGSS has an exclusively horizontal meaning for the legislator of Russia, i.e. the prohibition of discrimination implies equal treatment of only external applicants. This hinders the introduction of competition between JSC Gazprom and independent undertakings in the upstream and downstream markets.

III. For the purposes of regulation, the legislator of Russia opted for the classification of gas pipelines not according to pressure levels, like in cases in the EU and Germany, but based on the identity of the owner of the pipelines. This has led to a gap in the regulation of access to gas networks. Most noticeably, the high pressure gas pipelines that do not belong to the GTS-UGSS are not subject of regulation, and the distribution pipelines that are not part of the gas distribution systems do not fall under the provisions regulating access to local distribution networks.

IV. In Germany, a so-called entry-exit model of gas network access is applicable at the moment. This model of network access grants gas suppliers the possibility to arrange network access based on only two contracts, entry and exit contracts, irrespective of the quantity of networks concerned by the transport. On the contrary, there is no concept of network access model as such in force which would make the arrangement of gas network access faster for gas customers and independent gas suppliers, and thus contribute to the enhancement of competition. In order to be able to deliver gas to their customers and therewith fulfil gas supply contracts, Russian gas suppliers have to negotiate and conclude contracts for gas transportation with each operator of each part of the network through which they intend to transport their gas. Moreover, the operators of gas networks do not have any obligation to cooperate with each other at any level of the supply chain in order to facilitate the arrangement of network access for the gas customers and suppliers wishing to transport gas through their networks.

V. Even though contractual congestion is generally the main problem for competition-aimed regulation of gas network access, the legislation of Russia does not provide for any rules in relation to congestion management and does not prescribe the procedures for enhancing the usage of gas networks. Moreover, the capacity rights may not be traded on a secondary market in Russia. On the contrary, in Germany and in the EU this option is considered to be means of contributing to the better exhaustion of physical network capacities and thus increased competition.

VI. The legislation of Russia does not prescribe any potential grounds for refusal of network access, neither in relation to the transmission infrastructure, nor for local distribution networks. This constitutes another principal difference from the energy law of Germany. Moreover, the legal acts regulating the access to the pipelines do not define the criteria according to which a contested refusal should be measured. Even though the courts and the Federal Anti-monopoly Service often assume that a legitimate refusal ground has to be contained in the respective legal act regulating access to the network (the Regulation on access to the GTS-UGSS and the Provisions on access to distribution networks), such a provision is not included in any of these legal acts and therefore creates room for different interpretations.

VII. Further, in the energy law of the EU and Germany the entitlement to the network connection, as well as charges for connection services are considered to be one of the essential ways of making non-discriminatory access technically enforceable. On the contrary, the approach followed by the legislator of Russia leads to an ambiguous picture. It only entitles the gas customers and suppliers seeking connection to distribution networks to such connection but does not prescribe any other rules for the regulation of the procedure. Moreover, neither grounds for refusal to connect nor conditions for providing connection services are foreseen by the legislation. This gap leads to the problem that even if access to the network is rendered legally possible, its practical implementation remains questionable, giving the monopolist a ground for evading the obligation of granting access through a legitimate way due to the non-existence of the relevant legal base.

VIII. The legislation of Russia concerning access to networks covers exclusively access issues that concern the gas transportation infrastructure. The issues in relation to the 'non-transportation' infrastructure, e.g. access to liquefied natural gas (LNG) and storage facilities, are not regulated. Since LNG does not play a significant role in supplying the domestic market, leaving access to the LNG-pipelines without regulation may be acceptable transitionally. However, this cannot be the case for access to storage facilities. Currently, all underground storage facilities in Russia are owned and operated by JSC Gazprom's subsidiary, JSC Gazprom UGS. All existing gas storage facilities are parts of the United Gas Supply System, which is owned and operated only by JSC Gazprom. Moreover, the fact that the United Gas Supply System is indivisible by virtue of law, leads to the situation where JSC Gazprom has the exclusive right to build and operate such storages. However, neither access nor tariffs for using storage facilities are regulated.

IX. In contrast to the legislation of the EU and Germany, the rules of access to gas networks in Russia do not include any mechanism for the promotion of the construction of new infrastructure. On the contrary, the building of new infrastructure (e.g. underground storage facilities) is discouraged since only JSC Gazprom is entitled to construct such new infrastructure. The major legislative initiative concerning the rules for creating new and expanding the existing GTS-UGSS was a draft Federal Law on Trunk Pipeline Transport presented to the State Duma back in 1999 which has still not been adopted.

X. Even though the legislation of Russia provides for the basic requirements for the transparency of information in relation to the regulated activities of undertakings providing gas transportation services, they appear to be ineffective, as there is no means of verifying the information provided by these undertakings. The legislation of Russia does not provide for any mechanism for an independent verification of the information concerning the existence of spare capacities in gas pipelines. Therefore, suppliers and customers, as well as authorities have to rely on the information provided by the dispatching departments of the respective undertakings providing gas transportation services (Central Operations and Dispatch Department for JSC Gazprom).

XI. Moreover, the existing transparency requirements in the legislation of Russia are one-sided. Since only the access of independent undertakings to the GTS-UGSS is regulated, the charges to be paid by the undertakings of the system of JSC Gazprom for transportation services of the transmission undertakings of the system of JSC Gazprom, as well as other conditions applied to them, are not concerned by the transparency requirements.

XII. A weakness of the judicial review of the infringements of third party access (TPA) rules is the non-consistency of the court practice in relation to the qualification of contracts for gas transportation. The case law in Russia is equivocal whether contracts for gas transportation constitute the so-called public contracts or not, thereby resulting in legal uncertainty in the field. Since the obligation to contract specifies only public contracts according to the legislation of Russia, the qualification is decisive for ascertaining the obligation to contract of gas transmission and distribution undertakings. This problem does not exist in Germany partially due to the fact that the right of access to gas networks constitutes a statutory right and is not considered to be an obligation to conclude a contract. Furthermore, even if TPA was considered to be a type of obligation to contract in Germany, it is still not characteristic of certain types of contracts only (i.e. public contracts in this case) and rather results from the existence of other, objective criteria (e.g. the essential facilities doctrine).

Lastly, under the law of the EU and Germany, national regulatory authorities are legally distinct and functionally independent from any other public or private entity. In Russia on the contrary, the anti-monopoly bodies undertake the tasks of regulatory authorities too. Moreover, in Germany the tendency of the division of the competences between the competition authority and sector-specific energy regulation gradually shifted towards the regulatory bodies. This development has contributed to relieving the workload of the competition authority. In Russia on the contrary, the national regulatory body, the Federal Tariff Service, was recently abolished at the cost of the anti-monopoly organs, which assumed the responsibilities of the Federal Tariff Service. The resulted overload of the anti-monopoly bodies with the ex post functions of sector-specific regulation is not compatible with the competition-aimed regulation as it undermines the actual tasks of the competition authorities on the one hand, and decreases the level of independence of the body fulfilling regulatory functions on the other hand.

Zusammenfassung

Aus der Untersuchung lassen sich im Wesentlichen folgende Ergebnisse ableiten:

I. Die Regulierung des Zugangs zu Erdgasnetzen in Russland unterscheidet sich von den Vorschriften in Deutschland und denen der EU in entscheidenden Punkten.

II. Ein wesentlicher Unterschied zwischen den Jurisdiktionen besteht darin, dass durch die russischen Vorschriften der Zugang zum Gastransportsystem des einheitlichen Gasversorgungssystems (nachfolgend GTS-UGSS) allein für solche Unternehmen reguliert wird, die von der Gazprom AG unabhängig sind. Beim GTS-UGSS handelt es sich um das größte Gasfernleitungsnetz des Landes, das fast alle Hochdruckgasleitungen Russlands abdeckt. Es steht im Eigentum der Gazprom AG. Für Tochterunternehmen der Gazprom AG, die auf allen Stufen der Wertschöpfungskette tätig sind, wird der Zugang hingegen nicht reguliert. In Anbetracht der Tatsache, dass es sich bei der Gazprom AG um ein vertikal integriertes Unternehmen handelt und in Russland, anders als in der EU und in Deutschland, keine rechtliche oder anderweitige Entflechtung durchgeführt worden ist, erscheint es fragwürdig, ob das grundsätzlich höchste Ziel der staatlichen Zugangsregulierung von Gasnetzen – die Schaffung von Wettbewerb – erreicht wird. Nicht nur kann der Gasfernleitungsbetreiber die russischen Vorschriften über den Zugang zum Hauptgasfernleitungsnetz des Landes zum Nachteil Dritter anwenden, sondern die Vorschriften wirken schon selbst diskriminierend gegenüber solchen Gasversorgern, die in keiner Verbindung zur Gazprom AG stehen. Ein diskriminierungsfreier Zugang zum GTS-UGSS hat für den russischen Gesetzgeber ausschließlich horizontale Bedeutung, d.h. das Diskriminierungsverbot hat nur die Gleichbehandlung von externen Antragstellern zur Folge. Dadurch wird die Entstehung von Wettbewerb zwischen der Gazprom AG und den von ihr unabhängigen Unternehmen auf den vor- und nachgelagerten Märkten gehemmt.

III. Im Gegensatz zu den Vorschriften in der EU und in Deutschland hat sich der russische Gesetzgeber zum Zweck der Regulierung dafür entschieden, die Eingruppierung der Gasleitungen nicht anhand des Druckniveaus, sondern in Abhängigkeit des Eigentümers der Leitungen zu unterscheiden. Dies hat zu einer Lücke bei der Zugangsregulierung der Gasnetze geführt. So unterfallen die Hochdruckgasleitungen, die nicht Teil des GTS-UGSS sind, nicht der Regulierung. Auch unterfallen solche Verteilleitungen, die nicht Teil des Gasverteilungsnetzes sind, nicht den gesetzlichen Zugangsbestimmungen zu lokalen Verteilernetzen.

IV. In Deutschland gilt zurzeit das sogenannte Entry-Exit-Modell des Gasnetzzugangs, das Gasanbietern/Versorgern die Möglichkeit gewährt, das Gasnetz zu nutzen, indem sie nur zwei Verträge abschließen (unabhängig von der Zahl der für den Transport tatsächlich benötigten Netze). Im Gegensatz dazu gibt es in Russland kein Zugangskonzept als solches, das die Gestaltung des Gasnetzzugangs für unabhängige Gasabnehmer und Versorger beschleunigen und so zur Stärkung des Wettbewerbes beitragen würde. Um ihre Kunden beliefern und damit ihre Verträge erfüllen zu können, müssen Gasversorger in Russland Gastransportverträge mit jedem einzelnen Netzbetreiber, durch dessen Leitungen sie Gas transportieren wollen, aushandeln und abschließen. Für die einzelnen Netzbetreiber besteht in diesem Zusammenhang keinerlei Verpflichtung zur gegenseitigen Kooperation innerhalb der Lieferkette, um dadurch den Zugang für Gasabnehmer und Versorger, die Gas durch ihre Leitungen transportieren wollen, zu erleichtern.

V. Obwohl vertraglich bedingte Engpässe das größte Problem für die auf Wettbewerb abzielende Zugangsregulierung der Gasnetze sind, hält die russische Gesetzgebung keinerlei Regelungen bezüglich eines Engpassmanagements bereit und scheibt auch keine Maßnahmen zur Verbesserung einer verstärkten Nutzung der Gasnetze vor. Darüber hinaus dürfen die Kapazitätsrechte in Russland nicht auf einem Sekundärmarkt gehandelt werden. In Deutschland und der EU wird diese Option hingegen gezielt als Mittel zur besseren Ausschöpfung der physischen Netzwerkkapazitäten angesehen, das einen gesteigerten Wettbewerb zur Folge hat.

VI. Die russische Gesetzgebung schreibt keine potentiellen Verweigerungsgründe für den Zugang zum Fernleitungsnetz und zu den lokalen Verteilernetzen vor. Auch dies ist ein wesentlicher Unterschied zum deutschen Energierecht. Zudem werden die Kriterien an denen eine beanstandete Verweigerung gemessen werden soll, in den Rechtsakten zur Regulierung des Zugangs zu den Gasleitungen nicht näher definiert. Obwohl die Gerichte sowie die staatliche Antimonopolbehörde davon ausgehen, dass ein rechtmäßiger Verweigerungsgrund in dem jeweiligen Rechtsakt zur Zugangsregulierung (Verordnung über den Zugang zum GTS-UGSS sowie die Bestimmungen über den Zugang zu Verteilernetzen) enthalten sein muss, sieht keiner der russischen Rechtsakte eine derartige Regelung vor, sodass an dieser Stelle Raum für unterschiedliche Auslegungen besteht.

VII. Darüber hinaus werden im deutschen und europäischen Energierecht ein Anspruch auf den Netzanschluss sowie Gebühren für die Anschlussdienste als unerlässlich erachtet, um einen diskriminierungsfreien Netzanschluss technisch umsetzbar zu machen. Der vom russischen Gesetzgeber verfolgte Ansatz führt an dieser Stelle hingegen zu einem unklaren Bild. Dieser räumt nur den Verteilernetzzugang begehrenden Gasabnehmern und Versorgern ein solches Recht ein, schreibt darüber hinaus jedoch keine weiteren Regelungen zum Ablauf des Prozesses vor. Zudem sind weder Anschlussverweigerungsgründe noch die Bedingungen für eine Anschlussgewährung vom Gesetzgeber vorgesehen. Dies führt dazu, dass selbst dann, wenn die Netzanbindung rechtlich möglich ist, die tatsächliche Gewährung des Netzzugangs fraglich bleibt, da für den Monopolisten die Möglichkeit besteht, sich seiner Pflicht zur Netzanbindung auf rechtmäßige Art und Weise zu entziehen, ohne dass es eine rechtliche Handhabe gäbe, mithilfe derer man sich gegen eine Verweigerung wehren könnte.

VIII. Die russische Gesetzgebung bezüglich des Gasnetzzugangs umfasst ausschließlich die Zugangsfragen, die die Gastransportinfrastruktur betreffen. Keine Regelungen bestehen z.B. in Bezug auf den Zugang zu LNG- und Speicheranlagen. Da LNG im Rahmen der Versorgung des inländischen Marktes keine bedeutende Rolle zukommt, scheint eine nicht regulierte Zugangsgewährung zu LNG-Leitungen zumindest vorübergehend hinnehmbar. In Bezug auf den Zugang zu Speicheranlagen kann dies jedoch nicht gelten. Denn in Russland gehören derzeit sämtliche unterirdische Speicheranlagen der Gazprom-Tochtergesellschaft Gazprom UGS, die diese Anlagen zugleich auch betreibt. Alle derzeit existierenden Gasspeicheranlagen Russlands sind Bestandteile des einheitlichen Gasversorgungssystems, das im alleinigen Eigentum der Gazprom AG steht und auch von ihr betrieben wird. Überdies führt die Tatsache, dass das einheitliche Gasversorgungssystem gesetzlich unteilbar ist, dazu, dass ausschließlich die Gazprom AG zum Bau und zum Betrieb derartiger Speicheranlagen berechtigt ist. Dennoch sind weder der Zugang noch die Gebühren für deren Nutzung reguliert.

IX. Im Unterschied zur Gesetzgebung in der EU und in Deutschland sehen die russischen Vorschriften über den Zugang zum Gasnetz keinen Mechanismus zur Förderung des Baus neuer Transportinfrastruktur vor. Vielmehr hält die Tatsache, dass einzig die Gazprom AG dazu berechtigt ist, beispielsweise vom Bau neuer unterirdischer Speicheranlagen ab. Die bedeutendste Gesetzgebungsinitiative im Hinblick auf Regelungen zur Schaffung eines neuen bzw. des Ausbaus des bereits bestehenden GTS-UGSS war der Entwurf eines Föderalgesetzes für einen Fernleitungstransport, der der russischen Staatsduma im Jahr 1999 unterbreitet, aber bis heute nicht verabschiedet wurde.

X. Obwohl die russische Gesetzgebung Grundregelungen für die Transparenz von Informationen bezüglich regulierter Tätigkeiten von Unternehmen vorsieht, die Gastransportdienstleistungen erbringen, gehen die Regelungen fehl; denn es besteht keine Möglichkeit, die bereitgestellten Informationen zu überprüfen. Die Vorschriften in Russland sehen keine unabhängige Überprüfung von Information bezüglich vorhandener Kapazitätsreserven in den Gasleitungen vor. Aus diesem Grund müssen Versorger, Gasabnehmer sowie Behörden auf die Informationen vertrauen, die ihnen von den zentralen Dispatchingabteilungen der jeweiligen Trans portdienstleistungsunternehmen zur Verfügung gestellt werden (Zentrale Betriebs- und Dispatching Abteilung für Gazprom AG).

XI. Darüber hinaus sind die Transparenzregelungen der russischen Gesetzgebung einseitig. Da nur der Zugang unabhängiger Unternehmen zu dem GTS-UGSS reguliert wird, sind die von anderen Unternehmen des Systems der Gazprom AG zu zahlenden Gebühren für Transportdienstleistungen von Fernleitungsunternehmen des Systems der Gazprom AG sowie andere auf sie angewandte Bedingungen von den Transparenzregelungen nicht erfasst.

XII. Eine Schwachstelle der gerichtlichen Überprüfung von Verstößen gegen die Vorschriften für den Zugang Dritter ist die Uneinheitlichkeit der Rechtsprechung hinsichtlich der Qualifizierung von Verträgen über den Gastransport. Die russische Fallpraxis hat noch nicht eindeutig festgestellt, dass Gastransportverträge als sogenannte öffentliche Verträge zu qualifizieren sind, was zur Entstehung von Rechtsunsicherheit führt. Diese Feststellung soll im russischen Recht für den Kontrahierungszwang von Bedeutung sein. In Deutschland besteht dieses Problem hingegen nicht, zum Teil aus dem Grund, dass das Recht auf Zugang zum Gasnetz gesetzlich verankert ist und nicht als Kontrahierungszwang ausgestaltet ist. Darüber hinaus, auch wenn das Gasnetzzugangsrecht als eine Art Kontrahierungszwang angesehen sein dürfte, kennzeichnet er trotzdem nicht nur die eine Sorte von Verträgen (d.h. die sogenannten öffentlichen Verträgen in diesem Falle) und wird eher durch andere, objective Kriterien begründet (z.B. das Essential Facilities-Konzept).

Zuletzt sind nationale Regulierungsbehörden nach deutschem und europäischem Recht rechtlich getrennt und funktional unabhängig von anderen öffentlichen und privaten Einrichtungen. In Russland hingegen werden die Aufgaben der Regulierungsbehörden von den Antimonopolbehörden wahrgenommen. Darüber hinaus hat die Entwicklung der Kompetenzverteilung in Deutschland zwischen der Wettbewerbsbehörde einerseits und der branchenspezifischen Energieregulierung andererseits zu einer schrittweisen Verlagerung in Richtung der Regulierungsbehörden geführt. Dies hat zu einer Entlastung der Wettbewerbsbehörden beigetragen. In Russland hingegen wurde die nationale Regulierungsbehörde erst kürzlich auf Kosten der Antimonopolbehörde abgeschafft, deren Organe nun die gesamten Zuständigkeiten der Föderalen Tarifbehörde übernommen haben. Die dadurch bewirkte Überlastung der Antimonopolbehörden mit branchenspezifischen Regulierungsaufgaben ist mit der auf Wettbewerb abzielenden Regulierung nicht vereinbar, da dies einerseits zulasten der eigentlichen Aufgaben der Wettbewerbsbehörde geht und andererseits das Maß an Unabhängigkeit bei der Wahrnehmung von Kontroll- bzw. Regulierungsaufgaben sinkt.

Annex: The most important relevant provisions of the energy law of Russia

Law on Gas Supply

[…]

Art. 2. Basic definitions

For purposes of the present Federal law, the following basic definitions apply:

gas – natural gas, petroleum (associated) gas, stripped dry gas, gas from gas condensate fields extracted and gathered by gas- and oil-producing undertakings, and gas produced by gas- and oil-processing undertakings;

supply of gas – a form of energy supply, constituting an activity for the purpose of providing consumers with gas, including the activity of creating a fund for exploration of gas fields, extraction, transportation, storage and delivery of gas;

[…]

independent undertaking – an undertaking, producing and supplying gas, which is independent from the undertakings owning gas supply systems and undertakings owning gas distribution systems;

gas transmission undertaking – an undertaking transporting gas and having gas trunk pipelines, spreaders of gas pipings, compressor stations and other industrial facilities at its disposal on the right of ownership or other legal grounds;

[…]

supplier (gas supply undertaking) – an owner of gas or a person authorised by the owner of gas, supplying gas to consumers on the basis of contracts;

consumer – a person acquiring gas for his own domestic needs, as well as for own industrial or other household needs;

Art. 5. Gas supply systems of the Russian Federation

The federal gas supply system consists of the following gas supply systems operating in the territory of the Russian Federation: the Unified gas supply system, regional gas supply systems, gas distribution systems and independent undertakings. The federal gas supply system is one of the federal power systems of the Russian Federation.

Irrespective of the type of the ownership and the organisational legal form, undertakings owning the Unified gas supply system, undertakings owning regional gas supply systems, undertakings owning gas distribution systems, and independent undertakings are subject to uniform legal principles of market design and pricing policy, uniform requirements of energy, industrial and ecological security, laid down by the present Federal law, other federal laws and legal acts of the Russian Federation adopted in compliance with them.

Art. 6. The Unified gas supply system

The Unified gas supply system constitutes a property and industrial complex, consisting of technologically, organisationally and economically interconnected and centrally managed industrial and other facilities for the production, transmission, storage and supply of gas, and owned by an undertaking having an organisational legal form established according to the civil law and having acquired the named facilities either through privatisation procedure or on other legal grounds, foreseen by the legislation of the Russian Federation. The Unified gas supply system is the fundamental gas supply system in the Russian Federation and its activities are regulated by the state as prescribed by the legislation of the Russian Federation.

Art. 7. Regional gas supply systems and gas distribution systems

Regional gas supply system constitutes a property and industrial complex, consisting of technologically, organisationally and economically interconnected and centrally managed industrial and other facilities for the production, transmission, storage and supply of gas, is independent from the Unified gas supply system and owned by an undertaking having an organisational legal form established according to the civil law and having acquired the named facilities either through privatisation procedure or on other legal grounds, foreseen by the legislation of the Russian Federation. Regional gas supply system is the fundamental gas supply system in the territories of the respective subjects of the Russian Federation; its activities are controlled by competent state authorities as prescribed by the legislation of the Russian Federation.

Gas distribution system constitutes a property and industrial complex, consisting of organisationally and economically interconnected facilities for the transportation and delivery of gas directly to the consumers in the respective territories of the Russian Federation, is independent from the Unified gas supply system and regional gas supply systems and owned by an undertaking having

an organisational legal form established according to the civil law and having acquired the named facilities either through privatisation procedure or on other legal grounds, laid down in the legislation of the Russian Federation and in the legislation of the subjects of Russian Federation.
[...]

[...]

Art. 8. Competencies of the federal bodies of executive power in the field of gas supply

The following powers constitute the competencies of the federal bodies of executive power in the field of gas supply:

[...]

to define the principles for the formation of prices for gas and tariffs for services of gas transportation through transmission and distribution networks, the order of the compensation for losses, borne by gas distribution undertakings for delivering gas to the population, considering the exemptions laid down by the legislation of the Russian Federation.

Art. 13. Competencies of the undertaking owning the Unified gas supply system

For purposes of ensuring the secure gas supply and compliance with the international treaties entered into by the Russian Federation, as well as agreements on gas supply, the undertaking owning the Unified gas supply system:

ensures the construction, exploitation, reconstruction and development of the facilities of the Unified gas supply system;

ensures uninterruptible dispatching control of the facilities of the Unified gas supply system as well as the connection points of the Unified gas supply system to other facilities;

manages the operation of the Unified gas supply system;

[...]

Art. 14. Indivisibility of the Unified gas supply system

For the purpose of reliability of the gas supply as well as secure and sustainable operation of the facilities of the Unified gas supply system related to the general technological regime of the production, transmission and supply of gas, the division of the Unified gas supply system is not allowed. The liquidation is only permitted on the basis of a federal law.

Technological and dispatching control of the facilities, connected to the Unified gas supply system, irrespective of who their owners are, is performed by the undertaking owning the Unified gas supply system. […]

Art. 15. Shares of the undertaking owning the Unified gas supply system and peculiarities of their turnover

The total amount of ordinary shares of the undertaking owning the Unified gas supply system, that are in ownership of the Russian Federation or the joint stock companies where the Russian Federation owns more than 50%, shall not constitute less than 50% plus one share of the total amount of the ordinary shares of the undertaking owning the Unified gas supply system. The sale or other means of alienation of these ordinary shares may only be implemented on the basis of a federal law.

Art. 21. Regulation of prices for gas and tariffs for services of gas transportation

Services of gas transportation through pipelines are provided under the conditions of a natural monopoly and are regulated in accordance with the legislation of the Russian Federation on natural monopolies, the present Federal law and other federal laws.

[…]

Art. 23. Regulation of tariffs for services of gas distribution undertakings

The federal body of executive power in the field of regulating tariffs approves the tariffs for services of gas transportation through gas distribution networks with a duration of not less than 3 and not more than 5 years and defines the order of their application. The tariffs may be differentiated considering economic and social conditions of the gas supply in various parts of the territory of the Russian Federation.

Art. 23.1. Federal state control (supervision) over fixing and/or applying state regulated prices (tariffs) in the field of gas supply and annulment of the decisions fixing prices (tariffs) in the field of gas supply

Federal state control (supervision) over fixing and/or applying state regulated prices (tariffs) in the field of gas supply is implemented by a competent federal

body of the executive power in the manner established by the Government of the Russian Federation.
[...]

Art. 23.2. State regulation of payments for the technological connection of gas-powered equipment to gas distribution networks

Payments for the technological connection of gas-powered equipment to gas distribution networks (hereinafter – technological connection) and/or standardised tariff rates, defining their amount, are subject to state regulation.
[...]

Art. 27. Access of undertakings to the gas transmission and distribution networks

Unless otherwise provided by the present Federal law, undertakings owning gas supply systems are obliged to grant to any undertaking operating in the territory of the Russian Federation access to the spare capacities of the gas transmission and distribution networks, belonging to them, in the manner established by the Government of the Russian Federation. Gas intended for transportation has to comply with the requirements which are approved in the manner provided by the Government of the Russian Federation.

In the first place, access to spare capacities of the gas transmission and distribution networks, belonging to the undertakings referred to in the first part of the present article, shall be granted to the suppliers applying for transportation of stripped dry gas gained after processing associated petroleum gas.

Regulation on access to the GTS-UGSS

[...]

1. Terms and definitions

1. In the present regulation, the following terms and definitions apply:

   [...]

   'undertakings of the system of JSC Gazprom' – open Joint Stock Company Gazprom, subsidiaries and dependent economic undertakings of JSC Gazprom, as well as other undertakings controlled by JSC Gazprom;

'independent undertakings' – undertakings, which are not part of the system of JSC Gazprom (independent producers, suppliers, customers of gas);

[...]

'spare capacity of the gas transmission system' – technically possible capacity of the system for the receipt and transport of gas, except for those volumes of gas transport, implemented for undertakings of the system of JSC Gazprom and independent undertakings under existing contracts at that certain moment, as well as for compulsory gas supplies by undertakings of the system of JSC Gazprom in accordance with the decisions of the President and the Government of Russian Federation;

'short-term contract' – a contract with a duration not exceeding 1 year;

'middle-term contract' – a contract with a duration from 1 to 5 years;

'long-term contract' – a contract with a duration of more than 5 years;

[...]

2. General provisions

2. The present Regulation, developed in accordance with the Decree of the President of the Russian Federation dated 28 April 1997 N 426 "On fundamental provisions of the structural reform in the sectors of natural monopolies" defines conditions and order of access of independent undertakings in the territory of the Russian Federation to the gas transmission system of JSC Gazprom for the supply of gas to consumers in the Russian Federation.

[...]

3. Conditions and the order of access to the gas transmission system of JSC Gazprom

4. Any undertaking in the territory of the Russian Federation is entitled to non-discriminatory access to the gas transmission system of JSC Gazprom for the purpose of transporting gas.
5. JSC Gazprom grants access to its gas transmission system to independent undertakings on the basis of contracts concluded between these undertakings and JSC Gazprom or its gas transmission undertakings on the behalf of JSC Gazprom, if the following requirements are met:

[a)] the existence of spare capacity in the gas transmission system from the connection point to the extraction point in the period of gas supply requested by the supplier;
[b)] the compliance of the quality and features of the supplied gas with the standards and technical requirements of the system of JSC Gazprom, as well as with other normative-technical documents;
[c)] the existence of the pipelines leading to the network and to the customers, the discharge pipes with data collection and quality control points at the disposal of the suppliers for the start date of gas supply requested by the supplier.

6. In order to be granted access to the gas transmission system of JSC Gazprom, independent undertakings submit an application to JSC Gazprom in a form approved by the commission of the Government of the Russian Federation for the issues of use of oil and gas high pressure pipelines (hereinafter Commission) on a submission of JSC Gazprom, which has to contain the following data:

    1) Information about the supplier;
    2) Sources of gas and their characteristics;
    3) A start and an end date of the gas supply;
    4) Volumes of the gas supplies for every quarter of the first year and for every year for the whole period of middle- and long-term contracts; for every month for the whole period of short-term contracts;
    5) Conditions of the gas supplies (firm and interruptible);
    6) Quality characteristics and parameters of the supplied gas;
    7) A connection point of the pipelines leading to the gas transmission system of JSC Gazprom;
    8) A point of the gas delivery to the customer;
    9) A confirmation of willingness to accept declared gas by the gas distribution network and the customer in the period of the gas supply;
    10) Documents certifying the right of ownership on the gas or the existence of contractual obligations on gas sales (purchase).

7. Requirements concerning the contents of the application have to be uniform for all applicants. Refusal to accept an application containing all data required in point 6 of the present Regulation is not allowed.
8. Deadlines for the submission of applications are:

    in the case of short-term contracts – not later than 1 month and not earlier than 3 months before the start date of the supplies;

in the case of middle-term contracts – not later than 3 months and not earlier than 1 year before the first year of the supplies;

in the case of long-term contracts – not later than 6 months and not earlier than 3 years before the first year of the supplies.

Applications are registered by JSC Gazprom with an indication of the date and time of arrival as well as the date of receipt of the application.

9. In a case where the volumes of gas transportation requested by independent undertakings and the volumes of gas transportation planned by JSC Gazprom for a certain time period exceed the spare capacity of the gas transmission network for this period from the connection point to the extraction point, independent undertakings, by virtue of a decision of the Commission, are entitled to use the existing technical possibility of the gas transmission network (considering the technological reserves in compliance with the applicable standards), but not exceeding the volumes of spare capacities in the requested period of gas supply.
10. In cases of lack of spare capacity in the gas transmission network, necessary for approving all applications, the priority should be given:

    in the first place – to the suppliers for communal and household needs of the population, to the suppliers of stripped dry gas, gained after processing of associated petroleum gas;

    in the second place – to the undertakings, which purchase and sell natural gas on the organised auctions;

    in the third place – to the gas suppliers planning supplies for a longer period as compared to other applicants.

    Applications of other independent undertakings are approved in compliance with the anti-monopoly legislation either proportionally according to the requested volumes of the gas transportation or based on an auction in the manner established by the Government of the Russian Federation.
11. Application for a short-term contract is subject of review by JSC Gazprom within a 15-days period, for a mid-term contract within 2 months, and for a long-term contract within 3 months from the day of receipt of the application.
12. As a result of examining an application, JSC Gazprom makes one of the following decisions:

consent to conclude a contract;

a consent to conclude a contract with a partial approval of the application in compliance with points 9 and 10 of the present Regulation;

a reasoned refusal to conclude a contract. The applicant is informed within 3 days about the decision made on the application.

13. Contracts for gas transportation are concluded within 1 month in the case of short-term contracts, within 2 months in the case of middle-term contracts, and within 3 months in the case of long-term contracts after the day of the decision on a full or partial access to the gas transmission system, in the form developed by JSC Gazprom in compliance with the legislation of the Russian Federation and the present Regulation. In these contracts, gas volumes, routes, tariffs and other conditions of gas transportation are defined according to the conditions of granting access and in compliance with the present Regulation.
14. In the case of a disagreement with the decision made by JSC Gazprom on a partial approval of the application or a reasoned refusal, the independent undertaking may submit the application for access, the decision of JSC Gazprom on the application and other necessary documentation to the Commission.
15. The Commission examines the materials with the participation of the representatives of JSC Gazprom and the independent undertaking within a month's period and makes a final decision.

4. Fundamental conditions of gas transportation

16. All expenses related to the connection of facilities of independent undertakings to the existing gas transmission network have to be borne by independent undertakings, unless a different condition has been defined in the contract with an undertaking of the system of JSC Gazprom, in the legislation of the Russian Federation or other normative legal acts.
17. The payment has to be made in compliance with the tariffs approved by the Federal energy commission of the Russian Federation.
18. Independent undertakings making use of the gas transmission network of JSC Gazprom are obliged to:

    1) ensure the level of preparedness of gas for transportation in accordance with applicable standards and technical conditions, as well as the data collection at the points of the delivery and receipt of gas;

2) present operative information about technological regimes of their facilities of gas industry and gas pipelines to JSC Gazprom within the prescribed time;
3) inform JSC Gazprom about accidents and extraordinary situations, planned preventive maintenance, other works on their facilities, as well as about possible alterations of the volumes of gas input into the gas transmission network as compared to the volumes stipulated in the contract;
4) agree with JSC Gazprom on the schedules of restoring the regime of gas supplies up to the level laid down by the contract;
5) comply with the norms and requirements of pipeline maintenance and security of gas transportation;
6) grant unrestricted access to the authorised representatives of JSC Gazprom for the purpose of controlling the data collection of volumes and quality of gas;
7) ensure a constant and stable radio or telephone connection between dispatching units of the gas supplier and JSC Gazprom.

19. A contract may be terminated before it is due to expire, in the following cases:

1) If the gas supplier culpably fails to deliver gas to the gas transmission network in the volumes and terms stipulated in the contract; in this case, a new contract with modified supply conditions may be concluded;
2) If the payment for gas transportation services is not made in the manner and within the time period prescribed by the contract;
3) If an independent undertaking culpably fails to fulfil any of those obligations stipulated under point 18 of the Regulation on access to the GTS-UGSS.

20. Undertakings of the system of JSC Gazprom are obliged to:

1) provide information about the availability of spare capacities in the transmission network and about their plans concerning the employment of the gas transmission network of JSC Gazprom in certain periods of time on certain sites as well as about applications received for access to these sites (to the extent of the mandatory data required for an application, stipulated under chapter 3 pt. 6 numbers 1, 3 to 5 and 7 to 10 of the present Regulation) and dates of their receipt;
2) provide information upon request of independent undertakings about the availability of spare capacities in the gas transmission network of JSC Gazprom in certain periods of time on certain sites as well as about applications received for access to these sites (to the extent

of the mandatory data required for an application, stipulated under chapter 3 pt. 6 numbers 1, 3 to 5 and 7 to 10 of the present Regulation);

3) provide gas transportation services to independent undertakings in a non-discriminatory manner in compliance with the present Regulation;
4) timely inform gas suppliers and customers about alterations of work regimes, accidents and extraordinary situations in the gas transmission network, as well as failures of the gas data collection system;
5) inform gas suppliers and customers in good time about planned maintenance and preventive works, influencing the fulfilment of gas suppliers' obligations and work regimes of gas customers;
6) grant unrestricted access to the authorised representatives of gas suppliers and customers of gas for the purpose of controlling the data collection of volumes and quality of gas.

21. Disputes concerning the conclusion, performance and termination of contracts are dealt by the Commission in the pre-trial order.
22. The Commission provides official clarifications on the application of the present Regulation.

Provisions on access to distribution networks

The Government of the Russian Federation determines to:

1. Approve the provisions on ensuring access of undertakings to local gas distribution networks.
2. Define that the Federal Energy Commission handles issues concerning the access of undertakings to local gas distribution networks.

[…]

I. General provisions

1. The present provisions define conditions and order of access of undertakings to local gas distribution networks in the territory of the Russian Federation and apply to legal relations arising between legal entities in relation to the gas transportation via local gas distribution networks.

   Any undertaking in the territory of the Russian Federation is entitled to have a non-discriminatory access to local gas distribution networks for transporting gas to customers.
2. Gas transport through local gas distribution networks is implemented on the basis of a contract between a gas distribution undertaking and a gas supplier

or customer, concluded in accordance with the legislation of the Russian Federation and the present provisions.

II. Definitions

3. In the present regulation the following terms and definitions are applied:

'local gas distribution network' – system of pipelines and equipment for the purpose of supplying customers with gas within a territorial unit (subject of the Russian Federation, cities, regions, etc.);

[…]

'spare capacity of local gas distribution networks' – technically possible capacity of the network for receipt and transport of gas, except for the volumes of gas transport, needed for the implementation of existing contracts in that certain time period;

[…]

III. Conditions and order of granting access to local gas distribution networks to undertakings

4. Access to local gas distribution networks are granted if:

there is spare capacity in the local gas distribution network (from the connection point to the extraction point) in the requested period of gas transport;

there are pipelines and discharge pipes leading to gas customers with the data collection and quality control points prepared for the start date of the gas supply;

the quality and features of the supplied gas comply with the requirements of normative-technical documents.

5. In order to conclude a contract for gas transportation, the supplier or customer shall submit to the gas distribution undertaking a copy of the gas supply contract and an application containing the following mandatory data:

information about the gas supplier and customer;

volumes and terms of gas transportation (including the regime and periodicity), as well as the suggested order of calculations;

start and end date of the gas transportation;

volumes of the gas transportation for every month of the first year and for every year for the following period;

the name of the producer of gas, quality and parameters of the supplied gas (to be presented in the case of transporting gas of local producers);

the connection point of the pipelines leading to the local gas distribution network;

the point of gas extraction or transfer for its further transportation through the networks of other undertakings;

the confirmation of willingness to accept gas in declared volumes by the gas distribution undertakings and the customers in the period of gas transportation.

6. The following terms of submitting applications on gas transportation shall apply:

   for the conclusion of contracts with a duration up to 1 year – not later than 1 month and not earlier than 3 months before the start date of transportation;

   for the conclusion of contracts with a duration from 1 to 5 years – not later than 3 months and not earlier than 1 year before the first year of the transportation;

   for the conclusion of contracts with a duration of more than 5 years – not later than 6 months and not earlier than 3 years before the first year of the transportation

   Applications on gas transportation are registered in gas distribution undertakings with a reference to the date of their receipt. A refusal to accept an application containing all data required in point 5 of the present provisions is not permitted.

7. In the case of lack of spare capacity of the local gas distribution network, necessary for approving all applications submitted, the priority is given to the applications of those undertakings, which ensure communal and household needs of the population at the location of the gas distribution network.

   Among suppliers of gas for different purposes, the priority is given to the applications of undertakings applying for a conclusion of a contract for a longer period of gas transportation. In the case of an equality of conditions, applications for access to local gas distribution networks are approved proportionally according to the requested volumes of gas transportation.

8. Applications on gas transportation for contracts to be concluded with a duration of up to 1 year are subject of review by gas distribution undertaking within 15 days.

   Applications on gas transportation for contracts to be concluded with a duration of more than 1 year have to be reviewed within 3 months from the moment of their registration, unless the parties have agreed on a different term.

   As a result of the examination of applications, gas distribution undertakings make one of the following decisions:

   consent to conclude a contract in compliance with the application;

   consent to conclude a contract with a partial approval of the application in compliance with the present provisions;

   a reasoned refusal to conclude a contract.

   Gas distribution undertakings inform applicants within 3 days about the decision made on the application. In the case of an approval of the application, gas distribution undertakings send a draft contract for gas transportation to the applicant within 10 days, unless the parties have agreed on a different term.

9. Within 1 month after the date of receipt of draft contract in compliance with point 8 of the present provisions, the applicant for gas transportation and the gas distribution undertaking conclude a contract for gas transportation. Essential terms of this contract are volumes and conditions of gas transportation (including the regime and periodicity), tariffs and order of calculations.

IV. Fundamental conditions of gas transportation

10. Payments by independent undertakings for gas transportation shall be made in compliance with the tariffs approved by the Federal Energy Commission of the Russian Federation.
11. Suppliers and customers of gas are entitled to the connection of pipelines and discharge pipes to local gas distribution networks in the case of the existence of free capacities in its corresponding sites.

All expenses related to the connection of pipelines and discharge pipes of suppliers and customers of gas to local gas distribution networks are borne by suppliers and customers, as a rule.

12. A contract for gas transportation through local gas distribution networks may include a special condition about the limitation of offsetting payments for gas transportation services on the account of the repayment of debts of the gas distribution undertakings towards the gas suppliers.
13. Suppliers and customers of gas making use of local gas distribution networks (or gas transportation undertakings on their behalf) are obliged to:

    ensure the preparedness of gas for transportation in accordance with the requirements of applicable normative-technical documents as well as the data collection at the points of the delivery and receipt of gas;

    present operative information to the gas distribution undertaking within the prescribed time about technological regimes of a gas pipeline or a system of gas pipelines leading to the gas distribution undertaking;

    inform gas distribution undertakings about accidents on their facilities, ongoing and capital repair works, and a possible alteration of the volumes of gas input into the local gas distribution network as compared to the volumes stipulated in the contract;

    agree with the gas distribution undertaking on the schedules of restoring the regime of gas supplies up to the parameters laid down by the contract;

    comply with the norms and requirements of pipeline maintenance and security of the gas distribution network during gas transportation;

    grant unrestricted access to the points of control and data collection of gas volumes and quality to the authorised representatives of gas distribution undertakings;

    ensure a constant and stable radio or telephone connection between dispatching units of the supplier and customer, and the gas distribution undertaking.

14. Gas distribution undertakings are obliged to:

    provide information upon request of the Federal energy commission of the Russian Federation, suppliers and customers of gas about the availability of spare capacities in the local gas distribution networks in certain periods of time on certain sites of the network as well as about applications received for transportation through these sites;

timely inform gas suppliers and customers about alterations of work regimes, accidents in the local gas distribution networks, failures of the data collection system of gas, repair and preventive works, influencing the fulfilment of duties concerning transportation of gas;

grant unrestricted access to the authorised representatives of suppliers and customers of gas for controlling data collection of volumes and quality of gas.

Rules on Gas Supply

[...]

II. Terms and definitions

3. In the present Rules the following terms and definitions are applied:

[...]

'gas distribution undertakings' – specialised undertakings of republics, territories, regions, cities, inter-regions and villages, developing and exploiting gas supply systems of these territories, ensuring gas supply, as well as providing services of gas transportation through their networks;

'gas transmission undertaking' – an undertaking transporting gas and having the gas trunk pipelines, compressor stations and other industrial facilities at its disposal on the right of ownership or other legal grounds;

'gas transportation system' – system of pipelines connecting gas producers with gas consumers, including gas trunk pipelines, discharge pipes and gas distribution networks owned by transmission and distribution undertakings, as well as by customers;

[...]

'transportation of gas' – movement and transfer of gas through gas transportation system;

[...]

III. Order of concluding contracts

4. Before starting to use gas as fuel, the customer has to fulfil the technical conditions for the connection of the gas-powered equipment to the gas distribution system. The technical conditions for the connection to the gas transmission and distribution system are issued accordingly by the gas transmission or distribution undertaking. […]

[…]

7. A customer or supplier of gas is entitled to have its gas transported in compliance with the regulations approved by the Government of the Russian Federation on ensuring access to independent undertakings to the gas transmission network of JSC Gazprom as well as to gas distribution networks.
8. The conditions and order of transportation of gas through gas transmission system are determined by the gas transmission or distribution undertaking and stipulated in a contract in compliance with the present Rules.

[…]

10. An offer to conclude a contract for gas transportation is sent by the gas transmission or distribution undertaking to the supplier (customer), together with the permission of access to the transmission system, issued in the manner established by the Government of the Russian Federation.
11. The party, which received an offer, has to consent on the conclusion of the contract within 30 days from the moment of receipt of the offer, unless a different term has been set in the offer itself.

In the case of a dissent with the offered conditions, the party, which received the offer, has to submit a report of disagreement to the other party. In case there is no feedback within 30 days after sending the report of disagreement, the party may refer to the commercial court or to the arbitration and may stop extracting gas on gas transportation after the expiry of the duration of the existing contract.

Extraction (continuation of extraction) of gas after the expiry of the mentioned 30 days and/or after the expiry of the duration of the contract, is considered as a consent on the conclusion of the contract for supply (transportation) of gas with the conditions offered by the supplier (gas transmission or distribution undertaking). […]

[…]

IV. Conditions, terms and order of implementation of contracts

[…]

19. […]

Guidance on the Implementation of the mentioned schedules and the corresponding changes in the daily volume of gas transferred to customers is issued by the Central Operations and Dispatch Department of open joint stock company Gazprom.
[…]

V. Gas accounting

22. […]
A contract for gas transportation may also oblige and entitle gas transmission and distribution undertaking to fulfil the duty of data collection at the points of the delivery and receipt of gas on behalf of the supplier (customer). […]

VI. Payments for gas and its transportation

31. Conditions of the payment of gas transportation are determined by contract for gas transportation based on the tariffs for its transportation, defined in the manner set out by federal bodies of executive power.
[…]

Law on Competition[597]

[…]

Article 2. Anti-monopoly legislation of the Russian Federation and other statutory legal acts on protection of competition

1. The anti-monopoly legislation of the Russian Federation (further on referred to as anti-monopoly legislation) is based on the Constitution of the Russian Federation, the Civil Code of the Russian Federation and consists of this Federal Law, other Federal Laws regulating relations stated in Article 3 of this Federal Law.
2. Relations stated in Article 3 of this Federal Law may be regulated by Regulations of the Russian Federation Government, statutory legal acts of the Federal Anti-monopoly body in cases directly provided for in the anti-monopoly legislation.

597 An unofficial translation of the Law can be downloaded from the FAS website under: http://en.fas.gov.ru/documents/documentdetails.html?id=14737, last accessed on 16.11.2017.

3. If an International Treaty of the Russian Federation establishes different rules than those provided for by this Federal Law, the rules provided for by the International Treaty of the Russian Federation are applied.

Article 3. Area of application of this Federal Law

1. This Federal Law is applied to the relations which are related to the protection of competition, including prevention and restriction of monopolistic activity and unfair competition and in which Russian legal persons and foreign legal persons, organisations, federal executive authorities, public authorities of the subjects of the Russian Federation, bodies of local self-government, other bodies or organisations exercising the functions of the above-mentioned bodies, as well as public extra-budgetary funds, the Central Bank of the Russian Federation, physical persons, including individual entrepreneurs are involved.
2. Provisions of this Federal Law are applicable to the agreements reached between Russian and/or foreign persons or organisations outside the Russian Federation, as well as to actions performed by them, if such agreements or actions affect the state of competition in the Russian Federation.
3. Provisions of this Federal Law are not applicable to the relations regulated by common rules of competition on trans-border markets, compliance with which is controlled by Eurasian Economic Commission in accordance with the international treaty of the Russian Federation. Criteria of trans-border markets are established in accordance with international treaty of the Russian Federation.

[…]

Article 5. Dominant position

[…]

5. The position of an economic entity – subject of a natural monopoly – in a goods market, which is in a state of natural monopoly, is considered to be dominant.

[…]

Article 10. Prohibition of abuse of a dominant position by an economic entity

1. Action (omission) of an economic entity occupying a dominant position, which results or can result in prevention, restriction or elimination of competition and/or infringement of the interests of other persons (economic entities) in the area of entrepreneurship, or of that of an indefinite number of consumers, are prohibited, including the following actions (omissions):

1) establishing and maintaining monopolistically high or monopolistically low price for a commodity;
2) withdrawing goods from circulation, if the result of such withdrawal is an increase of price of the commodity;
3) imposing contractual terms upon a counteragent which are unfavourable for the latter or not related to the subject of agreement (economically or technologically unjustified and/or not provided for directly by the Federal Laws, statutory legal acts of the President of the Russian Federation, statutory legal acts of the Government of the Russian Federation, statutory legal acts of the authorised federal executive authorities or judicial acts, requirements for transferring financial assets, other property, including property rights, as well as a consent to conclude a contract concerning the goods in which the counterparty is not interested, and other requirements);
4) economically or technologically unjustified reduction or cutting off the production of goods if there is demand for the goods or orders for their delivery are placed and there is possibility of their profitable production, as well as if such reduction or cutting off the production of goods are not provided for directly by the Federal Laws, statutory legal acts of the President of the Russian Federation, statutory legal acts of the Government of the Russian Federation, statutory legal acts of the authorised federal executive authorities or judicial acts;
5) economically or technologically unjustified refusal or evasion from concluding a contract with individual purchasers (customers) in the case where there are possibilities for the production or delivery of the relevant goods, as well as if such a refusal or evasion is not provided for directly by the Federal Laws, statutory legal acts of the President of the Russian Federation, the Government of the Russian Federation, authorised federal executive authorities or judicial acts;
6) economically, technologically or otherwise unjustified establishment of different prices (tariffs) for the same goods if not otherwise provided by the law;
7) establishment of unjustifiably high or unjustifiably low prices for a financial service by a financial organisation;
8) creation of discriminatory conditions;
9) creation of entry barriers into the goods market or foreclosing the goods market for the other economic entities;
10) violation of the procedure for pricing established by statutory legal acts.
11) manipulating prices on wholesale and/or retail markets of electric power (capacity).

2. An economic entity has the right to provide evidence that its actions (omissions) stated in Part 1 of this Article (except for actions indicated in Clauses 1, 2, 3, 5, 6, 7 and 10 of Part 1 of this Article) can be recognised as eligible in accordance with the requirements of Part 1 of Article 13 of this Federal Law.
3. To prevent discriminatory conditions, a federal law or a normative legal act of the Government of the Russian Federation can establish the rules of non-discriminatory access to the goods markets and/or the goods produced or sold by natural monopolies, whose activities are regulated in accordance with N 147-FZ Federal Law "On Natural Monopolies" of 17th August 1995, as well as infrastructure facilities used by these natural monopolies directly for providing services in the field of activities of natural monopolies. [...]

[...]

Article 23. Powers of the anti-monopoly body

1. The anti-monopoly body fulfils the following powers:
   1) initiates and examines cases of violation of the anti-monopoly law;
   2) issues binding instructions to economic entities in the cases stated by this Federal Law:
      a) on the termination of concerted practices restricting competition and/or termination of agreements restricting competition and fulfilment of actions aimed at ensuring competition;
      b) on the termination of abuse of a dominant position by an economic entity and fulfilment of actions aimed at ensuring competition;
      c) on the termination of violation of rules of non-discriminatory access to products;
      d) on the termination of unfair competition;
      e) on the prevention of actions which can hinder the introduction of competition and/or can lead to prevention, restriction or elimination of competition and violation of the anti-monopoly legislation;
      f) on the elimination of the consequences of a violation of the anti-monopoly legislation;
      g) on the termination of other violations of the anti-monopoly legislation;
      h) on the restoration of the situation that existed prior to the violation of the anti-monopoly legislation;
      i) on the conclusion of contracts, change of contractual terms or abrogation of contracts if in the course of an examination into a violation of the anti-monopoly legislation by the anti-monopoly body, the persons whose rights were breached or can be breached, lodged a petition, or

in the case when the anti-monopoly body exercises state control over economic concentration;

j) on transferring the profit gained as a result of a violation of the anti-monopoly legislation to the federal budget;

k) on the change or restriction of use of a brand name in the case where, in the course of examination into a violation of the anti-monopoly legislation by the anti-monopoly body, the persons whose rights were breached or can be breached lodged a petition, or in the case where the anti-monopoly body exercises state control over economic concentration;

l) on the fulfilment of economic, technical, informational, and other requirements for the elimination of discriminatory conditions and prevention of their creation;

m) on the fulfilment of actions aimed at supporting competition, including actions on ensuring access to production facilities or information according to the procedures established by the Federal Law or other statutory legal acts, on granting rights to facilities of industrial property protection according to the procedures established be the Federal Law or other statutory legal acts, on transferring property rights or prohibiting the transfer of property rights, on informing the anti-monopoly body in advance about the intention to undertake the actions prescribed in the instructions, on selling particular volume of products through commodity exchange, on preliminary approval by the anti-monopoly authority of specifics of determining initial prices for the products to be sold through commodity exchange in accordance with the procedures established by the Government of the Russian Federation;

[…]

3.2) issues notices of warning to terminate actions (omissions), specifying the violation of the anti-monopoly law, in the cases prescribed by this Federal Law;

[…]

5) holds commercial organisations, non-commercial organisations, their officials, officials of the federal executive authorities, of the bodies of executive authority of the constituent territories of the Russian Federation, of the local self-government bodies, and of other bodies or organisations exercising the functions of the said bodies, as well as other officials of the public extra-budgetary funds, physical persons, including individual entrepreneurs, liable for a violation of the anti-monopoly legislation in the cases and in accordance with the procedure established by legislation of the Russian Federation;

[…]

10) establishes a dominant position of an economic entity in the course of an examination into a violation of the anti-monopoly legislation and while exercising control over economic concentration;
11) oversees the compliance with the anti-monopoly legislation by commercial organisations, non-commercial organisations, federal executive authorities, bodies of public authority of the subjects of the Russian Federation, bodies of local self-government, other bodies or organisations exercising the functions of the above-mentioned bodies, as well as by public extra-budgetary funds, physical persons; requests necessary documents, as well as information, explanations in written or verbal form from such parties, and in accordance with the procedure established by the legislation of the Russian Federation; applies to the agencies discharging operative investigatory activities with the request to carry out operative investigations; [...]

[...]

Article 24. The rights of the officers of anti-monopoly bodies during the inspections regarding compliance with the anti-monopoly legislation

When exercising the control over the compliance with the anti-monopoly legislation, officers of an anti-monopoly body, in accordance with their powers and upon presenting their certificates of employment and the order of the Head of the anti-monopoly body about organising an inspection regarding compliance with the anti-monopoly legislation (further on referred to as an inspection), have the rights of unimpeded access to the federal executive bodies, the executive bodies of the constituent territories of the Russian Federation, local self-government bodies, other agencies and organisations exercising the functions of the above bodies, as well as state extra-budgetary funds, and non-profit organisations in order to obtain documents and information required by the anti-monopoly body.

Article 25. Obligation to provide information to the anti-monopoly body

1. Commercial and non-commercial organisations (their management), the federal executive bodies (their officials), executive bodies of the constituent territories of the Russian Federation (their officials), local self-government bodies (their officials), other agencies or organisations exercising the functions of the above bodies, as well as state extra-budget funds (their officials), physical persons,

including individual entrepreneurs, are obliged to provide to the anti-monopoly body, upon its reasonable request within the established period, and in accordance with its scope of the reference, documents, explanations, and information, orally or in writing (including information constituting commercial, official, other legally protected secrets), including acts, contracts, certificates, business correspondence, other documents and materials in the form of digital recording or in electronic format.

[...]

Article 37. Liability for violations of the anti-monopoly legislation

1. Officials of federal executive authorities, public authorities of the subjects of the Russian Federation, bodies of local self-government, other institutions or organisations discharging the functions of the aforementioned authorities or bodies of local self-government, officials of other bodies or organisations exercising the functions of the above-mentioned bodies, as well as officials of public extra-budgetary funds, commercial and non-commercial organisations and their officials, physical persons, including individual entrepreneurs can be held liable as provided for by legislation of the Russian Federation.
2. Holding persons stated in Part 1 of this Article liable do not exempt them from the duty to fulfil the decision and instruction of the anti-monopoly body, to submit to the anti-monopoly body an application or notices for the examination or carry out other actions provided by the anti-monopoly legislation.
3. Persons whose rights and interests are infringed as a result of a violation of the anti-monopoly law, can file lawsuits under the established procedures, particularly, lawsuits to restore the violated rights, including lost profit, compensation for harm caused to their property.

[...]

Article 39. Grounds for initiating a case on violating the anti-monopoly legislation, location of examination of the case, and the consequences of revealing the signs of an administrative offence in course of the case examination

1. The anti-monopoly body initiates and reviews the cases of a violation of the anti-monopoly legislation, adopts decisions on these cases and issues instructions based on these decisions within the scope of its powers.

2. The basis for the initiation and review of the cases of a violation of the anti-monopoly legislation (further on referred to as the case) by the anti-monopoly body are:
   1) the receipt of documents (further on referred to as documents) specifying a violation of the anti-monopoly legislation from state bodies or bodies of local self-government;
   2) a petition from a legal person or a physical person denoting signs of violating the anti-monopoly law (further on referred to as a petition);
   3) the detection by the anti-monopoly body of the signs of violation of the anti-monopoly legislation;
   4) mass media reports, natural and legal persons' reports pointing out the signs of violation of the anti-monopoly legislation
   5) findings of an inspection, that revealed the facts of violating the anti-monopoly legislation by commercial organisations, non-commercial organisations, federal executive bodies, the authorities of the constituent territories of the Russian Federation, local self-government bodies, other agencies or organisations exercising the functions of the above bodies, and state extra-budgetary funds.
3. A case of a violation of the anti-monopoly legislation can be considered by the anti-monopoly body of the territory where the violation was committed or at the location (residence) of the person against whom the complaint about the anti-monopoly violation is lodged. The federal anti-monopoly body can process the above case regardless of the location where the violation was committed or the location or place of residence of the person against whom the claim or materials are filed.

[…]

Article 39.1. Notice of warning to terminate actions (omissions) specifying the violation of the anti-monopoly law

1. To suppress actions (omissions) that lead or can lead to preventing, restricting, eliminating competition and/or infringing the interests of other persons (economic entities) in the field of business activities or infringing the interests of an indefinite number of consumers, the anti-monopoly authority issues a written notice of warning to an economic entity, a federal executive body, an authority of a constituent territory of the Russian Federation, a local self-government body, other bodies and organisations exercising the functions of the above bodies, an organisation involved in rendering state or municipal services, an extra-budgetary fund to terminate actions (omissions), abolish

or amend acts that have elements of a violation of the anti-monopoly law, or eliminate the cause and conditions that facilitated such a violation, and to undertake measures to eliminate the consequences of the violation (further on referred to as a notice of warning).

2. A notice of warning is issued to the persons listed in Part 1 Article 39, if elements of violating Clauses 3, 5, 6 and 8 Part 1 Article 10, Articles 14.1, 14.2, 14.3, 14.7, 14.8 and 15 of the Federal Law "On Protection of Competition" are revealed. The anti-monopoly body cannot make a decision to initiate a case of the violation of Clauses 3, 5, 6 and 8 Part 1 Article 10, Articles 14.1, 14.2, 14.3, 14.7, 14.8 and 15 of the Federal Law "On Protection of Competition" without issuing a notice of warning and before the deadline for executing the notice of warning.
3. In the course of the investigation of a case of a violation of the anti-monopoly law, a notice of warning is issued by a commission that investigates the anti-monopoly case if in course of the case investigation the signs of violating Clauses 3, 5, 6 and 8 Part 1 Article 10 and Articles 14.1, 14.2, 14.3, 14.7, 14.8 and 15 of this Federal Law are revealed, that were not known at the moment of initiating the case.

[...]

7. If a notice of warning is executed, the anti-monopoly case shall not be initiated and the person that executed the warning shall not be subject to administrative liability for violating the anti-monopoly law due to its elimination.

[...]

Article 51. Fulfilment of the instruction on the case on violating the anti-monopoly legislation. Consequences of non-fulfilment of the instruction on recovering the revenue gained through a monopolistic activity or unfair competition to the federal budget

[...]

2. The failure to fulfil an instruction on the case of a violation of the anti-monopoly legislation in time entails the administrative liability.
3. The person, whose actions (omissions) in accordance with the procedures established in this Federal Law is considered to be a monopolistic activity or unfair competition and are impermissible according to the anti-monopoly legislation, is obliged to recover the revenue received from these actions (omissions) to the federal budget according to the instruction of the anti-monopoly body. In the case of failure to fulfil an instruction, the revenue received from the monopolistic activity or unfair competition is subjected to collecting into the budget at the suit of the anti-monopoly body. The person,

to whom an instruction on the recovery of the revenue received from monopolistic activity or unfair competition to the federal budget is issued, may not be held administratively liable for the violation of anti-monopoly legislation in relation to which this instruction is issued if such an instruction is executed.

[...]

Article 52. The procedures for appealing decisions and instructions of the anti-monopoly authority

1. A decision and/or an instruction of the anti-monopoly authority can be appealed to a commercial court within three months from the day when the decision was made or the instruction was issued. Cases of appealing decisions and/or instructions of the anti-monopoly authority are subject to the jurisdiction of commercial courts. A decision and/or instruction of the regional anti-monopoly body could be appealed to a collegial body of the federal anti-monopoly body.
   1.1. In case a decision and/or instruction of anti-monopoly body is appealed to the collegial body of the federal anti-monopoly body, acts determined with regard to the case of a violation of the anti-monopoly legislation could be appealed to a commercial court within one month from the moment when decision of the collegial body of the federal anti-monopoly body entered into force.
2. If a commercial court initiates proceedings on an appeal against an instruction, execution of the instruction of the anti-monopoly body shall be suspended until the day when the judgment of the commercial court becomes effective.

[...]

Law on Natural Monopolies

[...]

Article 3. Definitions of fundamental terms

For the purposes of the present Federal law, the following definitions of fundamental terms apply:

natural monopoly – a state of the market of commodities, in which demand is more efficiently satisfied when due to technological peculiarities of the production there is no competition (due to substantial reduction of the production costs per unit of the commodity as a result of increasing output), and the commodities manufactured by natural monopolies cannot be substituted with other commodities in the market, thus causing the demand in the given commodity market to be less responsive to changes in price compared to the demand for other types of commodities;

subject of natural monopoly – engaged in the production (sales) of commodities under the conditions of natural monopoly;

[...]

Article 4. Areas of activities of subjects of natural monopolies

1. The present Federal law regulates activities of subjects of natural monopolies in the following areas:

    transportation of oil and oil products through high pressure pipelines;

    transport of gas through pipelines;

    rail transport;

    services in transport terminals, ports and airports;

    public telecommunications services and public postal services;

    services for transmission of electric energy;

    services for operational dispatch management in the electric power industry;

    services of heat transfer;

    services on the use of the inland waterway infrastructure;

    radioactive waste;

    water supply and sanitation with the use of a centralised system of municipal infrastructure systems;

    icebreaking ships, ice pilotage of vessels in the waters of the Northern Sea Route.

[...]

Article 5. Bodies regulating activities of subjects of natural monopolies

1. For the regulation and control of activities of subjects of natural monopolies federal bodies of executive power (hereinafter – regulatory bodies of

natural monopolies) are formed in the manner established for federal bodies of executive power.

[...]

Article 8. Obligations of subjects of natural monopolies

1. Subjects of natural monopolies are not entitled to refuse to conclude a contract with consumers on the production (sales) of the goods, which are subject to regulation pursuant to the present Federal law, in case the subject of natural monopoly has a possibility to produce (sell) such goods.

[...]

3. Subjects of natural monopolies are obliged to provide access to the markets and/or offer goods and services, which are subject to regulation based on the present Federal law, in a non-discriminatory manner in compliance with the anti-monopoly legislation.
4. Subjects of natural monopolies are obliged to keep separate accounts of their income and expenditure according to the types of activities. Keeping separate accounts of income and expenditure by a subject of natural monopoly is carried out in the manner approved by the Government of the Russian Federation and/or the federal executive body authorised by the Government of the Russian Federation.
5. For the purpose of ensuring transparency of the activities of subjects of natural monopolies, openness of regulation of activities of subjects of natural monopolies and protection of interests of consumers, subjects of natural monopolies are obliged to grant free access to the information concerning their activities, which are regulated pursuant to the present Federal law (hereinafter – regulated activity of subjects of natural monopolies).

Free access to the information concerning regulated activities of subjects of natural monopolies shall be provided by subjects of natural monopolies in accordance with information disclosure standards, approved by the Government of the Russian Federation, through publishing information in the media, including internet, and providing it on the basis of written requests of consumers.

The following types of information concerning regulated activities of subjects of natural monopolies are subject to free access:

information about prices (tariffs) for regulated goods (works, services) of subjects of natural monopolies (hereinafter also – regulated goods (works, services));

[...]

information about existence (or lack) of the technical possibility of access to the regulated goods (works, services) of subjects of natural monopolies and the progress of processing of applications for technical connection to the infrastructure of natural monopolies;

information about conditions of the supply of regulated goods (works, services) by subjects of natural monopolies and conditions of technical connection to the infrastructure of subjects of natural monopolies;

[...]

Article 8.1. Standards of information disclosure

1. Standards of information disclosure shall ensure:

accessibility of disclosed information to the general public, including peculiarities of information disclosure in the territories where there is no access to internet;

transparency of the activities of subjects of natural monopolies in relation to production of regulated goods (provision of services, performance of works);

[...]

Article 9. Regulatory bodies of natural monopolies

1. Bodies of regulation of natural monopolies are formed according to the areas of activities, set out in article 4 of the present Federal law.
[...]

Article 10. Functions of regulatory bodies of natural monopolies

Regulatory bodies of natural monopolies fulfil the following principal functions:

to establish and manage the registers of subjects natural monopolies, which are subject to state regulation and control;

[...]

Apart from the obligations of natural monopolies on the provision of the information listed in the respective legal acts, on more general terms natural monopolies are also obliged to deliver all documents, information and explanations to the executive bodies regulating natural monopolies needed for the fulfilment of their functions, as per Art. 13 para. 2 of the Law on Natural Monopolies.

Article 13. Right of access to information concerning activities of subjects of natural monopolies

1. For the purpose of fulfilling their functions, the employees of the executive bodies regulating subjects of natural monopolies are entitled to have unrestricted access to the information concerning the activities of subjects of natural monopolies, other undertakings, which is in the possession of bodies of executive power and local authorities, subjects of natural monopolies or any other undertakings.
2. Subjects of natural monopolies, other undertakings, bodies of executive power and local authorities are obliged upon request of regulatory bodies of natural monopolies to deliver valid documents, explanations in written and oral form and other information, necessary for fulfilling the functions of regulatory bodies of natural monopolies, prescribed by the present Federal law.

[...]

Civil Code of Russia

[...]

Article 426. Public contract

1. A public contract is a contract concluded by a commercial organisation and establishing its obligations for the sale of goods, performance of works, or rendering of services that this organisation by the nature of its activity must exercise with respect to everyone who applies to it (retail trade, carriage by transport for common use, communications services, energy supply, medicine hotel service, etc.).

   A commercial organisation does not have the right to provide a preference to one person before another with respect to the conclusion of a public contract, except in the cases provided by a statute or other legal acts.
2. The price of goods, works, and services, and also other terms of a public contract shall be established equally for all consumers, with the exception of cases when a statute or other legal acts allow the granting of privileges for individual categories of consumers.
3. A refusal of a commercial organisation to conclude a public contract if there is the possibility of providing the consumer with the respective goods or services, or to perform for it respective works, is not allowed.

In the case of an unjustified refusal by a commercial organisation to conclude a public contract, the provisions provided by paragraph 4 of article 445 of the present Code shall be applied.

4. In the cases provided by a statute, the Government of the Russian Federation as well as the federal bodies of executive power authorised by the Government of the Russian Federation may issue rules which are obligatory for parties for the conclusion of public contracts and their performance (model contracts, provisions, etc.).
5. Terms of public contract which do not meet the requirements established by paragraphs 2 and 4 of the present article are void.

Article 445. Conclusion of a contract by the obligatory procedure

[...]

4. If a party for whom, in accordance with the present Code or other statutes, the conclusion of a contract is obligatory, has refused to conclude it, the other party shall have the right to go to a court with a demand for compulsion to conclude a contract.

   A party who has unjustifiably refused to conclude a contract must compensate the other party for the damages caused by this.

[...]

Article 446. Pre-contract disputes

In the cases where disagreements arisen during the conclusion of a contract are brought to a court on the basis of article 445 of the present Code or by an agreement of the parties, the terms of the contract on which there were disagreements among the parties shall be defined in accordance with a decision of the court.

Bibliography

Ahrend, R./Tompson W., Russia's Gas Sector: The Endless Wait for Reform? OECD Economics Department Working Papers, N 402, 2004 (available at: http://dx.doi.org/10.1787/735153733318).

Artemyev, I. U./Sushkevich, A. T. (eds.), Konkurentnoe Pravo Rossii (Uchebnik) [Competition Law of Russia (Textbook)], Moscow, 2012.

Baur, J./Salje, P./Schmidt-Preuß, M. (eds.), Regulierung in der Energiewirtschaft. Ein Praxishandbuch [Regulation in the energy industry. A practice handbook], Cologne, 2016.

Belyi, A. V., Trends of Russia's Gas Sector Regulation, Fourth Annual Conference on Competition and Regulation in network industries, Brussels, 2011 (available at: http://www.crninet.com/2011/a4a.pdf).

Boesche, K. V., Die zivilrechtsdogmatische Struktur des Anspruchs auf Zugang zu Energieversorgungsnetzen. Eine Untersuchung der Zugangsregelungen der §§6, 6a EnWG und 19, 20 GWB [Civil dogmatic structure of the access right to energy supply networks. A study of access provisions sec. 6, 6a EnWG and 19, 20 GWB] (diss.), Baden-Baden, 2002.

Böhme, D., EU-Russia Energy Relations: What chance for solutions? A Focus on the natural gas sector (diss.), Potsdam, 2011.

Boute, A., Russian Electricity and Energy Investment Law, Leiden, 2015.

Britz, G./Hellermann, J./Hermes, G. (eds.), Energiewirtschaftsgesetz. Kommentar [German Energy Act. Commentary], Munich, 2015.

Brodt, E. T., Das Gasnetzzugangsmodell des §20 Abs. 1b EnWG und seine Auswirkungen auf integrierte Gaslieferverträge [Gas network access model of sec. 20 para. 1b of the EnWG and its impacts on integrated gas supply contracts] (diss.), Baden-Baden, 2008.

Büdenbender, I., EnWG. Kommentar zum Energiewirtschaftsgesetz [EnWG. Commentary on German Energy Act], Cologne, 2003.

Busche, J., Privatautonomie und Kontrahierungszwang [Private autonomy and obligation to contract], Tübingen, 1999.

Constantinesco, L. J., Rechtsvergleichung, Band II, Die rechtsvergleichende Methode [Legal comparison, tom II, The comparative law method], Cologne, 1972.

Ebert, K. H., Rechtsvergleichung. Einführung in die Grundlagen [Legal comparison. Introduction to basic principles], Bern, 1978.

EBRD, EBRD energy sector assessment, 2010 Final Report (available at: http://www.ebrd.com/downloads/legal/irc/assessment.pdf).

Ehricke, U. (ed.), Das neue Recht für die Energiewirtschaft. Ziele und Herausforderungen [The new law of energy industry. Objectives and challenges], Speeches from the 33rd event of the Institute of Energy Law in Cologne held on 18 November 2004, Baden-Baden, 2005.

Ehricke, U. (ed.), Erwartungen an das neue Energierecht im nationalen und europäischen Kontext [Expectations towards the new energy law in the national and European context], Speeches from the 34th event of the Institute of Energy Law in Cologne held on 10 November 2005, Baden-Baden, 2006.

Emch, A./Regazzini, J./Rudomino, V. (eds.), Competition Law in the BRICS Countries, 2012.

Falter, M., Russlands natürliche Monopole, Deregulierung am Beispiel der russischen Stromwirtschaft [Russia's natural monopoly, deregulation on the example of the Russian electricity industry] (diss.), Berlin, 2008.

FAS, The FAS offers to deprive Gazprom of the monopoly right on gas storage [FAS predlagaet lishit Gazprom monopolii na khranenie gaza], news release of 11.04.2014 (available at: http://izvestia.ru/news/569047).

FAS, Analytical report on the results of the analysis of the competitive situation on the wholesale market of natural gas in 2011–2014 (available in Russian at: http://fas.gov.ru/documents/documentdetails.html?id=14100).

Fehling, M./Ruffert, M. (eds.), Regulierungsrecht [Regulatory Law], Tübingen, 2010.

Golomzin, A., Obzor praktiki primeneniya antimonopolnogo zakonodatelstva na rinkakh gaza [Overview of the practice of application of the anti-monopoly legislation to the gas markets], presentation of the Deputy Head of the Federal Anti-monopoly Service of Russia, 2005 (available at: http://www.fas.gov.ru/analytical-materials/analytical-materials_2149.html).

Grigoryev, Y., The Russian gas industry, its legal structure, and its influence on world markets, ELJ, vol. 28, p. 125, 2007.

Gudkov, I. V., Transportirovka gaza v Rossii: tekushchee sostoyanie i perspektivi normativno-pravovogo regulirovaniya [Gas transportation in Russia: Current situation and perspectives of legal regulation], NiG, 3-4, 2009, pp. 35–47.

Höffler, F., Engpassmanagement und Anreize zum Netzausbau im leitungsgebundenen Energiesektor. Wirtschaftstheoretische Analyse und wirtschaftspolitische Handlungsempfehlungen [Congestion Management and incentives to network expansion in grid-bound energy sector.

Economic-theoretical analysis and recommendations for economic policy actions], Baden-Baden, 2009.

Höppner, T., Netzveränderungen im Zugangskonzept. Verpflichtungen zur Anpassung der Infrastruktur im Rahmen des Essential Facilities-Konzepts unter Berücksichtigung US-amerikanischer Erfahrungen [Network changes in access concept. Obligations to adapt the infrastructure within the framework of the essential facilities concept taking into consideration US American experiences] (diss.), Baden-Baden, 2009a.

Höppner, T., Die Regulierung der Netzstruktur. Elektrizität, Gas, Telekommunikation, Eisenbahn [Regulation of network structure. Electricity, gas, telecommunication, railway], Baden-Baden, 2009b.

International Energy Agency (IEA), Russia Energy Survey, 2002 (available at: http://www.iea.org/publications/freepublications/publication/russia_energy_survey. pdf).

Johnston, A./Block, G., EU Energy Law, Oxford, 2012.

Kemper, S., Gasnetzzugang in Deutschland und in Spanien [Access to gas networks in Germany and in Spain] (diss.), Frankfurt, 2012.

Kment, M. (ed.), Energiewirtschaftsgesetz [German Energy Act, Commentary], Baden-Baden, 2015.

Koenig, C./Kühling, J./Rasbach, W., Energierecht [Energy law], Baden-Baden, 2013.

König, C., Engpassmanagement in der deutschen und europäischen Elektrizitätsversorgung [Congestion management in the German and European electricity supply] (diss.), Baden-Baden, 2013.

Korepanov, K. V., Dogovori transportirovki magistralnim truboprovodnim transportom [Contracts for gas transportation through high pressure pipelines], Moscow, 2013.

Körting, J., Geschichte der deutschen Gasindustrie [History of the German gas industry], Essen, 1963.

Kruimer, H., The Non-discrimination Obligation of Energy Network Operators, Cambridge, 2014.

Larin, I. G., Truboprovodniy transport vnuzhdaetsya v regulirovanii [Pipeline transport is in need of regulation]. Opinion on the website of the journal 'Ekonomika i TEK segodnya', 27.06.2009 (available at: http://www.rusoil.ru/opinions/o09_06_27.html).

Makovsky, A. L./Khokhlov, S. A., The Civil Code of the Russian Federation, Parts 1 and 2, edited and translated by Peter B. Maggs with A. N. Zhiltsov, M. E. Sharpe, London, 1997.

Mechetny, B. S., Pravovoye regulirovaniye gazosnabzheniya naseleniya v rosiyskoy federatsii: kompleksnoye issledovaniye [Legal regulation of gas supply to the population in Russian Federation: a complex research], Norma, Moscow, 2008.

Monopolkommission, Sondergutachten der Monopolkommission gemäß §62 Abs. 1 des Energiewirtschaftsgesetzes. Strom und Gas 2007: Wettbewerbsdefizite und zögerliche Regulierung [Special Report of the Monopolies Commission pursuant to sec. 62 para. 1 of the EnWG. Electricity and Gas 2007: lack of competition and hesitant regulation], BT-Drs. 16/7087, 20.11.2007.

Monopolkommission, Strom und Gas 2009: Energiemärkte im Spannungsfeld von Politik und Wettbewerb. Sondergutachten der Monopolkommission gemäß §62 Abs. 1 EnWG [Monopolies Commission, Electricity and Gas 2009: Energy markets at the crossroads between politics and competition. Special Report pursuant to sec. 62 para. 1 of the EnWG] (available in German at: http://www.monopolkommission.de/index.php/de/gutachten/sondergutachten/248-liste-sondergutachten).

OECD, OECD Review of Regulatory Reforms, Russia, Building rules for the market, 2005 (available at: http://www.keepeek.com/Digital-Asset-Management/oecd/governance/oecd-reviews-of-regulatory-reform-russia-2005_9789264011236-en#page1).

Olbricht, T., Netzzugang in der deutschen Gaswirtschaft [Network access in the German gas industry], Essen, 2008.

Pashchenko, T./Rachkov, I., Gaswirtschaft in Russland – Rechtliche Rahmenbedingungen [Gas industry in Russia – legal framework], WiRO, 6/2006.

Perchik, A. I., Truboprovodnoe pravo [Pipeline law], Moscow, 2002.

Pisal, R., Entflechtungsoptionen nach dem Dritten Energiebinnenmarktpaket [Unbundling options according to the third energy package] (diss.), Baden-Baden, 2011.

Roggenkamp, M. M./Barrera-Hernandez, L./Zillman, D. N./Del Guayo, I. (eds.), Energy networks and the law, Oxford, 2012.

Säcker, F. J. (ed.), Berliner Kommentar zum Energierecht [Berlin Commentary on energy law], Frankfurt, 2014.

Säcker, F. J., Der Independent System Operator. Ein neues institutionelles Design für Netzbetreiber? [The independent system operator. A new institutional design for network operator?], Frankfurt, 2007.

Säcker, F. J. (ed.), Handbuch zum deutsch-russischen Energierecht [Handbook of German-Russian energy law], Munich, 2010.

Salaschek, R. U., Die kartellrechtlichen Sanktionssysteme der USA und der EU vor dem Hintergrund ihrer jeweiligen Sanktionsumfelder [The antitrust sanctions systems of the USA and the EU in light of their sanctioning peripheries], Baden-Baden, 2016.

Salje, P., Energiewirtschaftsgesetz. Kommentar [German Energy Act. Commentary], Cologne, 2006.

Schneider, J. P./Theobald, C. (eds.), Recht der Energiewirtschaft [Law of energy industry], Munich, 2013.

Smirnova, O. O., Antimonopolnoye regulirovaniye rinkov gaza [Anti-monopoly regulation of gas markets], presentation of the Deputy Head of the Department for control over fuel-energy complex of the Federal Anti-monopoly Service of Russia, 2012 (available at: http://www.fas.gov.ru/analytical-materials/analytical-materials_30845.html).

Stern, P. J., The future of Russian gas and Gazprom, Oxford, 2005.

Stuhlmacher, G./Stappert, H./Schoon, H./Jansen, G. (eds.), Grundriss zum Energierecht. Der rechtliche Rahmen für die Energiewirtschaft [Outline of Energy law. Legal framework for the energy industry], Frankfurt, 2015.

Sukhanov, E. A. (ed.), Grazhdanskoye Pravo, Tom III, Obyazatelstvennoye Pravo (Uchebnik) [Civil Law, vol. III, Law of Obligations (Textbook)], Moscow, 2008.

Timofeeva, E., Unbundling in der russischen Elektrizitätswirtschaft im Vergleich zum deutschen und europäischen Energierecht [Unbundling in the Russian electricity industry in comparison with the German and European energy law] (diss.), Frankfurt, 2012.

Theobald, C./Nill-Theobald, C., Grundzüge des Energiewirtschaftsrechts. Die Lieberalisierung der Strom- und Gaswirtschaft [Fundamentals of law of energy industry. Liberalisation of electrcity and gas industry], Munich, 2013.

Varlamova, A. N., Konkurentnoye Pravo Rossii [Competition Law of Russia], Moscow, 2009.

Varlamova, A. N., Pravovoye obespecheniye razvitiya konkurentsii (Uchebnoye posobiye) [Legally ensuring the development of competition (Textbook)], Moscow, 2010.

Vinois, J. A. (ed.), EU Energy Law, vol. VIII, The Energy Infrastructure Policy of the European Union, Deventer, 2014.

Waloszyk, M., Law and Policy of the European gas market, Cheltenham, 2014.

Wendt, H., Kapazitätsengpässe beim Netzzugang. Engpassmanagement, Ausbaupflichten und Engpassvermeidungsanreize im Energie-, Eisenbahn- und Telekommunikationsrecht [Capacity Congestions in the case of Network Access. Congestion management, obligations of extension and incentives to avoid congestions in energy, railway, and telecommunication law], Tübingen, 2012.

Zweigert, K./Kötz, H., Einführung in die Rechtsvergleichung auf dem Gebiet des Privatrechts [Introduction to legal comparison in the field of private law], Tübingen, 1996.

Veröffentlichungen des Instituts für deutsches und europäisches Wirtschafts-, Wettbewerbs- und Regulierungsrecht der Freien Universität Berlin

Herausgegeben von Franz Jürgen Säcker

Band	1	Franz Jürgen Säcker (Hrsg.): Deutsch-russisches Energie- und Bergrecht im Vergleich. Ergebnisse einer Arbeitstagung vom 31. März/1. April 2006. 2007.
Band	2	Franz Jürgen Säcker/Walther Busse von Colbe (Hrsg.): Wettbewerbsfördernde Anreizregulierung. Zum Anreizregulierungsbericht der Bundesnetzagentur vom 30. Juni 2006. 2007.
Band	3	Dirk Zschenderlein: Die Gleichbehandlung der Aktionäre bei der Auskunftserteilung in der Aktiengesellschaft. Zum Problem der Zulässigkeit der Weitergabe von Informationen an einzelne Aktionäre und Dritte. 2007.
Band	4	Simone Kirchhain: Die Anwendung der Vertikal-GVO auf innerstaatliche Wettbewerbsbeschränkungen nach der 7. GWB-Novelle. 2007.
Band	5	Franz Jürgen Säcker: Der Independent System Operator. Ein neues institutionelles Design für Netzbetreiber? 2007.
Band	6	Stefanie Otto: Allgemeininteressen im neuen UWG. § 1 S. 2 UWG und die wettbewerbsfunktionale Auslegung. 2007.
Band	7	Jochen Eichler: Vertragliche Dritthaftung. Eine Auseinandersetzung mit der Frage der Dritthaftung von sogenannten Experten und anderen Auskunftspersonen im Rahmen des § 311 Abs. 3 BGB. 2007.
Band	8	Markela Stamati: Die Anforderungen der operationellen Entflechtung nach den Beschleunigungsrichtlinien der Europäischen Kommission. Umsetzung in Deutschland und Griechenland. 2008.
Band	9	Franz Jürgen Säcker: The Concept of the Relevant Product Market. Between Demand-Side Substitutability and Supply-Side Substitutability in Competition Law. 2008.
Band	10	Renate Rabensdorf: Die Durchgriffshaftung im deutschen und russischen Recht der Kapitalgesellschaften. Eine rechtsvergleichende Untersuchung. 2009.
Band	11	Franz Jürgen Säcker: Der beschleunigte Ausbau der Höchstspannungsnetze als Rechtsproblem. Erläutert am Beispiel der 380-kV-Höchstspannungsleitung Lauchstädt – Redwitz – Grafenrheinfeld mit Querung des Rennsteigs im Naturpark Thüringer Wald. 2009.
Band	12	Helen Mahne: Eigentum an Versorgungsleitungen. 2009.
Band	13	Franz Jürgen Säcker (Hrsg.): Russisches Energierecht - Gesetzessammlung. 2009.

Band 14 Franz Jürgen Säcker/Maik Wolf: Integrierte Energieversorgung in geschlossenen Verteilernetzen. Zum Gestaltungsspielraum des Gesetzgebers zur Neuregelung des § 110 EnWG im Lichte des Dritten EG-Energiepakets. 2009.

Band 15 Franz Jürgen Säcker (Hrsg.): Das Dritte Energiepaket für den Gasbereich. Deutsch-Englische Textausgabe mit einer Einführung. 2009.

Band 16 Franz Jürgen Säcker (Hrsg.): Das Dritte Energiepaket für den Elektrizitätsbereich. Deutsch-Englische Textausgabe mit einer Einführung. 2009.

Band 17 Thomas Dörmer: Die Unternehmenspacht. Rechtsstellung der Vertragsparteien unter besonderer Berücksichtigung der Pflicht des Unternehmenspächters zur ordnungsgemäßen Unternehmensführung sowie der Rechtslage bei Vertragsbeendigung. 2010.

Band 18 Klaas Bosch: Die Kontrolldichte der gerichtlichen Überprüfung von Marktregulierungsentscheidungen der Bundesnetzagentur nach dem Telekommunikationsgesetz. 2010.

Band 19 Geng-Sook Leem: Einheitliche Corporate Governance-Grundsätze für die Europäische Aktiengesellschaft (SE). Eine rechtsvergleichende Untersuchung anhand der Ausgestaltung der SE im deutschen und britischen Recht. 2010.

Band 20 Wiebke Gebhardt: Gentechnik und Koexistenz nach der Gesetzesnovelle von 2008: Zivilrechtliche Haftung im Vergleich Deutschland und USA. 2010.

Band 21 Cathrin Isenberg: Die Geruchsmarke als Gemeinschaftsmarke. Schutzfähigkeit und Einsatzmöglichkeiten. 2010.

Band 22 Franz Jürgen Säcker/Jochen Mohr/Maik Wolf: Konzessionsverträge im System des europäischen und deutschen Wettbewerbsrechts. 2011.

Band 23 Judith Antonia Loeck: Die unzumutbare Belästigung nach der UWG Novelle 2008 und dem Gesetz zur Bekämpfung unerlaubter Telefonwerbung und zur Verbesserung des Verbraucherschutzes bei besonderen Betriebsformen. 2011.

Band 24 Jörg Jaecks: Konzernverrechnungsklauseln und verwandte einseitige Verrechnungsbefugnisse im Mehrpersonenverhältnis. 2011.

Band 25 Franz Jürgen Säcker: Marktabgrenzung, Marktbeherrschung, Markttransparenz und Machtmissbrauch auf den Großhandelsmärkten für Elektrizität. 2011.

Band 26 Susanne Wende: Die einheitliche Auslegung von Beihilfen- und Vergaberecht als Teilgebiete des europäischen Wettbewerbsrechts. 2011.

Band 27 Leonie Kempel: Die Anwendung von Art. 102 AEUV auf geistiges Eigentum und Sacheigentum. Die Voraussetzungen des Kontrahierungszwangs nach Art. 102 AEUV und der Essential-Facility-Doktrin unter besonderer Berücksichtigung der Unterschiede zwischen geistigem Eigentum und Sacheigentum. 2011.

Band 28 Christoph Schuldt: Werbejingles – schützenswerte Kompositionen!? Die urheberrechtliche und markenrechtliche Schutzfähigkeit von Werbejingles vor unbefugter Nachahmung. 2012.

Band 29 Lydia Scholz: Die Rechtfertigung von diskriminierenden umweltpolitischen Steuerungsinstrumenten. Eine Untersuchung der Reichweite der Warenverkehrsfreiheit und ihrer Begrenzung durch den Umweltschutz als Vertragsziel am Beispiel der deutschen Energiefördergesetze EEG und KWKModG. 2012.

Band 30 Franz Jürgen Säcker: Investitionen in Kraftwerke zur Sicherung einer zuverlässigen Elektrizitätsversorgung nach der Energiewende. Rechtliche und ökonomische Rahmenbedingungen. 2012.

Band 31 Florian Leib: Kartellrechtliche Durchsetzungsstrategien in der Europäischen Union, den USA und Deutschland. Eine rechtsvergleichende Darstellung. 2012.

Band 32 Holger Hoch: Marktverschlusseffekte und Effizienzen vertikaler Zusammenschlüsse. Kartellrechtliche Beurteilung nach europäischem und deutschem Recht. 2012.

Band 33 Sebastian Kemper: Gasnetzzugang in Deutschland und in Spanien. 2012.

Band 34 Elena Timofeeva: Unbundling in der russischen Elektrizitätswirtschaft im Vergleich zum deutschen und europäischen Energierecht. 2012.

Band 35 Gisela Drozella/Harald Krebs: Marktbeherrschung im Bereich Stromerzeugung/Stromgroßhandel. Eine kritische Analyse der neueren Sicht des Bundeskartellamts. 2013.

Band 36 Christian Rehm: Die Einzel- und Gesamtverantwortung der Vorstandsmitglieder der Aktiengesellschaft. Die Verantwortung für die Leitung und Geschäftsführung im mehrköpfigen Vorstand in der unabhängigen und der herrschenden AG. 2013.

Band 37 Ann-Christin Richter: Mengen- und umsatzbezogene Rabatte marktbeherrschender Unternehmen in den Grenzen des Art. 102 AEUV. 2013.

Band 38 Nikolaos Pitsos: Die erhebliche Behinderung des wirksamen Wettbewerbs (SIEC-Test) im Fusionskontrollrecht. Zugleich ein Beitrag zur Problematik der oligopolistischen Marktbeherrschung unter Vergleich mit dem amerikanischen SLC-Test. 2013.

Band 39 Mirko Heinemann: Das Markenzeichen als Anknüpfungspunkt des Markenimages. 2013.

Band 40 Sylvia Lorenz: Der Immaterialgüterschutz virtueller Ladengeschäfte. Ein Vorschlag für die rechtliche Erfassung virtueller Güter. 2014.

Band 41 Anke Reimers: Wettbewerbsrechtliche und regulatorische Analyse der Kapazitätenvergabe an Grenzkuppelstellen im Elektrizitätsbinnenmarkt. 2014.

Band 42 Franz Jürgen Säcker / Carsten König / Lydia Scholz: Der regulierungsrechtliche Rahmen für ein Offshore-Stromnetz in der Nordsee. 2014.

Band 43 David Preisendanz: Der Humor in der vergleichenden Werbung. 2014.

Band 44 Martin Gerig: Vollendung des EU-Energiebinnenmarktes vs. nationale Marktabschottungen. Europarechtskonformität mitgliedstaatlicher Fördermaßnahmen und Kapazitätsmärkte am Beispiel Deutschlands. 2014.

Band 45 Jan Patrick Ehinger: Dritthaftung für Kunstexpertisen und Aufnahmebestätigungen in den Catalogue raisonné. Ein Beitrag zur Expertenhaftung. 2014.

Band 46 Julia Gerzen: Das Recht der Gesellschafter-Fremdkapitalfinanzierung. Rechtsvergleichende Analyse der Behandlung von Gesellschafterdarlehen vor und in der Insolvenz der GmbH nach deutschem und russischem Recht. 2014.

Band 47 Laura Börger: Die gerichtliche Kontrolldichte bei der Überprüfung von Entscheidungen der Europäischen Kommission auf dem Gebiet der Fusionskontrolle. 2014.

Veröffentlichungen des Instituts für Energie- und Regulierungsrecht Berlin

Band 48 Daniel Simon Travers: Kopplungsangebote. Eine Studie zum Vertrags- und Lauterkeitsrecht. 2015.

Band 49 Anna Olbryś-Sobieszuk: EU-rechtliche Schranken der Glücksspielwerbung in Deutschland, Großbritannien und Polen. 2015.

Band 50 Franz Jürgen Säcker/Lydia Scholz/Thea Sveen: Renewable Energy Law in Europe. Challenges and Perspectives. 2015.

Band 51 Lina Berezgova: Festlegung von Stromnetzentgelten in Deutschland und Russland. Eine rechtsvergleichende Untersuchung der anreizbasierten Regulierungsvorgaben. 2015.

Band 52 Fengliang Jin: Aufgreifkriterien in der Fusionskontrolle. Eine rechtsvergleichende Untersuchung des europäischen (Art. 3 FKVO), deutschen (§ 37 GWB), taiwanesischen (§ 6 FHG) und festlandchinesischen (§ 20 AMG) Rechts. 2015.

Band 53 Vasileios Triantafyllidis: Die Einordnung der Passing-On-Defense in das allgemeine Schadensersatzrecht. Eine rechtsvergleichende, dogmatische Studie. 2015.

Band 54 Peipei Liu: Die Inhaltskontrolle von Allgemeinen Geschäftsbedingungen und formularmäßigen Vertragsklauseln im deutsch-chinesischen Vergleich. 2016.

Band 55 Evelyn Kozak: Zur Notwendigkeit eines arbeitsrechtlichen und haftungsrechtlichen Whistleblowerschutzes. 2016.

Band 56 Genevieve Baker: Der bereicherungsrechtliche Nutzungsanspruch. 2017.

Band 57 Maria Zaykova: Der rechtliche Rahmen für den bergbaulichen Zugang zu den Erdöl- und Erdgaslagerstätten in der Russischen Föderation im Vergleich zum deutschen Bergrecht. 2017.

Band 58 Qian Luan: Geldschöpfungsprozess und Geld als abstraktes Schuldversprechen. Die europäisch-verwaltungsrechtliche Betrachtung des Geldschöpfungsprozesses der EZB und die Rechtsnatur von Zentralbankgeld und Geschäftsbankengiralgeld. 2017.

Band 59 Sára Gabriella Hoffman: Regulation of Cloud Services under US and EU Antitrust, Competition and Privacy Laws. 2017.

Band 60 Matthias Schöpf: Das neue Planungsrecht der Übertragungsnetze: Vorgaben des deutschen und europäischen Rechts. 2017.

Band 61 İpek Çevik: Eine vergleichende Untersuchung der Joint Ventures – Gemeinschaftsunternehmen – nach europäischem, türkischem und deutschem Wettbewerbsrecht. Die Analyse von wettbewerbsrechtlichen Auswirkungen bei Gründung der konzentrativen und/oder kooperativen Gemeinschaftsunternehmen. 2017.

Band 62 Raffaele Mazza: Verbotsirrtum und Vertrauen auf Rechtsrat im europäischen Kartellrecht. Eine rechtsvergleichende Analyse des europäischen, des deutschen und des französischen Kartellrechts. 2017.

Band 63 Stavroula Antoniou: Die Kontrolle einseitiger Preisanpassungsrechte in Dauerschuldverhältnissen am Beispiel langfristige Energielieferverträge. Eine rechtsvergleichende Untersuchung nach deutschem und griechischem Recht. 2018.

Band 64 Lucas Noura de Moraes Rêgo Guimarães: Energieversorgungssicherheit im Europarecht mittels der Förderung erneuerbarer Energien und der Interkonnektion der Netze. 2018.

Band 65 Nino Kobadze: Regulation of Access to Gas Networks in Russia in Comparison with the Energy Law of Germany and the EU. 2018.